SHOOTING *for a* CENTURY

FINDING ANSWERS TO THE INDIA-PAKISTAN CONUNDRUM

STEPHEN P. COHEN

HarperCollins *Publishers* India

First published by The Brookings Institution Press, Washington, D.C., USA, 2013

First published in India by
HarperCollins *Publishers* in 2013
4th Floor, Tower A, Building No. 10, Phase II,
DLF Cyber City, Gurugram, Haryana -122002
www.harpercollins.co.in

4 6 8 10 9 7 5 3

P-ISBN: 978-93-5116-015-1
E-ISBN: 978-93-5116-016-8

Typeset in Minion

Composition by Cynthia Stock
Silver Spring, Maryland

Printed and bound at
Manipal Technologies Limited, Manipal

Again, for Bobby

Contents

If there were only two men in the world, how would they get on?
They would help one another, harm one another,
flatter one another, slander one another, fight one another, make it up;
they could neither live together nor do without one another.

—Voltaire

What keeps people apart? Their inability to get together.

—Mayor Richard J. Daley

PREFACE

The prospects of India-Pakistan normalization should be receiving greater world attention, especially in view of the many factors that make this an urgent issue: the rise of South Asia as a source for much global terrorism, the rise of India as a major economic power, the declining integrity of Pakistan, and problems within the Indian political order. It cannot be assumed that the recent lurch toward civility in India-Pakistan relations, notably the signing of trade and visa agreements, signifies stability between the two states, or that their nuclear capability makes war so costly that it will never happen in the subcontinent again. The presence of nearly 200 nuclear warheads has merely driven their conflict underground, with each side testing the patience of the other and the limits of deterrence.

One of this book's central observations is that the India-Pakistan rivalry is likely to endure for several more decades—even to 2047, a "century," to use the shorthand for a hundred runs in cricket, the most popular sport in both countries. Of course, this need not be the case if the two states took some steps toward high-level strategic accommodation or if contacts between the peoples of these two countries were to expand—both prospects seem unlikely now. Yet some external event or development might also change the context of the dispute. Alternatively, one of them—most likely Pakistan—might fragment or disintegrate, or the two might engage in a cataclysmic conflict, most likely growing out of a crisis that led to a war in which nuclear weapons were used in great numbers. Right now, full normalization seems unlikely, so this book is suffused with conditional pessimism: normalization would be desirable, but there are worse futures than a projection of the present rivalry for another thirty years or more.

This book explores the reasons for the enduring rivalry between Pakistan and India, with suggestions as to how it might end. I partially share the view, common in the strategic literature but anathema in the peace community, that stability on the subcontinent can only be achieved if strategic elites first recognize their overarching common interests: after this will come the people-to-people meetings, economic exchanges, larger volumes of mutually beneficial trade, cultural exchanges, and other interactions that solidify normalization. However, another difficult roadblock must also be surmounted: the clash of state and national identities between India and Pakistan.

Of course, normalization is not "peace." India and Pakistan may yet have crises; the road to normalization will undoubtedly be littered with them. Moreover, nothing may happen at all if the two political processes cannot, in the end, support it.

I use "normalization" in modified Westphalian terms. The Treaty of Westphalia of 1648 set forth standards for relations between sovereign states: their borders and their governments would be assured of legitimacy and integrity as long as they maintained political and physical control over their territories—hence the central role of armies in shaping states. A second Westphalian principle was that states should not actively try to transform or undermine each other. This principle can be said to apply particularly to neighbors, who find it easier to reach across borders by overt and covert means. No system is perfect: espionage and subversion do take place even between partner states—often in the guise of seeking information—and political subversion is common among hostile states. Another of the treaty's norms—that sovereign states have a responsibility to prevent their territory from being used to assault another state—is also frequently violated.

Force and violence are thus closely associated with the modern state: they determine the boundaries of states. Force is used to maintain order within a state, but it must be legitimate to be credible, accepted, and effective.

In their modern application, Westphalia's principles can be extended to any social, cultural, and political overlap between states. Many handle this overlap through peaceful means: for example, through regulations for trade, the movement of people, and sometimes the movement of ideas, which, however, is more difficult to standardize. All of these regulatory efforts are kept within the bounds of political acceptability. To do otherwise invites both retaliation in kind and the use of force of one sort or another.

However, notoriously in South Asia—but also in many other parts of the world—the state-to-state regulatory mechanism is absent. As a result, the domestic events in one state are in effect linked to the domestic events of another; there is no bright line here between foreign and domestic politics.

The linkage can be between ethnic groups, which in South Asia spill across borders, and it can be between separatist and autonomist groups, especially the survivors of a botched partition. As is often the end result, a sovereign border may mean nothing to important groups, and the state—usually via its intelligence services—may think it has the right to intervene in the affairs of another. Indeed, much foreign policy in South Asia is actually transborder interference in another state, with intelligence agencies or willing ethnic, religious, or linguistic assets being the preferred instrument of policy. In many cases, states allow groups to operate across formal borders; this passive policy may be calculated and deliberate if a weak government is unwilling to clamp down on its own citizens in the case of a politically popular cause, or if the government is incapable or ignorant. In a few instances, states themselves organize such groups, support them with training and logistics, and justify this action on the grounds that the alternative would be open war; some do so to allow a great injustice to continue.

State normalization may be conceived in several ways. It may be viewed from the top down as the accommodation of strategic relations between states.[1] At the other extreme, it may be viewed as the accommodation of abnormal economic, political, cultural, and social relations between two populations. In this case, it is thought that improving these ties will have an impact on strategic rivalries. I discuss this view at greater length in chapter 5. Both approaches are right, but both are incomplete. So is the view that "regional integration" is a feasible end point for South Asia, which can follow such models that are elsewhere successful. This approach is actually very Westphalian, in that it associates state insecurity with threats coming from within and outside the region.[2] It tends to overlook the fact that for most South Asian states the chief form of insecurity is domestic, often intensified by the meddling of one or more neighbors. The Westphalian model provided an admirable framework for the conduct of relations between European monarchies, but it broke down in the face of popular passions, often inflamed by insecure democratic governments or unstable authoritarian ones.

None of the approaches to normalization just mentioned measure relations between or among states. To my knowledge there has been no attempt to measure the degree to which states can be located on a cooperation-conflict spectrum in the separate arenas of social integration, economics, security relations, and diplomatic cooperation, although it could theoretically be done in several ways. Of course, one also needs to consider whether economic or cultural normalization can take place in the absence of strategic commonalities—a question that is taken up in several places in this book.

The policy implications of my analysis are evident and plentiful. For India and Pakistan, the first rule of holes is to stop digging. For the United States, its relationship with each of these two nuclear powers is arguably much less important than their relationship with each other. Despite Pakistan's importance in Afghanistan, India's potential as a balancer of the People's Republic of China, and the economic and political benefits that America derives from relations with each, these seem to be outweighed by both the risks and the benefits that would flow from a normal relationship between the two.

Broadly, this book is about the struggle of two states to create a normal relationship and the poor prospects of reaching that goal. History provides many examples of normalization, but in few of them has the process been so prolonged and so much in doubt. On another level, the discussion is about the origins (and costs) of India-Pakistan hostility, various explanations of why the dispute endures, past and current efforts to normalize the relationship, the consequences of nuclearization, and the rise of a shared external threat (Islamic extremism) to the two states. Two new factors are also taken into account: namely, Pakistan's slow coming apart and the possibility that normalization may take place in one or two spheres (at the moment economics and trade seem to be the leading candidates). The discussion closes with thoughts on the broader policy implications of enduring Pakistan-India hostility.

Because there is a vast literature on specific issues between the two states, notably Kashmir, it is surprising that no authoritative history of India-Pakistan relations yet exists.[3] This is not that book, but I do attempt to explain why and how these two states became, and remain, hostile. I hope that others will attempt a large-scale history; the subject deserves it.

The argument in this book opens by "sizing" the relationship between India and Pakistan: their present and past ties, the degree of hostility and of cooperation, and the opportunity costs of hostility. This overview follows the course of their relationship since independence—indeed, even before independence, when ideas regarding the structure of the subcontinent after the British departure were widely debated. Some comparisons with other regions are also drawn.

Chapter 2 is about specific disputes between the two states. Chapters 3 and 4 turn to contemporary Indian and Pakistani narratives about their conflict. These narratives sustain the regional competition, and the more deeply embedded they are in culture and identity, the less likely is the rivalry to dissipate or disappear.

Explanations of the persistence of hostility between India and Pakistan are taken up in chapter 5. These can be grouped into several categories:

geostrategy (looking at the dispute in the classic realist and structuralist frameworks) and the view from within the state, including psychological and cultural explanations. No single theory explains the persistence in entirety, but in combination the ideas put forth in the literature provide insight and suggest some strategies for amelioration and resolution. It may even be possible to take advantage of "bad deeds" and thereby drive Indian and Pakistani strategic elites in the same direction.

Various attempts already made to normalize relations between India and Pakistan are examined in chapter 6. These include Track II diplomacy, back-channel contacts, and third-party interventions. The probable future of this hitherto intractable conflict is also discussed and compared with resolution attempts that have succeeded elsewhere. Although it is difficult not to be pessimistic in this instance, looking ahead may suggest opportunities (and costs) that are omitted in the usual narratives.

Chapter 7 focuses on America's ambivalent roles in the region. Clearly, the United States should not attempt to "solve" the Kashmir problem or become deeply involved in India-Pakistan normalization efforts, but it should recognize the extreme importance of normal relations between these two nuclear weapons states. In view of regional realities, the United States must recognize the Line of Control in Kashmir as the de facto and perhaps de jure boundary, and must help find a way to legitimize Pakistan's nuclear program, bringing that state—as well as India—into the web of obligations and commitments that are incumbent on responsible states with nuclear weapons. To take on such tasks, Washington must restructure its own approach to South Asia—the present arrangement does not encourage holistic thinking about this quarter of the human race.

I hope that this book will be of value not only to scholars who wish to probe more deeply into the causes and consequences of hostility between these two states but also to the policy community. It has been badly served by the often polemical nature of much of the literature on relations between India and Pakistan—each of growing importance for quite different reasons, and potentially constituting a dynamic and democratic region of the world.

Acknowledgments

I am especially indebted to Constantino Xavier who served as my prime research assistant during the writing of this book; Tino offered wise counsel and helped keep this project moving despite many administrative distractions. Kevin Grossinger, Shruti Jagirdar, Mishal Khan, Tarika Khattar, Elizabeth Phillip, and Jonathan Weatherwax all capably served as interns while this project was under way and contributed much in the form of draft text and good comments, with Shruti coming to the rescue as the manuscript was being prepared for publication.

I would also like to thank the Brookings Institution, which has provided a wonderful home for my work since 1998 and allowed me to write the books that are a capstone to my career. Support to Brookings from the Norwegian government has made this and other projects possible.

Many others have helped me over the years, notably Nisar A. Chaudhry and Rajesh Kadian, Americans from Pakistan and India, respectively, plus the exceptional community of South Asia watchers in Washington. Finally, I must express my gratitude to all of my former students, too numerous to mention, who remind me that "one learns by teaching." They have taught me much.

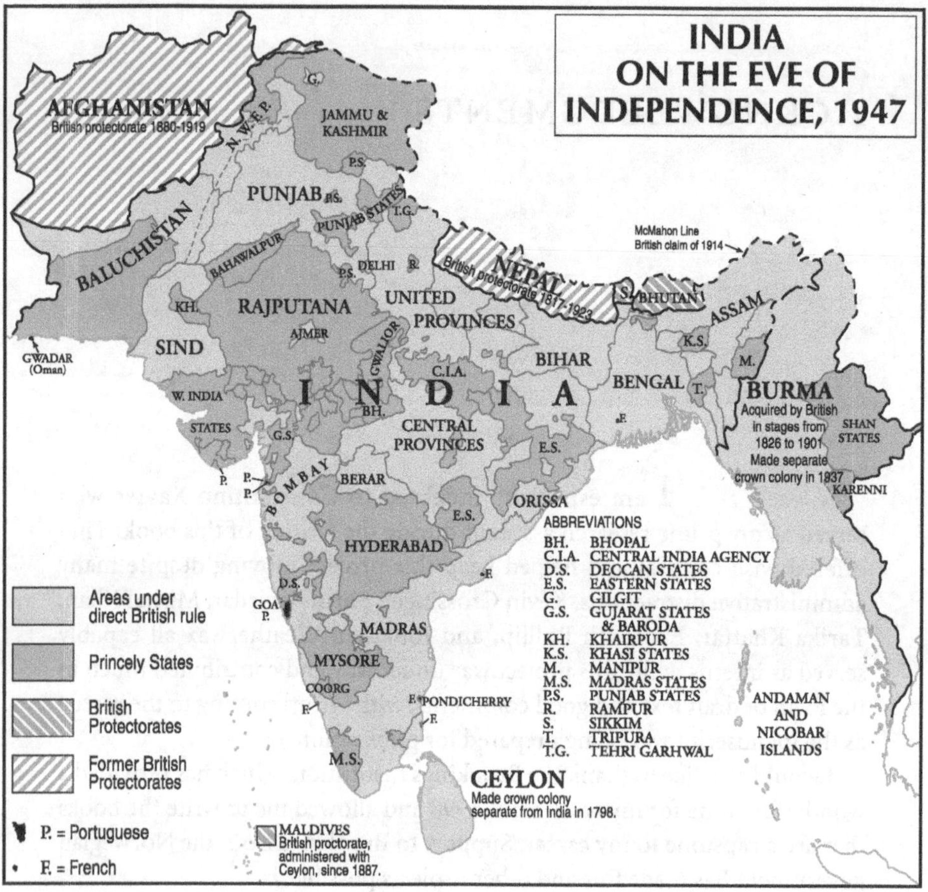
INDIA
ON THE EVE OF
INDEPENDENCE, 1947
AFGHANISTAN
British protectorate 1880-1919
N.W.F.P.
G.
JAMMU & KASHMIR
P.S.
PUNJAB
P.S.
PUNJAB STATES
T.G.
BALUCHISTAN
BAHAWALPUR
DELHI
R.
NEPAL
British protectorate 1817-1923
S.
BHUTAN
McMahon Line
British claim of 1914
ASSAM
KH.
RAJPUTANA
UNITED PROVINCES
AJMER
GWALIOR
SIND
GWADAR
(Oman)
K.S.
M.
BIHAR
C.I.A.
W. INDIA
STATES
I N D I A
BH.
BENGAL
T.
BURMA
Acquired by British in stages from 1826 to 1901
Made separate crown colony in 1937
SHAN STATES
KARENNI
G.S.
CENTRAL PROVINCES
E.S.
F.
P.
P.
P.
BOMBAY
BERAR
ORISSA
E.S.
HYDERABAD
ABBREVIATIONS
BH. BHOPAL
C.I.A. CENTRAL INDIA AGENCY
D.S. DECCAN STATES
E.S. EASTERN STATES
G. GILGIT
G.S. GUJARAT STATES & BARODA
KH. KHAIRPUR
K.S. KHASI STATES
M. MANIPUR
M.S. MADRAS STATES
P.S. PUNJAB STATES
R. RAMPUR
S. SIKKIM
T. TRIPURA
T.G. TEHRI GARHWAL
D.S.
F.
GOA
P.
MADRAS
MYSORE
COORG
F.
F.
PONDICHERRY
F.
M.S.
ANDAMAN AND NICOBAR ISLANDS
CEYLON
Made crown colony separate from India in 1798.
Areas under direct British rule
Princely States
British Protectorates
Former British Protectorates
P. = Portuguese
F. = French
MALDIVES
British proctorate, administered with Ceylon, since 1887.

CHAPTER ONE

CONTEXT

Since emerging as independent states in 1947, Pakistan and India have been engaged in one of the world's most complex and sharply contested rivalries. It is as long-lived as the Israeli-Palestinian-Arab dispute. Though the two states are similar in many ways, not least in their cultural closeness, they began with a basic clash of national identities, soon followed by border and territorial disputes. Each then went on to support separatist elements in the other country. Now, after four wars and numerous crises, they are nuclear rivals, and a deep and near-permanent diplomatic hostility shapes their relations with the rest of the world. The conflict continues to evoke international attention, although only rarely action. In comparative terms, it has the dubious distinction of being one of the few conflicts that are truly intractable, meaning conflicts that last more than twenty years despite multiple attempts to end them. As one student of the subject notes, 95 percent of the world's conflicts are resolvable, only 5 percent are not, the India-Pakistan dispute being the longest-lasting in the latter group.[1]

Relations between India and Pakistan, today the world's second and sixth most populous states, are far from static, however. They improve and deteriorate within a certain range—generating new aspects and complications, giving rise to cautious optimism, but also feeding uncertainty. The emergence of nuclear capability in both states after 1998 raised the stakes but also reduced the chances of a new conflict. Although going nuclear did not prevent a small war in 1999 and nearly a major one in 2001–02, it did show that these weapons affect the propensity for (and conduct of) war between nuclear-armed rivals. All the same, intelligence errors or a strategic misjudgment—of a kind common to all states, big and small, wise and stupid—could (and probably will) lead to another crisis.

History's Trajectory

In the wide view of scholars and policymakers, the rivalry between India and Pakistan is deeply rooted in the years 1858, when Great Britain assumed direct control over a large part of the subcontinent, taking over from the British East India Company, and 1947, when it partitioned India and decamped. During these years many princely states continued with ultimate authority resting in the British Crown and Parliament. Over half of territorial India (approximately two-thirds of the population) was ruled by British administrators, magistrates, and military forces—collectively known as the Raj—as well as a large army raised in India but officered by the British. The overall security of the subcontinent was enforced by the unchallenged sea power of the Royal Navy. The Indian military (later divided between the two successor states) tied the region together, its multiethnic, multireligious, and multicaste regiments reflecting the region's diversity as well as British expansion from the south and the east to the west and northwest.

Under the Raj's system of direct and indirect governance, South Asia became a strategically coherent region. It served as an important commercial and military gateway to East and Southeast Asia; then as a source of capital, technology, manpower, and investment for Britain's African and Mideast possessions; and later as an imperial police force in two world wars.

Even before 1947, conflict arose as a result of the intertwining of two competitions. The first competition was between the nascent visions of India and Pakistan, epitomized respectively by the Congress Party and the Muslim League. Both wanted independence from Britain; the Muslim League also wanted independence from a perceived Hindu dominance. The second was the multisided rivalry between and among the princely states, the British Raj, and the leaders of these two competing nationalist movements. The visions of the Muslim League and Congress also differed in the disposition of the princely states; the rivalry was further complicated by their different military, strategic, and economic visions.

The Indian National Congress, formed as a lobbying group in 1885, was initially sympathetic to British rule (one of its founders was an Englishman). Until the group's Lahore session in 1929, it regarded itself as a loyal opposition movement, seeking not independence but reform. By 1930 the Congress was transformed into a mass movement seeking independence—albeit one still led by elites—and included such notable Muslims as Mohammed Ali Jinnah and Maulana Azad. Still other Muslims called for a renaissance, leading to the foundation of the Muslim League in Dhaka in 1906. The close analogy with the Middle East has often been noted; there the concept of Israel as a homeland for the Jewish people and that of Palestine as an Arab-dominated but multiethnic state was intensified and enlarged by their incompatible territorial claims.

In response to pressure, the British introduced the elective principle in the governance of India under the Morley-Minto reforms of 1909 and acceded to demands for separate electorates for Muslims, a step that was strongly criticized both by Hindu-oriented parties and by secular groups such as the Indian National Congress. By 1940 the Muslim League, now with Jinnah at its head, was openly advocating a separate Muslim-dominated and -oriented state, to be called Pakistan.

Despite the rivalry between the ideas of India and Pakistan, supporters on both sides agreed on one major point: all wanted to rid India of the British, although the two differed in the proposed timing of the break. Note, too, that many prominent Muslims were members of the Indian National Congress, though the League ultimately claimed to speak on behalf of all of Indian Muslims. When partition finally took place, it drove the greater population into disastrous turmoil: hundreds of thousands lost their lives and millions became refugees. About 7.2 million Indian Muslims migrated to Pakistan, forming about one-fourth of the population of West Pakistan.[2] On the other side, about 5.5 million Hindus and Sikhs left Pakistan for India.

The two states subsequently acquired extraregional, mutually exclusive allies, became ideological rivals, and were shaped by quite different organizing principles. All of this happened despite a common history and geography, very similar cultural roots and economic systems, and a strategic environment that had been shared for centuries.

Partition was made even more complicated by the existence of a third vision of South Asia, that of the hundreds of princely and autonomous states, although only a half dozen really counted. Though nominally independent, even the major ones—Jammu and Kashmir, Hyderabad, Junagadh—were bound to New Delhi by treaty and by their inferior military capability.* The British saw to it that no princely state acquired modern military hardware in any significant amount and that the princely armies were deployed and manned in such a way as to ensure that they would never serve as the basis for a breakaway movement. This control strategy was applied during World War II when many of the princely armies were brought into the regular Indian army. The British exerted similar control through their treaties with the princes and attendant political advisers residing in the state capitals. These ensured that the rulers did not stray in the direction of independence

*In this book I usually refer to the state simply as Kashmir, or J&K. It is now divided into Indian-controlled and Pakistan-controlled administrative units in the respective countries.

and that affairs of state remained within boundaries tolerated by the British. The quid pro quo was that when a ruler got into trouble, he (or rarely she) could usually count on British military and political support. By and large the system worked at very little cost to the British, as exemplified by Hyderabad, a princely state larger than France with a predominantly Hindu population and a Muslim ruler, known as the nizam. The British provided advice and security to the (Muslim) nizam, who presided over a cluster of smaller Hindu rulers, who in turn governed a largely Hindu population, albeit one with a sizable Muslim minority in one of India's most stable regions—now the state of Andhra Pradesh.[3] Some of these princes, including the nizam at one point, had thoughts of independence, but the costs of challenging the British were steep, and the rewards for loyalty, both fiscal and symbolic, were substantial, as was the assurance of British support against any usurpers.

When partition did come, the Indian princes were strongly advised by the British to choose either India or Pakistan. The visions of a future India and Pakistan rubbed against the ambitions of some of the princes, with the result that the rush to force them to join one or the other ignited several significant conflicts.

Although technically the decision to accede was in the hands of the ruler, not the ruled, India used force to incorporate Hyderabad and Junagadh (another largely Hindu state with a Muslim ruler). But it also proposed a plebiscite in the cases of Junagadh and Jammu and Kashmir, the latter a largely Muslim state with a Hindu ruler. The offer to Kashmir, subsequently regretted by Indian diplomats, came at a moment when the Indian and Pakistani armies were inconclusively battling for control of the state, and the stalemate has continued ever since.

The decision to coerce Hyderabad (in the middle of India) and Junagadh (on the western India-Pakistan border), both Muslim-ruled states with Hindu majorities, into joining India generated anger and unease about Indian intentions. Meanwhile, the handling of Kashmir, a Muslim-majority state with a Hindu ruler, sparked a conflict that would become the focus of competition between India and Pakistan for the next sixty years. This dispute reinforced Pakistan's notion that the army was the most critical institution for the survival and advancement of the nation, which was to have a detrimental effect on Pakistan's political order.

In the short view, it seemed natural that the British Empire should be succeeded by only a few states. The Raj itself rose from the ashes of the Mughal Empire, which in turn was the heir to several regional empires. In the long view, stretching over two millennia, states of the subcontinent emerged in a pattern of imperial advance and retreat, of a single dominant power and then diverse and often competing centers of power. No iron law decrees that South Asia should be dominated by one state, or even two states. Indeed, other regions—China, Europe—have had their integrative moments as well, followed by long spells of competition and rivalry among the fragments.[4]

The periods of imperial retreat were not necessarily marked by stagnation; modern historiography points to important cultural, economic, and even military developments during the many hundreds of years when South Asia was politically less united. Of equal significance here, these years saw the rise of durable regional and subregional political, economic, and cultural alignments. Some of these endured for centuries, especially in South India and along India's western coast, while Afghanistan was under North India's thumb. As a result, even when South Asia was ruled from North India or Delhi, regional powers were usually in a bargaining position with the more powerful rulers.[5]

Bloodbath and Independence

On July 18, 1947, Britain's Parliament passed the India Independence Act and less than a month later, on August 14 and 15, respectively, declared India and Pakistan independent sovereign states. The dates were staggered to allow the last viceroy of India, Lord Louis Mountbatten, to travel from India to Pakistan for the transfer of power. He was then appointed governor-general of India, but in Pakistan the title was assumed by Jinnah to spite Mountbatten, who in his view was too pro-Indian and too much under the influence of Jawaharlal Nehru, the leading Indian politician of his generation.

The vast catastrophe called Partition was prefigured in the ghastly Calcutta riots of 1946. I deal with its impact on the memories of citizens of both states later in the book; suffice to say that it shaped the views of millions of Indians and Pakistanis, especially those who were forced to migrate from one state or another, or who were the victims (or perpetrators) of atrocities. Many of their memories, often in wildly distorted versions of the truth, have been passed on to second and third generations.

Important stories of members of both communities who helped or rescued members of a different faith are mostly undocumented. The great authors and cultural figures who recognized and opposed Partition go unmentioned. Even official history projects in both countries pay little attention to these stories and are devoted mainly to building national solidarity around negatives: distrust or hatred of another religious or ethnic community.

This is true of both countries, but not in equal measure. Taking the moral high ground, India has always seen itself as the regional power that does not need Pakistan and as the prime inheritor of the Raj's legacy of subcontinental dominance. Pakistan, as the smaller and militarily weaker of the two states, has assumed a more defensive and also a more assertive posture, strikingly reminiscent of Israel's stance. In keeping with these attitudes, India rejects outside support, whereas Pakistan cultivates it. In the case of Kashmir, Indians work hard to ignore what steps might change the status quo, whereas Pakistan is eager to seize upon them. India, which once sought UN intervention in Kashmir, now abhors it, and Indian diplomats scramble mightily to prevent it from being raised in *any* forum in the world, even as their government has been unable to accommodate or suppress Kashmiri separatists and pro-Pakistani factions. On the other side, generations of Pakistanis have been taught to believe that fundamentally India has not come to terms with Pakistan's existence. This overall narrative was reinforced and legitimized by the educational curricula in both countries, perpetuating the divide in successive generations, and the role of partition in feeding this narrative is well documented.

As for the more material consequences, the second partition (which gave East Bengal independence) was also important. In 1947 India and Pakistan constituted 94 percent of the South Asian land mass (not including Afghanistan) and 96 percent of its population. After the creation of Bangladesh out of the former East Pakistan in 1971 these figures changed: Pakistan was reduced by half in population and size. Today, with the loss of East Pakistan, Pakistan accounts for 12 percent of the total population of South Asia, 18 percent of the land mass, and 8.5 percent of the total economy. Its military spending remains very high, about 22 percent of government expenditure.[6] India spends much more on defense, about US$44.4 billion next to Pakistan's $5.6 billion, although as a proportion of GNP defense spending is about 2.7–2.8 percent for both. Nevertheless, Pakistan is falling behind India in terms of overall defense spending and conventional weaponry, which has propelled its nuclear acquisition program; it probably has more nuclear weapons than India, although exact figures are difficult to come by.

From the outset, both states benefited from institutions established by the British: a strong bureaucracy, a functioning judiciary, and a professional military. Contrary to its current status, however, Pakistan's army did not start out as the strongest institution in the state. Very few Pakistanis filled the ranks above colonel, and for a number of years key positions were held by British officers, who even served as the army's first two chiefs. At the same time, Pakistan had a uniting figure in a native son, Mohammed Ali Jinnah. Meanwhile, India had not only Nehru and Mahatma Gandhi but also a much stronger second and third tier of leaders.

Created in two parts or wings, with the more populous but militarily weaker East separated from the West by 1,000 miles of Indian territory,

Pakistan held a critically important strategic position. Yet the chaos of partition left it with a proportionately weaker state capacity than India's, as well as limited financial resources. Many Pakistanis also claimed that India had not fulfilled its part of the bargain when it came to sharing military assets, which quickly bred suspicion throughout official Pakistan, but especially the army—where it became one of the institution's treasured grievances. Thus right off the bat Pakistan viewed India as a hostile neighbor and considered itself vulnerable to India's malevolence, which meant that the Pakistan army's primary role from the beginning would be to counter India's enmity. Actually, the lesson drawn by both sides in the aftermath of partition and the ensuing wars and crises was that some military capability directed against the other was a prime necessity. Each saw the other as its most serious security threat, second only to the consolidation and absorption of the princely states.

Four Crises

India-Pakistan relations were greatly affected by four post-partition crises, three of them involving the princely states of Kashmir (see chapters 5 and 6), Hyderabad, and Junagadh. A fourth crisis revolved around the 1950 communal riots in East Bengal, which led the two rivals to sign the Nehru-Liaquat Pact protecting minority rights.[7]

In the case of Junagadh, trouble erupted when on August 15, 1947, its Muslim ruler acceded to Pakistan, which welcomed the move. Junagadh's largely Hindu public responded with massive protests, however, which prompted Indian forces to occupy the state on November 9, 1947, whereupon the ruler reversed himself and acceded to India (on the border, the weak Pakistani forces were unable to intervene in the state). On February 20, 1948, India held a referendum on the accession, and the state's population voted in favor of it.

As for Kashmir, its maharaja toyed with the idea of independence but changed his mind when the state came under attack from Pakistani raiders and was granted armed assistance from India. He then acceded to India, handing over powers of defense, communication, and foreign affairs. Both India and Pakistan agreed that the accession would be confirmed by a referendum once hostilities had ceased.

By May 1948 the Indian army had regained control over much, but not all, of Kashmir, and the regular Pakistan army was called upon to mount an offense. The war ended on January 1, 1949, when a cease-fire was arranged by the United Nations, which recommended that both India and Pakistan abide by their commitment to hold a referendum in the state. The two sides agreed to establish a cease-fire line where the fighting had stopped, which became a de facto border monitored by a UN peacekeeping force, but the referendum was never held.

Initially Hyderabad's ruler also believed that he could sustain an independent existence. Although the state was physically distant from Pakistan, he was assured its political and moral support. After months of negotiations with Indian officials, Nehru decided to use force to annex the state. Though a liberal internationalist, he was prompted by his tough home minister, Sardar Vallabhai Patel, who was less enamored of international mediation and peacemaking after the experience in Kashmir and who argued that India could not accept a hostile (and very large) independent state at its very core. In a police action termed Operation Polo, the Indian army swept through Hyderabad state, easily defeating the armed militias, known as Razakars.

The fourth crisis, centered in Pakistan's East Bengal, arose following the widespread massacre of its Hindu residents after partition, which sent thousands of Hindus fleeing to India. Reminded of the 1946 Calcutta bloodbath, Indians responded with a welling up of anti-Muslim feelings. A perplexed Nehru adopted a strategy of moving Indian armed forces closer to East Pakistan. Given the weakness of Pakistani forces in East Bengal, there was no realistic way Pakistan could stop them. After several crisis-filled months, Nehru and the Pakistani prime minister, Liaquat Ali Khan, agreed each country should protect its minorities and called for separate investigations of the communal situation on each side of their borders.

Throughout this crisis Great Britain was actively engaged on the diplomatic scene. Two of India's three service chiefs and all of Pakistan's were British—they provided London with up-to-the minute accounts of each government's policies, which were sometimes communicated to the other side. The United States regarded the conflict as tertiary, however, despite Prime Minister Liaquat's strong pitch to the Truman administration for military assistance.

Meanwhile, domestic public opinion on both sides became inflamed, nearly swamping the leadership with its rhetoric of crisis and war. Nehru and Liaquat agreed to a stopgap in the hope that a forthcoming UN mission might bring a resolution to the Kashmir conflict. Nevertheless, the overall pattern was by then set: *Pakistan concluded that its military weakness allowed India to push it around; India felt that the Pakistanis had not given up on the two-nation theory that had broken India up to begin with.*

These various conflicts, individually and collectively, drove home several "lessons" to Indian and Pakistani politicians, bureaucrats, and generals that have become embedded in their national narratives:

—The duplicity of the other side.

—The mixed role of international intervention—both sides sought it but only to pin the blame on the other.

—Indian eagerness to use force and coercion when it was in a dominant position, justified by alleged violations against Hindus in Pakistan.

—Pakistani willingness to play the Muslim card, especially the inflammatory idea of Hindus and Muslims constituting two separate nations.

—The tight link between domestic politics and foreign policy to the point where they were considered inseparable.

On both sides conservatives and fundamentalists egged on the leadership. Soon relations between India and Pakistan took on the qualities of a "communal riot with armor," a term I first heard from General "Monty" Palit, one of the ablest of the wartime entries into the Indian army.

More Wars and Crises

Pakistan's military vulnerability and the death by 1951 of its two dominant political figures, Jinnah and Liaquat Ali Khan, helped solidify army influence. Unlike India, with a strong Congress Party governing most of the country, Pakistan saw the Muslim League quickly deteriorate and the army (aligned with the bureaucracy) emerge as its most powerful institution. It then gained military hardware in the mid-1950s when it joined two U.S.-led treaty organizations—the Baghdad Pact (later the Central Treaty Organization, CENTO) and the Manila Pact (later the South East Asia Treaty Organization, SEATO). However, these failed to provide Pakistan the security guarantee it sought against India.

Instead, Great Britain and the United States maintained cordial ties with India until the mid-1960s, particularly from about 1959 onward when it actually moved close to the Western powers as a consequence of their shared fears of communist China.[8] Indeed, India bought significant weapons from America and even received some grant assistance for its military.

These foreign links may have facilitated the single most important peaceful agreement between India and Pakistan, the Indus Waters Treaty of 1960. The brainchild of the World Bank, the treaty contains a mechanism for arbitration and has worked—almost flawlessly—for fifty years, even though it has been a less-than-optimal solution to the problem of dividing the Indus waters between the two states. In the absence of any further agreements of this magnitude and because of a huge increase in demand, the 1960 treaty does not match up with contemporary demands.

When war broke out in 1965, this time it was triggered by the miscalculations of President Ayub Khan and his youthful foreign minister Zulfikar Ali Bhutto, who had become wary of India's growing military power, now fortified by American, British, and Soviet military hardware. The two tried to instigate a Kashmiri revolt and put pressure on India to negotiate on Kashmir, but the war ended in a stalemate. The United States suspended military aid to both countries and stood aside while the Soviet Union brokered a peace agreement in Tashkent. This reinforced the strategic status quo but was to have a deep effect on Pakistan's unity.[9] Ayub had declared during the war that East Pakistan could not be effectively defended (it was nearly encircled by India), which contributed to East Bengal's estrangement.

In 1971 East Bengali nationalism, fermenting for years, erupted into rebellion. Aided by a huge covert operation, in which Bengali-speaking Indian officers "resigned" their commissions to advise Bengali separatist forces, culminating in a direct Indian military intervention, the East broke away, forming the new state of Bangladesh. What remained of Pakistan came to be dominated by Punjabis, who made up almost 58 percent of the "new" Pakistani population, compared with 30 percent in undivided Pakistan. Coincidentally, they were also the largest ethnic/linguistic group in the army, thus bringing Pakistan's center of political power into alignment with its center of military power. More worrisome from a strategic perspective, the army and the political leadership, humiliated by India's victory, were bent on revenge, something blissfully ignored by victorious India.

For its part, New Delhi assumed that Pakistan was no longer a serious rival. When Prime Minister Indira Gandhi made peace with Bhutto, she failed to resolve still-remaining differences over Kashmir and a host of minor disputes, although in 1983, just before she was assassinated, she did establish a joint commission with Pakistan supposedly outside the political and military arenas. Its four subcommissions were to explore a host of items: trade, health, sports, science, consular issues, travel, and tourism.[10] She also agreed to a declaration on the South Asian Regional Cooperation (SARC) organization, the predecessor to the South Asian Association for Regional Cooperation (SAARC), but Pakistan vetoed an Indian proposal for a ministerial-level council.

This movement toward cooperation subsided when Pakistani governments began meddling in Indian affairs, notably in Kashmir. Indians came to view Pakistan as the most significant destabilizing force in the region and as part of an encircling alliance of hostile powers, which included its sponsors in Beijing and Washington.[11] For at least a decade the Indians suspected that America, China, and Pakistan were fearful of a resurgent India. In fact, India's rise was being hampered by its own dysfunctional economy, its incapacity to come to grips with a still-recalcitrant Pakistan, and its continuing military dependence on the Soviet Union. The latter proved especially embarrassing when the Soviet Union invaded Afghanistan in 1979 without even informing India. This was the beginning of a long Indian search for an alternative friend among the world's great powers.

Between 1987 and 2002 India and Pakistan faced another four crises, made a few aborted moves toward normalization, and saw the derailment of the Joint Commission.[12] No crisis evolved into a major war, and even the Kargil War of 1999 remained limited. At the same time, none of the steps to mitigate their rivalry were noticeably effective, including the Composite Dialogue introduced to address issues of terrorism. Moreover, the acquisition of nuclear weapons in both countries by the early 1980s added a new dimension to the rivalry. Yet both sides had also learned valuable lessons about the limits of conflict in attempting to achieve national objectives. The result was a period of relative stability and maturity in bilateral engagement, although not necessarily irreversible progress.

This cursory overview of the India-Pakistan relationship sets the stage for two central themes of this book. First, both India and Pakistan are modeled upon the modern nation-state, a model that is in some cases being imposed on peoples who share a weak national identity and marginal allegiance to the central state, as compared with their regional and linguistic affiliations. Second, the very legitimacy or "idea" of India and Pakistan as constituted at present is challenged by some, but not all, in the other country, a challenge that has deep roots in prewar relations between contesting images of the subcontinent's future.

These factors led the two states to become enduring enemies, each considering itself vulnerable to the other. Their shared and contested origins as modern states have also sparked the fear on both sides that their populations are not entirely loyal and that there are outsiders who do not mean them well. This thinking in turn makes it tempting to entertain the idea of turning unhappy populations against their neighbor's center. The view in Pakistani security circles is that even if Kashmir cannot be wrested from India, Pakistan's support for the Kashmiris will force India to divert resources to containing Kashmiri discontent. Conversely, Indians are in favor of tacit or sometimes explicit support for dissident Pakistani minority groups, as epitomized in the massive support provided to the Bangladeshi separatist movement in 1970–71. In sum, fears echo back and forth between the two countries, reinforcing paranoia in both.

Expectations

That paranoia received an early spark from British expectations regarding the wisdom and consequences of creating a larger India and a smaller

Pakistan. Another contributing factor was Britain's timing of the split, which was not guided by a realistic assessment of the difficulties of simultaneously dividing British India and incorporating the princely states into one of the two successor states.

British Concerns

Britain's Labor government was primarily concerned with the possible loss of British lives and with Britain's feeble global position. If the Indians and Pakistanis really wanted independence, the British argued, they might as well get it sooner than they expected. This was the attitude of Lord Mountbatten, who had been made viceroy in part because of his closeness to Jawaharlal Nehru and other Indian leaders. Mountbatten's charm and British haste carried the day, with catastrophic results. Mountbatten's temperament and that of his political superiors could be gauged by the countdown calendar he commissioned and distributed to his staff: when August 15 came, the Raj would be gone.

The consequences of partition are the subject of hundreds of books, but they are nowhere better summarized than in "Partition," a poem by W. H. Auden describing the plight of Sir Cyril Radcliff, a British administrator having no familiarity with the Indian subcontinent who chaired the committees set up to define the boundaries of the new India and Pakistan. His lack of experience in South Asia, which was even less than Mountbatten's, and its bitter flavor are evident in the following excerpt:

Having never set eyes on the land he was called to partition
Between two peoples fanatically at odds,
With their different diets and incompatible gods.

He got down to work, to the task of settling the fate
Of millions. The maps at his disposal were out of date
And the Census Returns almost certainly incorrect,

But in seven weeks it was done, the frontiers decided,
A continent for better or worse divided.[13]

Those who knew the region's security problems were less optimistic. A few British generals thought that Pakistan could serve as India's bulwark, guarding the North-West Frontier Province as the British had for a century. Indeed, Pakistan Army Headquarters moved into the old Northern Command of the (British) Indian army. However, most British senior officers were skeptical. One of the Raj's greatest generals and its last commander in chief, Field Marshal Claude Auchinleck, was dubious about some of his subordinates' enthusiasm for Pakistan, which in his view would at best be a second-rate power, unable to cope with any serious threat: "From the purely military and strategical aspect, . . . it must be concluded that the provision of adequate insurance in the shape of reasonably good defensive arrangements for Pakistan would be a most difficult and expensive business, and that no guarantee of success could be given."[14]

Those who like Auchinleck opposed partition pleaded in vain for a more measured withdrawal. In the especially relevant view of most British Indian army generals, Auchinleck being the most experienced, the division of India into two states was not really necessary, and all were enraged over the way it was rushed. Thirty years after the event, he caustically referred to this period as the most difficult in his entire professional career.[15] This view was echoed by one of the most capable British civil servants of the period, Sir Philip Mason, author of several classic studies of India, its bureaucracy, and army.

Among outside observers, the United States was sympathetic to the Indian nationalist movement but gave little thought to the prospect of Pakistan. Washington—especially President Franklin D. Roosevelt—saw British India as an unsustainable manifestation of colonialism, although he tempered his views to avoid alienating America's British ally during World War II (India was the site of several major bases for American forces that operated in Burma, resupplied the Chinese Nationalists, and gained access to Southeast Asia). After partition, America believed the United Nations should be the mechanism used to resolve the Kashmir issue but avoided taking sides, and eventually the Truman administration resigned itself to the situation on the ground.

Stalin's Soviet Union at first saw India as ripe for revolution, although its support for communists in India soured Nehru and other Indian leaders. Later, the Soviet Union supported India's position on Kashmir and provided massive military aid for this campaign. Soviet policy, like that of the United States, was driven by the need to gather allies in South Asia for the larger cold war struggle.

Indian and Pakistani Views

The impending partition of British India met with differences of opinion throughout the subcontinent, with strong pro-Pakistani sentiments in some regions, opposition in others. The demand for an independent Pakistan (which did not really acquire much political weight until the late 1930s) was strongest in areas of greatest Hindu-Muslim tension, notably the northern Indian plains, parts of the Bombay Presidency, and Bengal. In these regions the "two-nation theory" was a rallying cry for Muslims, a notable proponent being the poet-philosopher Allama Iqbal. In this view, Hindus and Muslims were two separate "nations," each deserving its own state.

Aligarh Muslim University, founded in 1875 by Sir Syed Ahmed Khan, the first major Muslim reformist-educationalist in British India, was a center of pro-Pakistan thought, and a large number of Pakistani politicians and soldiers studied there. These included Iqbal, whose writings inspired the Pakistan movement in the 1930s; Pakistan's first two prime ministers; its second and third governor-generals; and even, briefly, Ayub Khan, who later seized power in a military coup. Some Indians regarded Aligarh with suspicion (and still do) and moved to establish another "nationalist," that is, explicitly pro-Indian, Muslim university, Jamia Milia, in New Delhi.

Ironically, the Pakistan movement was weakest in several provinces that became part of the new state of Pakistan, notably the North-West Frontier Province, Baluchistan, and Sindh. This meant that the most enthusiastic supporters of Pakistan, many of them migrants to the new state, found themselves living in a population that was less than dedicated to the idea of a new, Islamic state. But its supporters were not of one mind in their vision. Iqbal, for example, saw Pakistan as a step on the road to a greater Muslim South Asian community. The far more secular Jinnah, whose brilliance and acumen actually brought about Pakistan's independence, wanted a homeland for Muslims, but not necessarily a nation made up entirely of Muslims. He, and many of the important Muslim landed gentry, considered themselves binational; they would live in "Pakistan" but retain homes in what was to become India, and they envisioned normal relations between the two successor states. Indeed, one of Jinnah's proposals was that Pakistan would become a province within a larger Indian entity, not a separate state.

Some proponents of independence favored a very loose political order with a high degree of regional autonomy and with some ties to India, as reflected in the actual Pakistani constitution, which envisions the country as a federation. By contrast, India's central government—the Union—has the power to create or alter individual states. The possibility of a "Pakistan" existing within India was always considered an option, but in the end the terms and conditions of such an arrangement were beyond agreement. The critical point insisted upon by Jinnah and the Muslim League was a separate army—something that the British had not planned for.

Many did not subscribe to Jinnah's latter-day moderate vision of Pakistan, however, especially Islamists such as Maulana Maudoodi and other leaders of the militant Jamaat-i-Islami (JI) movement.[16] A few regional leaders saw the British departure as an opportunity to gain or keep provincial autonomy and never subscribed to the idea of a strong central government in Pakistan; others wanted a more orthodox and Islamic Pakistan—Iqbal's model. After years of wrangling, Pakistan acquired a constitution that was in theory federal but in fact had strong centralizing tendencies, although it lacked the kind of political and cultural movement that would create the social basis for a centralized state. In particular, it had a weak civil service and increasingly powerful military, while the landlords and the "feudals" wanted to be left alone, secure in their regional position. Pakistan has since been ruled by an alliance between this conservative establishment and the army.

Because Muslims were not well represented in British India's civil and military bureaucracies—they had not turned to education as fervently as had Hindus—and their overall number was far lower, most supported partition. It would, they argued, provide jobs and promotions faster than an undivided India. This was especially the view of Muslim army officers, most of whom held a lower rank than their Hindu counterparts.

For India's large Sikh community, which lived primarily in the Punjab, the prospect of partition was alarming—and rightly so. It was devastated by partition, suffering more than any other community forced to migrate in vast numbers to India. The dream of an independent Sikh state mirroring Muslim Pakistan lingered and later burst out (with Pakistani help) in the form of a Khalistan movement in the 1980s. This was eventually contained by the Indian government.

Indian Hindus had mixed views of the wisdom of creating a separate Muslim state in South Asia. A few, such as B. R. Ambedkar, a prominent leader of the lowest Hindu castes (known variously as untouchables, scheduled castes, and now Dalits), welcomed an independent Pakistan on the grounds that Muslim soldiers and officers would then be concentrated in the new state rather than in India, where they would be a political threat to the government. His logic was forceful: get the most powerful element of the army (Punjabi Muslims) out of India, where they would cause political mischief; without them the Indian army would be easier to control. It was also prescient: the army became a major force in Pakistan, rising to dominance in large part because Punjab was both the political and military center of the country. By contrast, India's Punjab—split again by the creation of Haryana in 1966—was neither a military nor a political center of power.

Mahatma Gandhi and Jawaharlal Nehru did not see eye to eye on the creation of Pakistan, Gandhi calling it a disaster (he was willing to make Jinnah the prime minister of an undivided India to avoid partition). He was later reviled by Hindu extremists for urging India to be more responsible in the division of assets between the two countries—this "softness" toward Pakistan may have been the motive behind his assassination in 1948. Nehru, who did become the new India's first prime minister, agreed to partition but assumed that Pakistan, divided by a thousand miles of India, was not a permanent fixture. As the eminent social psychologist Ashis Nandy has written, Nehru expected Pakistan to collapse within months, thinking that a theocratic state could not survive in the contemporary world.[17] Like Israel, it was a historical aberration, argued Nehru and other Indians, a throwback to the religious states of the eighteenth and nineteenth centuries. Nehru had little reason to offer concessions to Pakistan, especially over Kashmir, which was for him an emotional as well as strategic issue. This was the general view held in the dominant Indian National Congress, with Sardar Patel being the most pessimistic about Pakistan's chances and the need for India to cooperate with the new state.

Hindu conservatives harbored more visceral anti-Pakistani attitudes, which partition only intensified. Veer Savarkar, then the leader of the militant Hindu revivalist group Rashtriya Swayamsevak Sangh (RSS), had opposed partition on the grounds that India was a cultural and religious entity with a Muslim minority that did not merit the privilege of becoming a separate state. Although he agreed with the "two-nation" theory, he did not believe that Muslims deserved any such reward, especially since RSS hagiography indicated they had conquered an innocent and vulnerable India by military oppression and forced conversions. A later faction of Indian political conservatives supported normalization with Pakistan, arguing that a religious state was not anathema, and that a Muslim Pakistan could exist alongside a Hindu India. However, the large numbers of Hindu refugees, especially from Sindh and Punjab, strengthened the anti-Pakistani sentiments of the militant RSS and later its associated political parties, the Jana Sangh Party and the Bharatiya Janata Party (BJP).[18]

These diverse views about the creation of Pakistan and partition can be summed up as follows:

—The two entities could live as separate if not quite equal states, as pragmatic rivals that might be able to cooperate (the view of Jinnah and of Gandhi).

—Pakistan could be the forerunner of a larger Islamist awakening, one that would eventually affect India's Muslim population (Iqbal's view and, to some extent, that of today's Jamaat-i-Islami).

—Pakistan could not be sustained as a modern state; its Islamic identity was an anomaly, and it would eventually be absorbed into India or broken up (Nehru's view and that of many Congress Party members).

—An independent Pakistan would represent a civilizational challenge to India and thus be an unacceptable entity (the RSS view).

—Pakistan's ethnic balances (the dominance of the Punjab) would present a political problem to democratic India, and separate but unequal status was desirable (Ambedkar's view).

The differences between India and Pakistan at partition were important, although sometimes ignored amid the rhetoric of a shared culture, geography, climate, and geostrategic location, or the manufactured myth of eternal Hindu-Muslim conflict. For one thing, the division of British India's two major provinces, Punjab and Bengal, produced very different successor provinces (in Pakistan) or states (in India). First, East Pakistan retained a large Hindu population, whereas West Punjab purged its Hindu minorities. Second, Pakistan's Punjab was the heartland of the increasingly powerful army, but very few soldiers came from the predominantly Bengali East Pakistan. Third, East Pakistan was largely rural, having been cut off from the great metropolitan area of Calcutta, once India's most industrialized city. As a result, there was a vast economic gap between East and West Pakistan, notably the prosperous Punjab.

The formal identities of the two new countries differed markedly as well, with Pakistan considered an Islamic republic and India a secular state. Of course, from the very beginning there were and still are many secular elements in the state of Pakistan, while religious identity is an important factor in India's politics and society; Pakistan has struggled longer and with greater difficulty to translate these overarching "ideas" into a workable reality, in the form of practical educational and political principles. Although both began life as poor states, with pockets of wealth and rudimentary industrial capabilities, they followed very different development philosophies. Nehru and the Congress Party set India on the road to modernization by engaging in modest land reform and increasing the power of the state in promoting industrial development. Fatally, Pakistan neglected land reform, largely because the leadership of the Muslim League was drawn from the landed aristocracy. On balance, however, West Pakistan became far more prosperous than most parts of India.

Mind the Gap

The surprise of India-Pakistan relations is how little they have changed over six decades, with the notable exception of the separation of East Pakistan (which some still feel portends the eventual breakup of the rest of the state). Relations between states are often summarized as "up" or "down," "better" or "worse," or, invoking a climatic metaphor, "cooler" or "warmer." Such terms are often wheeled in to describe complex trends, but they are unable to capture the full range of relations between states. To illustrate, how should relations between democracies be summarized when some may have strained political or strategic relations at the governmental level, for example, yet have lively cultural links or ideological ties? The complexities are even greater in the case of India and Pakistan, where numerous factors are in play, from the physical, sociocultural, and economic attributes of the overall region to the attitudes, some of which generate violence while others produce attempts at formal and informal cooperation.

Perhaps there is no better example of "distant neighbors" than these two states. To invoke Winston Churchill's comment about America and Britain, one might say India and Pakistan are divided by *several* common languages. Officials on both sides speak the same words but frequently mean different things. Even more important, there is no single axis around which the relationship can pivot. Instead, suspicion and hostility fill the space. The pathologies of India-Pakistan relations are well captured in the authoritative study of Pakistan's negotiating strategies with New Delhi carried out by the experienced American diplomats in South Asia, Ambassadors Howard and Teresita Schaffer.[19]

If intraregional trade in "goods, capital, and ideas" is taken to mean regional integration, as defined by the World Bank, South Asia is one of the least integrated areas of the world.[20] In 2004 it was the only developing region (as also defined by the World Bank) in which intraregional trade accounted for less than 5 percent of its world trade. In this definition, the flow of ideas is crudely measured by the cross-border movement of people, the number of telephone calls, or the purchase of technology and royalty payments. In South Asia, for example, only 7 percent of international telephone calls are regional, compared with 71 percent in East Asia.

As countries attempt to ensure their competitiveness in an increasingly globalized economy, they form regional trading blocs as a preferred strategy. By some estimates, more than 100 regional trading arrangements are in effect today.[21] Although South Asia has progressed significantly in integrating with the global economy, its regional integration has been negligible.

The first attempt at a regional grouping in the region was the Colombo Plan, developed after the 1950 Commonwealth Conference of Foreign Ministers and designed to improve regional living standards. A number of countries, including two dozen non-Commonwealth states, are members. The plan facilitates modest bilateral assistance for regional states and is devoted by and large to social and economic development.

The first truly regional organization grew out of the signing of the 2004 South Asian Free Trade Area (SAFTA) agreement, which led to the creation of the South Asian Association for Regional Cooperation (SAARC) in the same year. Despite these moves, South Asia's most important export markets remain in North America and the European Union.[22] In fact, Nepal is the only South Asian country with a substantial intraregional trade presence: just under 55 percent of its exports and imports by value are traded intraregionally, almost all with India. (See chapter 2 for further discussion of regional economic development and chapter 5 for the prospects of enhanced trade.)

One of the reasons for South Asia's weak integration is its relatively protectionist stance, as evidenced by the ratios of its exports and imports to GDP, which are lower than the world average, as well as its import tariffs, which are the highest of any developing region in the world.[23] South Asia is also weak in facilitating trade. Compared with East Asia, it registers the worst performance in every major category of trade facilitation, from ports to customs to regulations to services.[24]

On the other hand, informal or illegal trade is high and is widely assumed to represent an unlocked potential for trade—a signal that the countries' economies are complementary.[25] According to some estimates, the value of goods smuggled from India to Pakistan ranges from $200 million to $10 billion.[26] Implicitly, a high volume of illegal trade due to a lack of regional integration can be remedied by state measures designed to remove artificial barriers to trade.

The positive scenario for South Asia is that when regional integration and cooperation increase, connectivity will improve, restrictions on trade will be reduced, landlocked countries will be given full access to markets, energy shortages will be eased, and growth and investment will rise. It is widely assumed that this bottom-up approach would help improve the environment for regional politics, increase welfare, and promote peace and stability.[27] In the real world, however, this scenario's arrival date is always in the future.

The Violence Factor

South Asia—led by India and Pakistan—is also one of the most violent (or least peaceful) regions of the world, whether because of the states' internal disorder or turbulent relations between them. According to the Global Peace Index (GPI), an authoritative comparison of violence within and between states, South Asia (including Afghanistan, Bangladesh, Bhutan, India, Nepal, Pakistan, Sri Lanka) is the third most violent region in the world.[28] The GPI, which is developed by a web-based think tank called Vision of Humanity, applies to a UN-defined list of nineteen regions. South Asia ranks behind only Middle Africa and Northern Africa (GPI 2.387) on the violence scale. At the other end of the spectrum, Northern Europe ranks as the most peaceful

(GPI 1.474). The index is based on domestic violence and the prevalence of violence between states. Within South Asia, Afghanistan is the least peaceful, followed by Pakistan and then India. The most peaceful state in the region is Bhutan (GPI 1.481). Former British India—today's India, Pakistan, and Bangladesh—has a GPI of 2.484, which is higher than that of even Northern Africa. Although one may disagree with how the index is defined, it points to clear trends for each state (and for pairs of states). Given their several wars and multiple crises, India and Pakistan ranked with the most dangerous pairs in the world, and the nuclearization of their conflict makes the stakes attending their rivalry even higher.

Polls and Public Attitudes

Not surprisingly, most polls show that Pakistanis and Indians are suspicious of each other and diverge in their approach to governance and politics. But polling often provides a limited measure of public opinion, as suggested by some differences in polling results regarding the attitudes of these two publics. A 2011 Pew poll, for example, indicated the Pakistani public's historic hostility toward India, whereas other polling has shown a large pro-India swing. India used to be identified as Pakistan's greatest threat, greater than al Qaeda or the Taliban, but recent polls indicate greater support for normalization: in a 2012 poll 62 percent of Pakistanis thought it important to improve relations with India.[29] And roughly two-thirds supported more bilateral trade and further talks to try to reduce tensions between the two nations. On the other hand, Pew's 2012 polling shows that 72 percent of Pakistanis see India in an unfavorable light, with more than half (55 percent) feeling *very* unfavorable toward their neighbor. Furthermore, 57 percent of Pakistanis see India as a *very* serious threat.[30]

According to other polls, Pakistanis are keenly aware that they are lagging behind India in terms of economic growth, while 44 percent consider India's increasing importance in world affairs a "critical threat."[31] These sentiments might suggest a heightened sensitivity to their military vulnerability, or possibly even a recognition of Pakistan's own mismanaged priorities, although when it comes to India's treatment of Muslim minorities—a traditionally sensitive issue for Pakistanis—opinions on Kashmir would suggest otherwise. In a 2008 World Public Opinion poll designed to measure public attitudes toward Kashmir, Pakistanis questioned the Indian government's ability to treat its Muslim populations responsibly. More than half of all Pakistanis polled recently viewed India as negligent in this regard.[32] Indeed, this theme has been a mainstay of the Pakistani press since 1947, rising to the fore again in late 2012 when the liberal English-language Pakistan press frequently cited the reelection of Gujarat's BJP minister Narendra Modi as evidence of the communalism of Indian politics.[33] As the polls also show, most Pakistanis disagree that their own government is supporting Islamist militancy in Kashmir or in India in general, or is to blame for terror in Pakistan. If anything, conservative Pakistanis freely accuse India of fomenting communal and sectarian violence in its neighbor.

Indian polls are a mirror image of those conducted in Pakistan, although they reflect somewhat reduced anger. When asked in 2011 to identify the biggest threat to India, 45 percent responded Pakistan, 19 percent Lashkar-e-Taiba (the terrorist Islamist organization), 16 percent the Naxalites (militant communist groups), and 7 percent China.[34] Indians widely believe the Pakistani government bears responsibility for terrorist attacks (not without a basis in fact): according to some polls, 47 percent believe that Pakistan has provided support to militant groups that attack civilians in Indian Kashmir, while 53 percent think it supports groups that attack Indians in general.[35] When polled about Kashmir, 45 percent of Indians believe Kashmiris want to stay within India, while only 10 percent think they desire independence.[36] As I discuss later in the book, Kashmiris themselves are far more in favor of autonomy or independence.

On a more positive note, the 2011 survey also found that 70 percent of Pakistanis and 74 percent of Indians consider improved relations important and support greater diplomatic and economic ties across the border on the assumption that this would promote economic development for both nations. This and the expressed support for increased bilateral trade (among 69 percent of Pakistanis and 67 percent of Indians) may mean that individual economic priorities outweigh the impact of political hostilities and may be a major test of any normalization process that attempts to work from the bottom up.[37] Although 2012 polls of nine countries show India has the lowest attitudes toward Pakistan, an overwhelming majority of respondents (77 percent) think it is important to resolve the Kashmir dispute, and 58 percent favor further talks to reduce India-Pakistan tensions.

When it comes to Pakistani views on the use of violence, the majority polled denounced violence perpetrated against the Indian population: 64 percent said attacks against government institutions, such as parliament, were never justified, and only 12 percent felt they were sometimes justified. When asked about specific targets, 68 percent condemned "attacks conducted against Indian . . . subways, stock exchanges, and tourist sites," whereas only 12 percent said these attacks were sometimes justified.[38] More interesting, almost a year after the assassination of Osama bin Laden, a Pew Global Attitudes poll found a marked changed in attitudes: 55 percent of Pakistani

Muslims now held an unfavorable view of al Qaeda and only 13 percent a favorable view, whereas just a year earlier 21 percent had expressed "confidence in bin Laden."[39]

Equally notable, while both perceive each other as threats, the desire for greater defense spending is low.[40] In both populations only 31 percent wished to see greater allocations for defense spending as opposed to the two other options of maintaining or reducing arms levels. Furthermore, a Gallup survey in 2001 asking about hypothetically sending aid to India in the wake of the 2001 Gujerat earthquake found an encouraging 80 percent in favor of such aid.[41]

Although recent surveys neglect to ask Pakistanis directly about the comparative threat of the United States and India, a joint initiative by the World Opinion Poll and the United States Institute for Peace in 2008 found 78 percent considered the American military presence in Afghanistan a critical threat, whereas 54 percent named India a critical threat.[42] This anticipated the 2012 Pakistani shift in policy toward India, as tensions with the United States mounted. In fact, India is a distant concern in some parts of the country, such as the Federally Administered Tribal Areas (FATA). When asked to rank threats to their personal safety—choosing between the United States, India, the Taliban in Pakistan, al Qaeda, Pakistan's Inter-Services Intelligence (ISI) Directorate, the Afghan Taliban, and Israel—America was mentioned most often, in 38 percent of the responses, and India in only 12 percent.[43]

As already mentioned and revealed in a particularly penetrating opinion study, Indians and Pakistanis differ significantly in their attitudes toward governance.[44] The reasons for this are many: historical antecedents in the two states, changing attitudes of successive governments, and the rise of different political and social movements that placed different stress on democracy as opposed to authoritarian ("firm") government. All South Asian states bear elements of their Raj legacy, but the differences between India and Pakistan in this regard become clearer when pubic opinion is depicted in the form of a "funnel" or inverted pyramid that subtracts (from the overall support of democracy) elements that would prefer another kind of state (figure 1-1).

To illustrate, 95 percent of Indians and 83 percent of Pakistanis support the idea of democracy with elected officials. However, if one subtracts those who are either indifferent or who would "prefer dictatorship sometimes," the pro-democracy faction shrinks to 73 percent for India and 45 percent for Pakistan. If those who prefer army rule are excluded, the bar drops to 59 percent for India and 19 percent for Pakistan. Similarly, excluding those who would prefer being ruled by "a king" brings the bar to 55 percent for India and 13 percent for Pakistan. If those who want a strong leader without

Figure 1-1. *Support for Democracy in India and Pakistan*

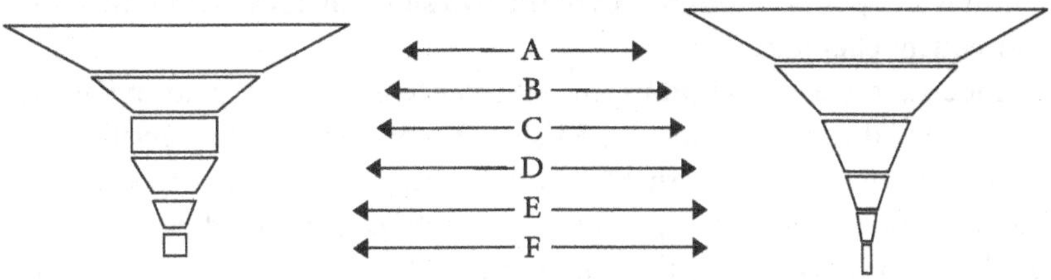

Source: Adapted from State of Democracy in South Asia project, 2008, p. 13; quoted in Philip Oldenburg, *India, Pakistan and Democracy: Solving the Puzzle of Divergent Paths* (New York: Routledge, 2010), p. 6.

A. Percentage of those who support government by elected leaders (India: 95 percent, Pakistan: 83 percent).

B. Excludes those who prefer dictatorship sometimes or are indifferent between democracy and dictatorship (India: 73 percent, Pakistan: 45 percent).

C. In addition, excludes those who want army rule (India: 59 percent, Pakistan: 19 percent).

D. In addition, excludes those who want rule by a king (India: 56 percent, Pakistan: 13 percent).

E. In addition, excludes those who want a strong leader without any democratic restraints (India: 40 percent, Pakistan: 10 percent).

F. In addition, excludes those who want rule by experts rather than politicians (India: 19 percent, Pakistan: 7 percent).

any democratic restraint are further excluded, the bar of support for democracy drops to 40 percent for India and 10 percent for Pakistan. Finally, when approval of the role of experts rather than politicians is excluded, Indian support for democracy falls to 19 percent and Pakistani support to only 7 percent. Drawing on these data, scholar Philip Oldenburg concludes that only 20 percent of Indians and 7 percent of Pakistanis support government by elected leaders without qualification. In other words, "the idea that the country should be governed by the army was endorsed by six out of every ten responses in Pakistan . . . [which is] one of the highest levels of support for army rule recorded in any part of the world."[45]

What most baffles outsiders (as well as Pakistanis) about both public opinion and policies in Pakistan is that they reflect a country aspiring to be a liberal democracy despite being part military autocracy. It seems that a neighbor's hostility has shaped Pakistan's domestic structure more than that of India, enabling the military to rule Pakistan for more than half of its life, while India has opted for a federalized, liberal democracy committed to secularism (most of the time). These differences are important not only as a springboard of attitudes on both sides but also as a barrier for some Indians who would like to normalize with a Pakistan that was in many respects close to it in ideology and purpose, although one cannot ignore the cultural and political differences of the two sides, themes that I return to in subsequent chapters.

Indeed, it is hard to find much congruence in Pakistani and Indian attitudes toward normalization. As Krishna Kumar puts it, their relations are divided by an iron curtain that "discourages any serious desire to know how the other thinks. And it keeps the two countries from building a common pool of knowledge about themselves and the world."[46] This mutual blind spot renders both populations vulnerable to being easily influenced by the limited and unchallenged narrative in the public consciousness about the other. With both publics greatly influenced by the media, biased educational curricula, and decades of observing hostile relations between the regimes, they hardly feel pressed to confront that narrative.

Writing on national cinema in India, culture and media expert Sumita Chakravarti explains that it may "be more a term of convenience, one that orients foreign audiences rather than reflects the social realities of the nation-group so designated."[47] This thought makes clear that discussions, programs, movies, and news reporting in both Pakistan and India should not be taken as a mirror of societal attitudes. On the other hand, the level of media attention does demonstrate which issues cause the most public consternation. When India or Pakistan show a miniseries on partition, for example, "millions in both countries are glued to their television sets and for weeks local newspapers are filled with letters and articles.[48]

Of course, a few commentators in Pakistan have appeared ready to criticize the media's obsession with mass-producing images of atrocities committed against Muslims in Kashmir, for instance.[49] The underlying intention of repeating these stories endlessly, they argue, is to highlight India's unreasonableness and lack of genuine interest in the well-being of Kashmiri citizens, as was the case in 1999 during the limited war between Indian and Pakistani forces in the Kargil region. The truth, however, is that the Pakistani media withdrew their support for the campaign once Pakistan was condemned by the international community, and that very few saw it as morally illegitimate in the first place.

Up until the late 1980s Pakistan's media were under tight state control, so their only option was to promulgate state narratives of India or revert to the legacy of pre-partition politics, spreading culpability to the British and their role in uprooting the Muslims of the subcontinent from their position of power.[50] With new and independent news channels arriving on the scene recently and foreign media sources more available, the public in both states is gaining greater access to information. Modern communications systems, including personal networking, now available cheaply and widely, have helped expand avenues of information as well. Nonetheless, preexisting stereotypes remain difficult to dispel, particularly when groups with anti-Indian political agendas have equally free reign to address the public. No good deed goes unpunished, however: in giving extremists as well as moderate voices electronic loudspeakers, the widespread democratizing of the media in both states has had the downside of making governments less able to govern.

In India the situation is complicated by the presence of a large Muslim minority, about 14 percent of the population. If the media portrayal of Muslims is taken to provide a good measure of how Pakistan is viewed, it may not be altogether evident that India seems to be dealing more constructively with its minorities than Pakistan, which is still focused on stereotypes.[51] This is partly because Muslims constitute an important market in the Indian economy and a growing force in Indian politics—offending almost one-fifth of consumers or voters is not a shrewd market strategy. The electronic media industry, in particular, has a considerable educated Muslim presence in urban areas.[52] Even so, Pakistan remains a negative presence—a causal factor in the identity crisis that Indian Muslims must deal with equally as much as with India's imperfect identity as a secular and inclusive state. In times of political tension, Indians are apt to distrust the Muslim community, on the assumption that if it undermined India's unity once, history may repeat itself. In the treatment of terrorists, for instance, even if the mention of Pakistan is taboo, the association is automatic, largely because a vocal segment of the public believes that Pakistan is a threat.[53] Discussions on the radio and letters to newspaper editors tirelessly reinforce the popular theory that Pakistan wants to dismember India.[54]

While Pakistanis are aware of India's economic progress, Indians are aware of its absence in Pakistan to the point of harboring "a coarse almost sordid image of day-to-day reality in Pakistan."[55] Even educated, liberal-minded Indians think the military's grip on the country is a reflection of a population prone to violence and narrow-mindedness. Kargil again serves to demonstrate public opinion. The Indian media were highly critical of the government's apparent "softness" in dealing with Pakistan's military incursions across the Line of Control.[56] But likewise, many Pakistanis, even those who are highly educated, exaggerate and distort the discrimination against Muslims that sometimes occurs in India.

Cooperation

With a few exceptions, the absence of deep and meaningful formal cooperation between New Delhi and Islamabad is a good measure of the region's weak integration (as already mentioned, the lowest in the world). No one expects them to cooperate, so it is surprising when they do.

Yet both sides agreed early on to avoid "any propaganda" regarding the amalgamation of Pakistan and India, including the establishment of any organization for this purpose. In 1950 Nehru and Liaquat Ali Khan signed an agreement further extending this commitment, specifying that it should apply to "terrorists" and support for secessionism. These agreements have never been operative, nor have subsequent agreements by the information ministers on both sides to refrain from hostile propaganda.

Forty years later they are still criticizing each other's positions on terrorism, propaganda, and support for separatists. When still another round of foreign secretary talks began in July 1990, the Indian preconditions for normalization were to be Pakistani statements dissociating the country from subversive activities in Kashmir, extraditing fugitives, and ceasing funding for separatists' activities in Kashmir. Pakistan, of course, replied that discussions on Kashmir were its own precondition.

However, several notable attempts have been made to "reset" the dialogue, most of them occurring after 2003 when the two sides agreed to a cease-fire on the Kashmir Line of Control, which still holds today.[57] A "composite dialogue" process was established, following a statement by Prime Minister Atal Bihari Vajpayee that all subjects, including Kashmir, could be discussed. It focused on several problem areas, including water, trade, travel, Siachen, Sir Creek, terrorism, and Kashmir. India suspended the dialogue after the terrorist attack on Mumbai on November 26, 2008, demanding that Pakistan take action against those responsible. Upon subsequent limited actions by Pakistan, India announced on April 2010 that it would not insist that Pakistan had fully to satisfy Indian demands on terrorism as a precondition for talks (earlier, Pakistan had countered by questioning Indian responsibility for horrific attacks on the Samjhauta Express, the India-Pakistan train service). The two prime ministers agreed to revive the dialogue without precondition but also without the title "composite." The decision was implemented slowly, with foreign secretary meetings in March 2011, meetings of the home ministers, and then a visit of the Pakistani prime minister to India to watch the Cricket World Series Cup semifinal between India and Pakistan.

It is hard to find opportunities for each state's political and bureaucratic equals to talk to each other, and when they do the results have usually been nonproductive, so deep are the differences in their perspectives. Just as disturbing, these official talks have always been vulnerable to outside forces, notably attacks by extremists based in India and Pakistan. The Mumbai attacks were clearly designed to disrupt the dialogue; the same was probably true of the Samjhauta Express attack by Hindu fanatics.[58] It seems extremists on both sides are united in their desire to prevent normal dialogue between their respective countries.

There may be exceptions. Studies have shown that both sports and popular films have an integrating effect at the national level, at least within India.[59] Whether they have this impact between sovereign states is unknown. Both India and Pakistan are full and active members of the International Cricket Council (which manages the Cricket World Cup) and the Asian Cricket Council (which manages the Asia Cup). They play each other regularly in third countries, and when extremists do not threaten, their home-and-home matches are huge events. A few Pakistanis play in the Indian Premiere League, based in individual Indian cities, and there are Indian and Pakistani teammates in third countries. There are no interstate tours of club, college, or university teams, the life-blood of national cricket, and on several occasions cricket matches have been canceled because of the fear of terror attacks, both in India and Pakistan.

The most politically explicit sports partnership has been in men's tennis doubles, with an Indian and a Pakistani teamed up in 2010–11 boasting of their binational credentials, and offering to play a tennis match at Wagah on the India-Pakistan border. Their slogan was "Stop war, start tennis."[60] Balancing this—in terms of political impact—Sania Mirza, a talented Muslim Indian women's tennis player, has been roundly criticized for having married a Pakistani citizen and was under police protection in India for wearing normal women's tennis garb.

The singular exception to the overall lack of cooperation is the 1960 Indus Waters Treaty, historically reviled by Indian diplomats as a foreign (U.S.) imposition on India. It has operated uninterruptedly for more than fifty years, with some success, but is currently threatened by pressure on both states for increased water shares. There has been no serious discussion of bringing other countries into a region-wide water arrangement, and India has found its water relations with Bangladesh to be very strained. China remains aloof from the region in terms of water power, even though the source of most important Indian and Pakistani rivers (the Indus and the Brahmaputra in particular) lies in China.

Both India and Pakistan made an attempt at regional cooperation as founding members of SAARC, but the organization barely got off the ground. At its inception the Indians suspected that it was a Pakistani plot to undercut Indian dominance, and the Pakistanis thought it was an Indian plot to exercise hegemony—in reality it was a goodwill effort by Sri Lanka and Nepal. No less futile is the South Asian Free Trade Area, which still remains an agreement on paper only.

In keeping with their Raj origins, the militaries of both states are also members of various UN missions, and sometimes both are in the same peacekeeping force, although to my knowledge one has never served under the direct command of officers from the other. Recent UN operations include East Timor and Sudan.[61]

Nongovernmental organizations (NGOs) thrive in both states, partly because of international support but also because the burgeoning social media and the Internet are keeping them abreast of events within and outside the region. Yet there are few cross-border ties between these groups, the most important being the organization of journalists (South Asia Free Media Association), which meets regularly in South Asian states.[62] Because visas are an issue, hardly any students from one state study in the other. Although a 2012 agreement between India and Pakistan included some measures for liberalizing their visa regimes, they applied only to the elderly and businesspersons and not to students. As for tourist traffic, it consists mainly of Sikh pilgrims going to holy shrines in Pakistan and a few Muslims going to shrines in India.

Various crises have precipitated some cooperation. For example, the Simla Agreement (1972) ending the 1971 war laid down principles that theoretically govern relations today, although these are routinely bent by both states. In addition, the Lahore Declaration of 1999, issued following a historic visit to Pakistan by Prime Minister Vajpayee, a BJP leader, led to a bus service between Delhi and Lahore. However, the declaration is remembered more for the fact that the Pakistan army was planning a cross-border attack at Kargil while Vajpayee was in Pakistan.

After India and Pakistan became nuclear weapons states in 1998, they quickly and dutifully signed a group of agreements to notify each other of their respective civilian nuclear facilities and to provide lists of citizens kept in prison. They also agreed to a hotline between their armies, and also one between their political leaders.

As discussed in later chapters, talks are also under way about expanding trade and giving each state preferential treatment. The two national academies of science are reportedly engaging in some cooperation, and minor steps are being taken to deal with common agricultural problems, usually at the encouragement of some NGO or international organization that operates in both states. In early 2012 the Indian National Science Academy and the Pakistani Academy of Science signed a memo of understanding for possible joint projects, agreeing "to identify specialized institutions so that scientists in both the countries could collaborate in different fields including research projects; organisation of joint workshops, seminars and conferences and exchange of scientists, professors and students for higher education programmes."[63]

Although the business communities might be expected to show the most cooperation, they have been reluctant to go beyond the limits set by the army in Pakistan and the Home and External Affairs Ministries in India. Until quite recently, Indian governments have done little to assist economic normalization, while Indian firms on the whole have not found Pakistan to be a welcome place to do business. However, this represents the greatest area of potential growth and cooperation (see chapter 6), and the two business communities have already had a hand in the 2012 agreement to start discussions on reducing excess tariffs.

Rivalry outside the Region

For several generations, diplomats of India and Pakistan have regarded their overseas assignments and other postings to international organizations, including most UN bodies, as an opportunity to gain merit by denigrating the other. This has become a joke in the diplomatic community, which long ago tired of the incessant one-upmanship by each country. Furthermore, each state has blocked the other's membership in certain groups. Pakistan prevented India from joining the Organization of Islamic Cooperation (OIC), an association of over fifty-seven Muslim states that routinely criticizes Indian policy in Kashmir, while India has carefully excluded Pakistan from groups that it sponsors, such as the Bay of Bengal Initiative for Multi-Sectoral Technical and Economic Cooperation (BIMSTEC).

In response to a decision by the International Court of Arbitration, both countries agreed to abide by the UN peacekeeping mandate in Kashmir, but with reservations. India, for example, severely limited the UN presence in its territory after the 1971 war. Worse, neither state has been able to find (or seemed interested in) common ground where they might work together. Their strategic freedom of action is mightily constrained by their respective set of international friends, who provide diplomatic support to each on such well-worn issues as Kashmir or human rights violations.

The absence of cooperation is especially noticeable in the matter of Afghanistan, where both countries compete despite important and parallel security interests. When created, Pakistan was a neighbor of Afghanistan, but distracted by the greater Indian threat, Pakistani operations never went much beyond intelligence service and deliberately keeping the frontier regions backward: Pakistan did not have the depth and resources to do much more, so left these areas to their own devices. By contrast, India consolidated its position in its northeast, battling a series of tribal rebellions over the years with a mixture of force, bribery, and the Indian model of democratic governance. Similarly, China expanded into Tibet and its far west regions.

Elsewhere in South Asia and the Indian Ocean, a region once dominated by the Raj, India and Pakistan share the same choke points, the same overseas ethnic interests (especially in the Persian Gulf region), and the same concerns about piracy and smuggling, yet find it difficult if not impossible to cooperate directly. On the other hand, they do engage in some limited cooperation when warranted by a common interest in regional organizations such as the Shanghai Cooperation Organization or international bodies. Diplomats and strategists on both sides might attribute this general lack of cooperation to the rivalry in Kashmir, but in areas where they have a natural shared interest it goes beyond this. Countries that would like to encourage India-Pakistan normalization in UN forums for antipiracy, peacekeeping, and other operations have long since given up on enabling the two states to work together. Their bilateral relations also seem to be as impermeable as ever. Their hostility infiltrates almost all regional issues, from security to cross-border trade or cooperation. If held at all, regional summits mainly serve as an occasion for informal consultations between Indian and Pakistani diplomats—smaller countries like Bangladesh or Sri Lanka know full well that the proposals for a South Asian free trade zone or even economic union will remain on paper until the two agree. The centrality of the India-Pakistan dispute, playing itself out in regular wars, crises, and a near-total absence of cooperation defines South Asia. As a result, SAARC was comatose on arrival; it rules out bilateral issues, at India's insistence, and serves only to give the leadership of the two states a place to meet offline from time to time, and to provide smaller South Asian states—notably Bangladesh, Sri Lanka, and Nepal—the illusion of a regional organization that means something.

There is a paradox here: the two states are economically more prosperous *and* politically weaker than ever before. All governments in the modern world are challenged by their greater access to ideas from elsewhere, as well as the new means of communication within their states. Twitter, Facebook, the web, and other social media have made governance difficult. It is hard to build states, economies, and national identities in the face of an expansion of "people's power." These media have given large numbers of people the ability to interact with each other and with the outside world that was reserved for the upper classes in the nineteenth century and the middle classes in the twentieth century. Today's Indians and Pakistanis are better able to connect, to express their grievances, and to organize against the state. What is astonishing is that this functional fragmentation has not led to cross-border alliances or contacts between the two states, as it has in other regions. Though weak as states, they are nevertheless strong enough to prevent these ties from growing.

Since India and Pakistan never went through a "Pan Arab" moment or succumbed to the idea of collaboration, they have developed only feeble linkages between peace groups and the business communities, and no companies openly do business in both states. University students find it almost impossible to attend classes in each other's country, although a few elite colleges have established tentative linkages and some Pakistanis attend the new graduate-student-only South Asian University established by SAARC and located in New Delhi. The India-Pakistan divide is most apparent in the trade and investment sectors. While China's two-way trade with India ($74 billion in 2011) and Pakistan ($11 billion in 2011) is growing at high rates, total official trade between the two South Asian rivals remains minimal and stagnant ($3 billion in 2011). The same applies to investments, with China investing an average $2 billion in the Pakistani economy annually and $500 million in India, while India and Pakistan make hardly any significant mutual investments. India did not even permit Pakistani investments until 2012.[64] Yet the fringes of popular and mass culture abroad, in third countries, are now home to a community that has developed through joint contacts and business deals between entertainers and businessmen. An important but undocumented cultural exchange takes places in these areas. Back home, India and Pakistan remain comfortable in their "enemy-ness," although they are diverging in this sense in some important geostrategic ways. The dominant perceived threat in India is no longer Pakistan but China, while the great threat for Pakistan now is not India but domestic terror groups and abroad the United States.

The Wrong Metaphor

Because they are based on the calculations of humans, all nations rely upon simplifying metaphors to define themselves, their history, and guidelines for the future. Since 1940 the grand political metaphor for Americans has been Pearl Harbor, which stands for a sneak attack, a breakdown of intelligence, and a civilizational war. Many subsequent crises have been interpreted in the light of the original metaphor, especially the New York and Washington attacks of 9/11, which were as complex in civilizational and moral overtones as Pearl Harbor. A common metaphor in the India-Pakistan context is the communal or religious riot between Hindus and Muslims. The metaphor of the religious riot refers to the original partition of India and for many outsiders has become the implicit (if no longer accurate) explanation of Indian-Pakistani rivalry. "India and Pakistan would be at peace were it not for their dispute over Kashmir, desired by Muslim Pakistan and Hindu India," goes the refrain.

Besides being historically inaccurate, the metaphor is conceptually wrong. Most riots in India and Pakistan—religious and otherwise—are part of a complex bargaining relationship between two or more political communities. The riot itself is one stage in a long and complex game, and the purpose of the game is not only to gain the upper hand over the other side but also to influence the bystander—in the case of religious riots, the local police and military authorities. India-Pakistan relations have to be seen in this framework. Unless one side or the other collapses entirely, the game will continue, and nuclear weapons do not change this basic fact, although they do present an alternative and mutually undesirable end to the game. The nature of the game becomes clearer when one examines the major disputes between the two sides (chapter 2) and then sees how this powerful but historically flawed metaphor has been reified in the politics of both India (chapter 3) and Pakistan (chapter 4).

CHAPTER TWO

CONFLICTS

Physicists jest that often their theories fail to predict the results of experiments or their results fail to make theoretical sense, but that most experiments simply fail and no one knows why. The partition of India and Pakistan can be seen as a great experiment in political and human engineering that in large part went awry, with the successor states still trying to cope. Most of the key players in this gigantic drama assumed that the worst would not happen. With goodwill and common sense, problems could be managed over time. The worst did happen, and there has been a steep price for the errors of omission and commission perpetrated both by the British and by the nationalist leaders who accepted and tried to manage a flawed partition.

The two states form a peculiar complex in which fear, hatred, and a sense of persecution drive *both* sides, as discussed further in chapter 5. The only other disputes like this in recent history are those between Israel and the Palestinians or the Greeks and the Turks and several civil war conflicts, notably that between the Sinhala and Tamils of Sri Lanka.

While much of the India-Pakistan conflict lies in the realms of high strategy and identity, it also revolves around the absence of trade and normal discourse, size disparities, and three geostrategic issues: Kashmir, water, and the Siachen Glacier. These are matters in which the absence of a normal relationship hurts *both* states, making the disputes over them particularly puzzling. What theoretically might make this moment different from the past sixty-five years (as far as normalization goes) is the advent of a nuclearized South Asia and the rise of extremist Islam. Respectively, these raise the cost of conflict and provide new incentives for cooperation.

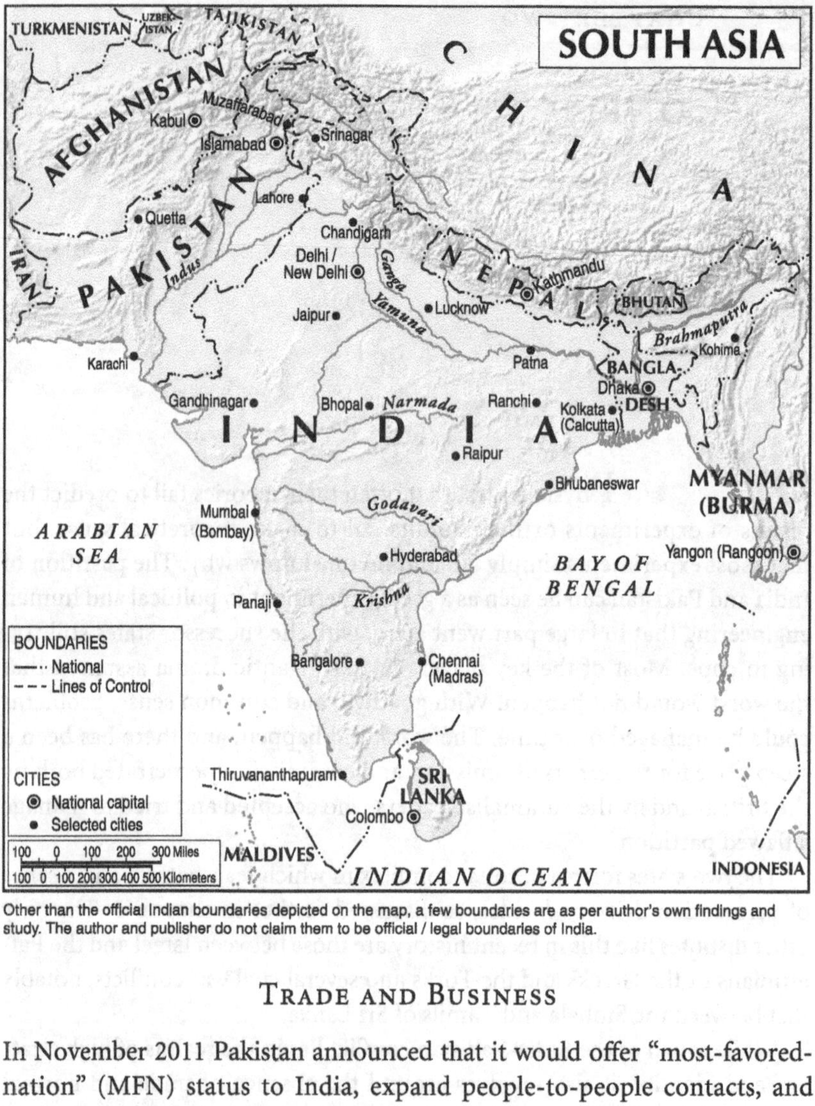

Other than the official Indian boundaries depicted on the map, a few boundaries are as per author's own findings and study. The author and publisher do not claim them to be official / legal boundaries of India.

Trade and Business

In November 2011 Pakistan announced that it would offer "most-favored-nation" (MFN) status to India, expand people-to-people contacts, and institute a new visa regime. This was hailed as a major breakthrough in India-Pakistan relations, paving the way for interaction on other issues and perhaps full normalization.[1] India in turn has promised to reduce nontariff barriers, cutting back drastically the number of items on a "positive list," over 800 items in April 2012.[2] The announcement was greeted warmly on both sides of the border, even by the traditionally anti-Indian Urdu press, perhaps because it had the backing of the Pakistan army.[3] Some, however, said that trade agreements without resolution of the Kashmir dispute and water problems would be problematic; otherwise "neither the history nor the future generations would forgive" the Pakistani leadership.[4] Others more darkly hinted that Pakistan had to take "extreme steps" instead of talks to resolve outstanding disputes.[5]

The response of most observers was "It's about time." In the years following partition, official trade between India and Pakistan was at an all-time high—a remnant of pre-partition economic integration. Pakistan's exports to India were at 56 percent, while 32 percent of its imports came from its neighbor. By 1950 this figure had dropped dramatically. The 1965 war further reduced trade between the two; before that war it was possible to purchase Pakistan magazines and books in New Delhi; afterward it was difficult. Ironically, the Internet, cable television, and mass piracy defeat efforts by both countries to protect their citizens from each other's press and entertainment.

In 1956 India and Pakistan signed a trade agreement stipulating the MFN clause for each other's goods. Specific agreements—allowing for limited trade in select items—would not be signed until the mid-1970s. In January 1986 Pakistan reversed its previous stance, agreeing to private sector imports of forty-two items from India. Then a series of crises beginning in 1987 ensured continued distrust and no serious movement on trade.

South Asia today is the least economically integrated region in the world, largely because India and Pakistan together account for 90 percent of the region's GDP yet remain rivals.[6] As pointed out elsewhere, the peace dividend of better relations between the two countries would be a 405 percent increase in bilateral trade.[7]

Pakistan and India have both been part of the South Asian Association for Regional Cooperation (SAARC) since its inception in 1985 and the South Asia Free Trade Agreement (SAFTA) of 2004. Yet according to all economic indicators, the increase in trade since these dates has been abysmally low.[8] India and Pakistan were once a single trade area, despite some minor internal barriers. As mentioned in chapter 1, however, trade does continue along "informal channels," the economist's euphemism for smuggling, often via traditional historical, geographic, and ethnic links.[9] The question then is whether directing such trade into formal channels would enhance regional economic cooperation. That is to say, if illegal trade is high, can it be assumed that there is unlocked potential for trade—a signal that the countries' economies are complementary?

Since both countries are members of the G77 block in the United Nations and of the World Trade Organization (WTO), they normally find themselves on the same negotiation team with other least developed and developing economies on issues such as global trade tariffs, agricultural and textile protections, new global labor standards, patent and intellectual property rights, or even the effect of climate change. At this international level, Pakistan and Indian negotiators thus share a surprising number of interests, most of them economic ones, which often lead to at least tacit cooperation.

While *economic* imperatives should tie India and Pakistan together, they have not done so. Instead of working toward regional integration, South Asia has focused on entering global markets, particularly North America and the European Union, and increasingly China.[10] Nepal is the only South Asian state that has a substantial intraregional trade presence, with just under 55 percent of its exports by value as well as imports by value traded intraregionally, almost all to and from India. Other regional states—India, Pakistan, Bangladesh, Sri Lanka, and the Maldives—trade less than 15 percent of their exports by value intraregionally and get less than 20 percent of their imports by value intraregionally. In fact, if the Maldives is disregarded, since virtually all of its exports go to Sri Lanka, the remaining four states—India, Pakistan, Bangladesh, and Sri Lanka—all trade less than 7 percent of their exports by value intraregionally. Afghanistan is a special case: goods shipped there often wind up in Pakistan's black market, and Pakistan's limits on transit trade to Afghanistan mean that it is hard for India to sell there. On the import side, Indian and Pakistani intraregional imports account for less than 5 percent of total imports by value.[11] This low level of intraregional trade has given rise to the term "inverse regionalism" to describe South Asia.[12]

One of the key reasons behind this state of affairs is that South Asia is still relatively protectionist, as evidenced by the ratios of exports and imports to its GDP, which are lower than the world average, as well as by its import tariffs, which are the highest of any developing region in the world.[13] Equally striking, in 2004 South Asia was the only developing region in which intraregional trade was less than 5 percent of its world trade. The region had previously shared this status with Sub-Saharan Africa, which since 1984 has displaced South Asia as the least integrated region in the world.[14] South Asia is also comparatively weak in facilitating trade. Compared with East Asia, South Asia has the worst average performance in every major category of trade facilitation, from ports to customs to regulations to services.[15]

The list of items that Pakistan illegally imports from India is fairly long. Cloth is the largest item, illegal imports in this category amounting to more than $185 million, twice as much as is exported to India. Other goods illegally imported from India include livestock, pharmaceutical machinery, cosmetics, jewelry, tires, and medicine.[16] Cattle are physically the largest smuggled item, some being moved underground via tunnels under the

Rajasthan/Sind border. Items smuggled from India to Pakistan range in value from $200 million to $10 billion; precise estimates are hard to come by, and of course these goods go untaxed, although their transit is usually associated with corrupt officials, sometimes the police or paramilitaries, on both sides of the border.

Hence powerful groups in both countries oppose trade just as much as others are interested in expanding it. And the members of the anti-trade camp—the smugglers, police, and politicians—have considerable resources, and illegal trade flourishes when normal channels are blocked. However, business associations and corporations on both sides favor normalization. On the Indian side, both major business associations advocate greater trade. The Federation of Indian Chambers of Commerce and Industry (FICCI), and the Confederation of Indian Industries (CII) each sent trade delegations to Pakistan in 2012. While some Pakistani companies fear Indian competition, others recognize that they stand to benefit. Indeed, companies and business and industry associations on both sides believe that greater cooperation would bring material gains to both countries. They are acquiring political influence in India, and whenever civilian governments have been in office, also in Pakistan. A number of highly visible meetings of businesspersons have been organized by the Punjab, Haryana, Delhi Chambers of Commerce and Industry (PHDCCI), the FICCI, CII, and the Karachi Chamber of Commerce. These efforts had an impact on relations between the two countries, especially when Nawaz Sharif (a businessman) was prime minister. Pakistan's decision to expand its import list for India in the early 1990s was arguably the result of ideas exchanged during these meetings as well as Pakistan's democratization, which brought into prominence Punjabi business families that stood to gain most significantly from direct trade between the two countries. In 2012 FICCI and CII delegations to Pakistan were greeted warmly, a visit made possible by the Pakistan army's breakthrough decision to allow the civilian government to grant MFN status to India.

The fact that some Pakistani companies would be strengthened by trade with India creates a natural affinity between them in certain areas. As pointed out by Warren Weinstein, the American aid and trade expert kidnapped by an unidentified group in Lahore in 2011, India's new ferrochrome industry could import chromite from Pakistan.[17] The two could market ferrochrome jointly in the world. Other potential Pakistani exports to India, according to Weinstein, are its thriving gems and minerals industries. Pakistan now exports cloth (the largest single item), dry fruit, bed sheets, prayer mats, video games and CDs, footwear, cigarettes, and surma, the eye cosmetic. Individual Indian companies have tried to make forays into Pakistan, and already a huge amount of goods (including the bulk of Pakistan's truck tires) are sold to Pakistan via Dubai and other cut-out locations.

But as just mentioned, the smuggling industry is powerful. Its operations make large use of containers that move through third countries, mainly Dubai. Officials at ports in Dubai assign the goods a false country of origin, and they are then shipped to Pakistan. These transactions are reflected in the United Arab Emirates balance of trade rather than that between India and Pakistan. In some cases goods from India that are technically banned in Pakistan do not even travel all the way to Dubai. False papers are manufactured before they leave their ports in India, and they sail directly to Karachi.[18]

Goods also travel across the India-Pakistan border, mainly through remote unfenced areas. Trenches and tunnels are dug with the assistance of local villagers, and border officials are routinely bribed. Goods are also transferred via train passengers traveling between Amritsar and Lahore who are looking for ways to subsidize their journey.

There are obvious tradeoffs between sectors, in addition to the potential for cooperation where they produce the same or similar items. India is strong in information technology, while Pakistan's agriculture is important, so theoretically, if the will were there, concessions could be swapped and thus the politically strongest sector on each side could be accommodated. In Pakistan this would include the many industries controlled by the military. Indian businessmen have suggested that this was an inducement on the Pakistani side to permit greater trade, arguing that the Pakistan military did not want to see the value of its real estate and manufacturing capabilities decline, and that this approach to normalization could have an impact on strategic relations between the two states.

Although hope for an expansion of India-Pakistan trade is now on the rise, hope is not a policy. Moreover, at least three obstacles stand in the way of enhancing trade and also have the potential to affect the overall relationship between the two countries.

First, there are many supporters of the status quo, notably among police and government officials. A recent report demonstrates the extent to which they themselves benefit from the black market.[19] Needless to say, they perpetuate illegal trade.

Second, although recent evidence shows a decline in illegal trade between India and Pakistan over the years, smuggling continues apace with goods from China, now a major trading partner with both countries. Some therefore believe that gains from liberalizing trade between India and Pakistan may not be as high as they would have been in the past.[20]

Third, ulterior motives may be lurking behind the new desire for a more liberal trade regime, especially on the Pakistani side. Pakistan is in deep economic disorder, in a position of sovereign debt, and in danger of defaulting on its International Monetary Fund (IMF) loans when they come due in 2013. In 2012 Pakistan admitted it was seeking the IMF's help once again to clear its debts. It was expected to repay a total of $7.82 billion for previous loans in four installments from 2011–12 to 2014–15.[21] Pointing to their country's internal economic failures and relations with a hostile America, Pakistani strategists argue that the opening to India makes good political as well as economic sense; it is much easier to let Indian investments revive the Pakistani economy than to carry out the kinds of tough reforms that are linked to IMF and other loans. Since Pakistan is still undertaxed and the military still controls a huge portion of the economy—with mostly inefficient industries—an injection of investment from India would be a quick fix, although it would not address the economy's deeper dysfunctionality.

This raises an obvious question, now being debated in India: why should India link its economy to a failing Pakistan? Some in India believe that New Delhi would be better off going slow, isolating Pakistan physically, economically, and politically. Others would go further, arguing this is the time to let Pakistan "crash" as India could survive a Pakistani economic disaster, plus it might bring down the country's regime and discredit the army, and thereby transform the India-Pakistan relationship.

Water

Water conflicts are endemic in South Asia, a region that is heavily dependent on monsoons and large-scale irrigation canals. Famine and flood are thus equal threats to hundreds of millions of Indians and Pakistanis (and Bangladeshis and Nepalis, who are part of regional hydrological systems).[22]

Under the British there were periodic water disputes between Sindh and undivided Punjab and between various South Indian provinces. These were mediated by the central government or by semijudicial commissions established to adjudicate such quarrels. Partition transformed what had been a localized disagreement into an international conflict.[23] Neither Pakistan nor India could agree on the division of the six main rivers of the Indus Basin—the Indus, Ravi, Sutlej, Chenab, Jhelum, and Beas. Even when the matter was taken up at the Inter-Dominion Conference in New Delhi in May 1948, little was resolved, although Pakistan was given time to find alternative water sources. India, however, demanded financial reparation for any allowance given to Pakistan during that time. In response, Pakistan in 1950 launched a formal complaint against India for the delimitation of its water supply and requested that the issue be submitted to the International Court of Arbitration, but India categorically rejected third-party intervention.[24]

Then in 1951 David Lilienthal, an expert on American water issues, wrote an article containing specific technical recommendations on developing the Indus Basin as a unit and suggesting that the World Bank be a financial contributor.[25] The bank's director at the time, Eugene Black, saw this as an opportunity to showcase the institution's ability to deal with international conflicts. Indian concerns were addressed when he assured India that the bank "would not adjudicate the conflict, but instead work as a conduit for agreement."[26]

After ten years of negotiations, proposals, and counterproposals, the Indus Waters Treaty was signed on September 19, 1960, backed by a commitment of immense financial assistance, perhaps a billion dollars, most of it to go to Pakistan to independently develop its own water resources. Major contributions came from Australia, the United Kingdom, and the United States, as well as the World Bank itself.[27]

As pointed out by John Briscoe, an expert on South Asia's water issues and former World Bank adviser, the "Indus Waters Treaty is widely and correctly considered to be the most important water treaty in the world, and has endured despite 50 years of hostility between India and Pakistan."[28] The treaty is a highly technical document, drawn up by engineers and technicians rather than diplomats and lawyers, and provides guidelines for developing water projects in India and Pakistan. The bank is also a signatory to the treaty, and in the words of two observers, it "did not have political power but its ability to bring several countries with the financial commitment was a kind of quasi-imperial third party inducement to the successful resolution of the dispute."[29] The treaty provides a rare example of economic incentives overriding political hostilities to make way for peaceful relations between the two states.

One important factor contributing to the Indus treaty's success was the purposeful depoliticization of the issue. Specifically, the World Bank's intervention was initially meant to follow Lilienthal's recommendation to develop the Indus Basin as a whole and thus increase the productive capacity of the region as a remedy to the situation, rather than simply allocating the water that was available at the time. Over the course of negotiations, this plan was abandoned in favor of dividing rights over the rivers, but the goal of aiding development on both sides of the border remained intact. The bank's approach was therefore to provide practical economic advice rather than resolve a political dispute.

Even though both sides started with mutually irreconcilable demands, Pakistan knew that negotiation was the only way it could sustain Punjab's economy, long considered India's breadbasket. India was similarly inclined to cooperate with the World Bank because Nehru desperately needed its financial support to sustain his second five-year plan.

In 1978 the two sides signed another water agreement, this time relating to the Salal Dam. Pakistan, which had objected to India building a water storage dam on the Chenab River in Jammu and Kashmir, sixty-four kilometers from the Pakistan border, agreed to India lowering the height of the dam and then using it only for power generation. The agreement was hailed as a shining example of the two countries being able to work out their problems peaceably. Further cooperation was halted in 1992, however, when India shared information with Pakistan on several dams it planned to build in Jammu and Kashmir. Matters came to a head in 2005, with Pakistan—for the first time in its history—invoking the arbitration provisions of the Indus Waters Treaty before a World Bank–appointed neutral expert in response to India's construction of the 450-megawatt Baglihar Dam on the Chenab River. The verdict on this particular dispute, announced in late 2011, was unfavorable to Pakistan.

In 2010 Pakistani militant organizations, traditionally focused on liberating Indian-held Kashmir, organized a march protesting India's control over Pakistan's water resources. Carrying signs and driving tractors, thousands of farmers protested India's plans for "water terrorism."[30] Army strategists echoed the theme, and it became a topic of analysis in Pakistan's Staff College and National Defense University.[31]

In 2011 the countries again went head to head at the International Court of Arbitration over yet another water project, India's 330-megawatt Kishanganga Dam in Jammu and Kashmir. The court has ordered India to temporarily stop some construction on the dam while assessments are being made.

Extremists in Pakistan have used the water disputes to argue that Pakistanis should not trust India, and that the government and bureaucracy are not defending Pakistan's best interests. In 2010 Hafiz Saeed, head of the Pakistani militant group Jamaat-u-Dawa, accused India of "water terrorism" using slogans such as "water flows or blood."[32] In denouncing India's "water aggression," Liaquat Baloch of the Jamaat-i-Islami charged that Pakistan's former technocrats on the Indus Water Commission and officials at the Foreign Ministry and Water and Power Ministry were secretly supporting India.[33] In a recent letter to the prime minister, energy expert Arshad H. Abbasi attacked the credibility of officials who appear to be paving the way for Indian projects while ignoring Pakistan's interests.[34]

The sense of victimhood is also present in India, where the Indus Waters Treaty and its provisions are considered detrimental to the country's interests and "water security." Similar sentiments are voiced in the state of Jammu and Kashmir, where the local government has contracted the services of a foreign consultant. As one Kashmiri official notes, "There is a feeling that the state is suffering on account of IWT [the Indus Waters Treaty]" and "a formula" needs to be worked out under which the state could "benefit by harnessing the water of its own rivers" without the constraints posed by Pakistan and the treaty.[35]

At India's national level, India's "soft stance" on the water disputes with Pakistan is blamed for delaying the country's dam projects and is thus said to be hampering its developmental and strategic needs. Indian concessions are described as coming out of "a sense of fairness or as a nation bound by the rule of law" but costing the country dearly because "arbitration is expensive, and India has more to lose than Pakistan in the wait."[36]

The repeated statements that "Pakistan gets more than the share it is entitled to" suggest a magnanimous India but, as in Pakistan, also imply that the government is unable to defend the country's best interests.[37] Ultimately, Indian criticism is directed not so much at a Pakistan that uses "every dam as a strategic weapon . . . to delay if not deny progress that primarily benefits J&K [Jammu and Kashmir]," but more at the Indian government for being "too soft" and compromising. As one analyst suggests, India should consider using the same "weapon" and denounce the Pakistani dam project at Skardu, in the Pakistani region of Gilgit-Baltistan claimed by India.[38]

Will the involvement of an international institution, the International Court of Arbitration, again lead to agreement? Although the Indus treaty has lasted without any major issues for half a century, it is sheer speculation to assess the likelihood of another agreement between the countries, but the stakes are as high today as they were fifty years ago. With the Pakistani public's dwindling interest in Kashmir, the apparent injustice of water policies has replaced Kashmir as a prime example of Indian duplicity, especially for the military and those close to it.

Analysts such as Briscoe have suggested that while Pakistan's fears are not entirely unwarranted, the likelihood that India's project will actually have an impact on Pakistan's water supply is slim if not unfounded. Although India has the potential to obstruct the flow of water into Pakistan, whether it would actually pursue such a course of action, given its likely illegality and a sharp response from Pakistan, is doubtful—an Indian diversion of water is one of Islamabad's nuclear red lines.

The water problem has received little comprehensive attention from non-governmental organizations in either state. Most are obsessed with a particular part of the puzzle: environmental issues in India and the exaggerated dangers of India shutting off the water in Pakistan. This is also true of the governments. Water in South Asia is linked to a myriad of issues, including energy, environment, and relations with China, but little attempt has been made to arrive at a comprehensive overview of how water problems can be addressed within a large framework.[39] Water is still a "national" issue, permeated with intense nationalism and subnational sentiments. For example, according to South Asia's leading energy NGO, TERI, fifteen Indian government departments have come up with fifteen different measurements of water flow, and South Asian states are reluctant to release data about water when it is regarded as a national security issue. In Pakistan the agencies that manage water, beginning with the Water and Power Development Authority (WAPDA), are considered pro-Punjabi by other provinces, and Punjab believes they are ganging up against it; there are parallel institutional and federal problems in India, where the provinces remain at odds because of agreements forged under the British; water tribunals come up with awards, but these are not acceptable to the states, and the aggrieved party goes to India's Supreme Court, which directs the prime minister to deal with the problem. But New Delhi has only limited leverage, especially when a political coalition partner is involved, as in the disputes between Tamilnadu and Karnataka or Punjab and Haryana. If neither India nor Pakistan finds it easy to manage water disputes within each of its own borders, how can they do so together?

Pakistan's fears stem from its marginal status as a water-short nation, its growing population, and its relatively inefficient agriculture, but also its failure to address the internal distribution of water between its provinces As for India, its booming economy is starved for power. Financial incentives might be a motivator, but the political nature of the problem is much sharper now than in the 1950s. The fact that the Islamists have taken up the cause is a concern, and there are groups in both states that use "water" as an excuse to whip up feelings against the other state; they are not interested in allowing the issue to deflate into an agreement. Either way, the fact that it is under consideration in an international court is a sign that negotiations have already failed to some degree.

Balancing legitimate concerns over water (its quality, quantity, cost, and timeliness, especially during the monsoon season) is difficult enough, but it has acquired an intensely emotional content as well. The Indus Waters Treaty viewed water as a technical problem. This allowed engineers and water experts to make the decisions, but the approach seems naive in the present highly charged, politicized context. Politicians and experts operate from quite different perspectives. The former are by and large uninfluenced by basic knowledge about water, dams, and power generation; along with NGOs, who are especially vulnerable to ideology and symbolism, they are suspicious of experts. As a result, expert voices are barely heard and foreign expertise is deeply discounted in the debate. Water issues in and between India and Pakistan are now literally the subject of a politicized science.

The Indus treaty once settled the water problem between India and Pakistan, but now it has a new dimension because of China's fast-paced development. If China should undertake engineering projects in the eastern part of Tibet, it would affect the Brahmaputra, while work of this nature in its western regions would impinge upon the Indus. India and Pakistan seem to have no mutual understanding of such developments, Pakistan being an ally of China and India using the same upper riparian arguments against Islamabad that China uses against it. Regional cooperation or a sense of a regional common interest in water matters is clearly wanting.

The new emotionalism embedded in water issues, especially in Pakistan, along with the fact that expertise is divorced from political decisionmaking and the international aspects of water are of little interest, makes the resolution of the India-Pakistan water problem difficult at best. Even if the International Court returns a verdict that is acceptable to all parties, in the long run the water issue will not go away, and there remains no regional institution capable of addressing it. In the short run, another technology fix may not be the optimum solution, but the good should not drive out the best.

Kashmir

As noted in chapter 1, those who oversaw the distribution of territories at partition failed to plan for the integration of Kashmir into the new two-state order, leaving both India and Pakistan with the impression that a massive injustice had been committed. Kashmir then came to play a role in the domestic politics of both states. For Pakistani leaders, both civilian and military, Kashmir was a helpful diversion from the daunting task of nation building. Also significant, powerful Kashmiri-dominated constituencies have a voice in major Pakistani cities. Even abroad, there have been strong Kashmir lobbies in some European states, especially in a few British cities with large numbers of Kashmiri or Mirpuri migrants. Because Pakistan's citizenship laws permit voting in two countries, many British and American Pakistanis try to play a political role in Pakistan. By contrast, Indian law prohibits dual

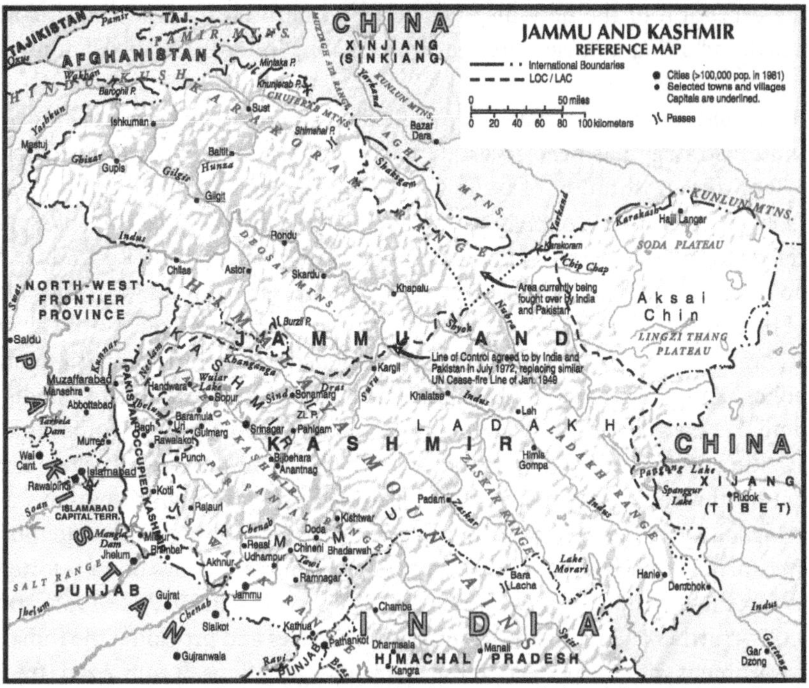

Other than the official Indian boundaries depicted on the map, a few boundaries are as per author's own findings and study. The author and publisher do not claim them to be official / legal boundaries of India.

citizenship. However, India has had a small but influential Kashmiri Hindu community, which early on was overrepresented in the higher reaches of the Indian government, not least in the presence of the Nehru family, a Kashmiri Pandit clan that had migrated to Uttar Pradesh from the Valley.

Over the years many solutions have been proposed for the Kashmir problem. These have included partition along the Line of Control, "soft borders" between the two parts of Kashmir (pending a solution to the entire problem), a region-by-region plebiscite of Kashmiris, a referendum, UN trusteeship, the "Trieste" and "Andorra" models (whereby the same territory is shared by two states, or a nominally sovereign territory that in fact is controlled jointly by two states), revolutionary warfare, depopulation of Muslim Kashmiris and repopulation by Hindus from India, patience, good government, a revival of "human values," and doing nothing. The dispute has not been resolved because of at least three factors.

First, the cold war led both American and Soviet administrations to see this regional dispute not for what it was but as part of the systemic East-West struggle. India and Pakistan were proxies, or treaty allies, and there was no incentive to look for regional solutions to regional problems, with the exception of the now-disputed Indus Waters Treaty. These efforts all failed, including a Soviet attempt to normalize India-Pakistan relations in the mid-1960s.

Second, both states have been inflexible where Kashmir is concerned. India's strategy has been to erode Kashmir's special status under Article 370 of the Constitution of India. India also pretends that the problem was "solved" by the Simla Agreement, and that it lies entirely with Pakistan, especially the Pakistan army. This dual strategy of no change within Kashmir and no discussion of it with Pakistan failed to prepare New Delhi for the events of the late 1980s. India rejected the political option, it rejected a strategy of accommodating Kashmiri demands, it excluded Pakistan from its Kashmir policy, and it has stubbornly opposed outside efforts to mediate the dispute. Yet New Delhi lacks the resources and a coherent strategy (other than awaiting others) to deal unilaterally with the Kashmir problem. The tepid, if not hostile, reaction of a major 2012 study on Kashmiri public opinion was evidence of an absence of useful ideas; it received no government attention and stirred up little debate.[40] Pakistan, on the other hand, has often resorted to force in attempting to wrest Kashmir from India—in 1947–48,1965, and 1999—further alienating the Kashmiris themselves and providing the Indian government with the perfect excuse to avoid negotiations. It runs Azad (free) Kashmir with an iron fist.

Third, it must be said that the Kashmiris, while patently victims, have not been reluctant to exploit the situation. The so-called Kashmiri Action Committee, a major lobbying effort on behalf of the Kashmir "cause" in the United States—with links to several other countries—was shown to be largely paid for by Pakistan's intelligence service, the ISI, and its American director was convicted and sentenced to prison.[41] Still, the committee pursues the goal of an independent Kashmir, oblivious to the wishes of most Kashmiris and certainly to the views of the Indian government. This remains a diaspora cause, and while the grievances in Kashmir that the committee highlights are real, it forwards no realistic strategy for resolution. Its counterparts in Europe are also reliably said to be funded by Pakistan's intelligence agencies. One credible international project to devise a normalization strategy for Kashmir—and therefore for India and Pakistan—the Kashmir Study Group, came up with many good ideas and important new ways of seeing the dispute, but its attempt at policy recommendations never caught hold in either India or Pakistan, let alone among Kashmiris.[42]

Opinions among Kashmiris are themselves varied, beginning with different understandings of India's original agreement to hold a referendum and Pakistan's insistence that a referendum be held (see box 2-1).[43] India has

Box 2-1. *What Do Kashmiris Think?*

After decades of insurgency (some initiated by Pakistan), several wars, and many crises, Kashmiris have become war-weary and disillusioned with both India and Pakistan. It was not until 2010, however, that a comprehensive survey of Kashmiri attitudes took place.[a]

The one point on which Kashmiris seemed to agree was that they were deeply dissatisfied with the status quo. When asked what they perceived to be the greatest problems in their daily lives, 81 percent pointed to the unemployment rate, 68 percent pointed to corruption, and 45 percent to poor economic development. Obviously, most people are more concerned with the day-to-day realities of their lives than with politics. However, 80 percent of respondents still claimed that the dispute was "very important" to them personally.[b] From these figures it seems that addressing the economic needs of Kashmiris is a necessary but not sufficient key to stopping violence, although a quarter of respondents (27 percent) said that war is the only solution.

What about the future? Of the combined population, 43 percent of respondents declared that they wanted Kashmir to be independent, and only 14 percent wanted the Line of Control (LoC) to be made a permanent border between the two countries, the latter being the preferred solution of the international community.[c] On further questioning, however, respondents made it clear that the border was not the issue so much as insecurity and the fact that it prevented the movement of people and goods, inhibiting all kinds of economic activity. When presented with the option of having no restrictions on the movement of people and goods, only 11 percent answered that they were not in favor of the LoC at all, and more than 85 percent were in favor of the LoC under freer circumstances.

Even if a referendum would have yielded a favorable result for Pakistan in 1949, the situation today is quite different. When the data for both Azad Jammu and Kashmir and Jammu and Kashmir districts were aggregated, the percentage of the population that opted for Pakistan was as low as 15 percent, and the percentage that opted to be part of India was only slightly higher, at 21 percent.[d] These figures would be significant if these were to be the only choices presented to Kashmiris in a referendum today.[e]

a. Robert W. Bradnock, "Kashmir: Paths to Peace," sponsored by Saif al Islam al Qadhafi, King's College London, Chatham House, May 2010 (www.chathamhouse.org.uk/publications/papers/view/-/id/881/).

b. Ibid., p. 4.

c. Arvin Bahl, *From Jinnah to Jihad: Pakistan's Kashmir Quest and the Limits of Realism* (India: Atlantic, September 2007), p. 29.

d. Ibid., p. 19.

e. Ibid., p. 17.

always held that the conditions for a referendum, including the withdrawal of Pakistani forces, were never met, and in any case that several elections in the parts of Kashmir that it controls are testimony to the Kashmiri desire to stay within the Indian Union. It has been difficult to prove conclusively what exactly the people of Kashmir, on both sides, wanted in the 1940s, or want now. A significant number of Kashmiris have always sought independence from India *and* Pakistan. The two states disagree as to *which* should control Kashmir and the mechanism for determining Kashmiri sentiment, but they are unified in their opposition to a truly independent state. Thus the seemingly well-intentioned proposal that Kashmiris be "consulted" or have a voice in determining their own fate is threatening to both Islamabad and Delhi.

Ironically, the prospect of an India-Pakistan normalization over trade and visas could be problematic for Kashmir, which itself is deeply divided. One Kashmiri consultant to the state government in Srinagar, Wajahat Qazi, has blogged that these are positive developments, but asks whether Kashmiris should accept the "unfurling amity" or continue to resist the Indian state. Qazi asks what role Kashmiri separatists would have in a world where India and Pakistan were at peace. The consequences of better relations, he concludes, would be that "the dispute over Kashmir will gradually whittle away as the core sticking point between the two countries.[44] This would be both a good and a bad development. Good because it potentially means the resolution of a complex issue and would allow both countries to focus on more pressing and urgent concerns. It would be bad because a core Kashmiri grievance—exclusion from the political process—would remain unaddressed. This would ignore the psychological dimension of the dispute as far as Kashmiris are concerned, and the state would "remain on the boil and can potentially erupt again." Thus for Kashmir normalization is good, but risky, and India and Pakistan—and outsiders—will have to take Kashmiri sentiments into account if the normalization process moves forward. One issue raised consistently by Kashmiris, especially in the Valley, has been unemployment, and the government has encouraged private enterprise to play a role in providing employment for Kashmiri youth. The scheme (Udaan) has had mixed results, as have attempts by the Congress Party to mobilize support for it. Knowledgeable Kashmiris have criticized these as artificial efforts. In one instant, student participants were handpicked to exclude those who might ask inconvenient questions.[45]

Given the difficulty that both parts of Kashmir have had in self-governance, there are other reasons for skepticism about genuine independence for Kashmir, whether united or divided. While it would be economically viable—given the area's desirability as a tourist destination and rich water and other resources—as an independent state Kashmir would be vulnerable to extremist Islamic pressures from the outside. Along with Palestine and Chechnya, it is already included on the list of jihadi targets. There are also deep divisions among Kashmiris, and thousands of Kashmiri Hindus have fled the Valley rather than stay on to be the target of extremist forces; the tiny Buddhist minority in Leh is also wary of dominance from Srinagar.

The Kashmir problem as a whole is so complicated that it is hard to say how a resolution might begin. Some still believe that Indira Gandhi failed to be tough enough on Pakistan at the Simla summit, others that India should have moved more quickly to a settlement instead of waiting—the delay gave the Pakistan army time to consolidate its power again and remove Bhutto. A completed Kashmir agreement might have been accepted then even by the Pakistan army—or perhaps it would not have. No one knows, but it is certain that after the 1971 defeat Pakistan's army harbored a deeper anger and a desire for revenge—both shared by many civilians.

Like the Middle East peace process, Kashmir elicits degrees of contentiousness. While the Valley Muslims feel aggrieved that they are dominated by India, other Kashmiri groups, especially the Pandits and the largely Buddhist population of Ladakh, fear having the state dominated by Muslims. Thus a number of proposals have suggested separating the Valley from other regions (Azad Kashmir, Ladakh, Jammu) and allocating parts of Jammu and Kashmir to India and Pakistan, leaving to the end the intensely disputed Valley. After reviewing several important books on Kashmir, distinguished American journalist Steve Coll is of the opinion that to be workable, an agreement must be favorable enough to Kashmiris for Pakistan's army to save face, but not so favorable as to provoke an unmanageable backlash from Hindu activists in India.[46] This will be hard to do.

Politically, "Kashmir" is not a homogeneous issue in India and Pakistan. During the height of the 1990 Kashmir crisis, it was clear that the further the distance from Delhi and Islamabad, the less the passion. In Chennai, Kolkata, Hyderabad (Deccan), and Mumbai, Kashmir was and is considered New Delhi's obsession; in Karachi, Quetta, Peshawar, and Hyderabad (Sindh), it is a secondary issue. In these provinces relations with Islamabad and the Punjab are more important than Kashmir. However, the enormous television coverage given to the Kargil episode in 1999 gave the Indian public a shared image of the Kashmir issue that was in direct contradiction to the one Pakistan's government-controlled media presented to its public over many years. By creating a generation of incensed Indians, this coverage also made compromise on Kashmir less likely.

Like proposals to resolve other complex disputes, such as those in the Middle East or China-Taiwan and the two Koreas, "solutions" to the Kashmir problem must operate at many levels. The examples of the Middle East, South Africa, and Ireland indicate that seemingly intractable disputes can be resolved, or ameliorated, by patience, outside encouragement, and, above all, a strategy that addresses their several dimensions. If such a strategy for Kashmir had been initiated in the early or mid-1980s, then some of the crises that arose later in that decade might have been averted, and it would not be seen as one of the world's nuclear flash points.

Any comprehensive solution to the Kashmir problem would involve many concessions and changes in relations between India and Pakistan (and within each state). A recent government-sponsored study of public opinion in Kashmir is the latest in a succession of government and private efforts to arrive at suggestions on how to approach the problem. Like all of its predecessors, it was quickly forgotten, and even some study contributors privately said that it was both premature and not comprehensive enough. As experts on the subject note:

> The interlocutors carried out their work conscientiously. They interviewed thousands of Kashmiris all over the Indian-controlled parts of the state, held public round-table discussions, and met with civil and military leaders. Although they were handicapped by the refusal of prominent separatists to meet formally with them, they did manage some informal contact. They could not, of course, sound out opinion in Pakistan-held areas. These were off-limits to them. Nor did their mandate include any invitation to make recommendations on how to engage the Pakistan government in bringing about a Kashmir settlement.[47]

The report was buried by the Indian Home Ministry, which waited several months before releasing it, with the result that it came out at just about the same time a more important study—of India's overall defense and security policy—was delivered to the prime minister. Those who were hopeful that relations with Pakistan and Kashmir might improve found little to be enthusiastic about just then, with a weak Indian government divided on Kashmir and struggling for its own survival.[48]

A settlement of Kashmir would require a number of measures: a change in India's federal system, changes in Kashmir's constituent parts, a reexamination of the military balance between India and Pakistan, and provisions that would prevent the two states from again turning to arms in Kashmir. Above all, it would require major concessions on the part of Pakistan—and

India might have to accommodate some Pakistani concerns in Kashmir itself. There also would have to be incentives for Pakistan to cooperate in such ameliorative measures, since its basic strategy is to draw outsiders into the region and to pressure India. For its part, India would have to demonstrate to Pakistan that it would be willing to make significant concessions, but also pledge that if Pakistan ceased its support for Kashmiri separatists, Delhi would not change its mind once the situation in the Valley had become more normal.

Doing nothing is the most likely option for Kashmir. At best, there might be an arrangement that would ensure that the state does not trigger a larger war between the two countries. However, it would do little to address Kashmiri grievances or the rights violations in both the Indian and Pakistani-controlled parts of the state. As pointed out in the next section, a settlement of Kashmir also has to take into account the interests of China, which actually controls an important part of the state and whose views on normalization between India and Pakistan are opaque at best.

One of the major obstacles to untangling Kashmir is the belief on all sides of the dispute that "*time* is on our side." Since the Kashmir problem has been mismanaged by several generations of Indians and Pakistanis (and Kashmiris have contributed their own share of errors), no age group thinks the time has come for a solution. As the two sides briefly pass through an equilibrium point when the time may be right for talks, neither one wants to negotiate since both believe that the present situation works to their advantage, or that they are just about to, or will after some time, regain the advantage. Moreover, both sides seem to assume that the other will not compromise unless confronted by superior force. The greater Kashmir problem lies in persuading both sides—and now the Kashmiris themselves (whose perception of how time will bring about an acceptable solution is not at all clear)—to examine their own deeper assumptions about how to bring the other to the bargaining table and reach an agreement.

The Kashmir issue inevitably comes back to the state of relations between India and Pakistan. The intellectually formidable retired admiral Verghese Koithara has argued that the context of the dispute is just as important as the specific Kashmir-related issues. The very process of reaching an agreement on Kashmir has become so convoluted and distorted, he points out, that the hard-core interests of both states, as well as the Kashmiris, have been ignored, and he offers a seemingly plausible path to normalization. I have elsewhere referred to the process-problem as the *pahelee aap* (please, you go first) syndrome, in which each side urges—begs—the other to go first, and nothing happens.[49]

It is not possible for one side to force the other into acceptance of a solution that the latter regards as detrimental to its interests and its sense of self-respect. Any outside attempt at mediation, or even arbitration, would be received with great suspicion in India—even though many Indians privately acknowledge that their relationship with Kashmir, and Pakistan, is pathological. But now even Pakistan has doubts about the wisdom of outside engagement, especially American—a fallout of the bitter relationship between the two that has arisen over Afghanistan. Much as India may feel convinced on legal and moral grounds that the Kashmir question is closed, it has still to tackle the supreme problem of living with Pakistan as a neighbor. Therefore the issue of Kashmir is likely to persist as long as Pakistan refuses to agree that it has been resolved. Likewise, Pakistan has to realize that it cannot successfully create situations that will force India to surrender its position in Kashmir.[50]

A Kashmir agreement must be 90 percent face-saving; it must find reasons for both sides to accommodate the intensely held fears and feelings of the other, as well as those of Kashmiris themselves. This would be difficult but not impossible. One strategy would be to develop common *criteria* for a settlement, rather than resorting to stale and unresolvable arguments based on mutually exclusive interpretations of history. As democracies, both India and Pakistan theoretically place high value on human rights, not just principles of national self-determination. The latter narrow vision would be destructive to Pakistan as well as India and would be an unacceptably dangerous basis for settling the future in a region where every state and province is vulnerable to the argument of self-determination. This means there must be concessions by Pakistan on one of the principles on which it was founded, but if these rights can be effectively protected in other ways, then Pakistani concerns can be met. India must then treat its own Kashmiri population as if it had the rights and freedoms of all Indians, not just as an exceptionally troublesome province. In turn, India needs assurances that a more "independent" or "autonomous" Kashmir would not fall under the sway of Islamic extremists or separatists. In their two-day 2001 Agra summit, the countries made considerable headway on the terms of a Kashmir agreement, but on these basic concerns—minority rights on the Pakistani side and the preservation of the basic political order on the Indian side are minimum conditions for an agreement—the two sides are still far apart.

Siachen

Siachen would seem to be an easy dispute to resolve. Kanti Bajpai, the Indian scholar and analyst, has urged both sides to do so, as it "has already been resolved once."[51] Drawing on comparisons with the Falklands, I once termed the dispute "two bald men fighting over a comb," but conversations with Indian military officers and their strong public opposition to a settlement on present terms indicate that unlike the Falklands case, where symbolism was the primary interest on both sides, Siachen may have critically important strategic dimensions.

The Siachen dispute arose in 1984 when the Indian army seized the glacier's heights, fearing that recent Pakistani expeditions might lead to an expansion of the latter's position. The general in charge of the operation in the world's highest battlefield has since expressed public remorse over his actions, but the army remains firmly committed to holding the high ground, even though it has suffered enormous casualties there, mainly due to frostbite. However, the construction of a helipad near the glacier and other logistic improvements have made the cost bearable for the Indian army.

In this case, India and Pakistan may have reached agreement during the prime ministership of Rajiv Gandhi—this is the view of many Indians and Pakistanis. Yet "almost" is not the same as "actually." According to one Indian official involved with Pakistan affairs, the agreement was first postponed to the time Rajiv was reelected (he was assassinated, however), was deferred by Pakistan after Hindu mobs attacked a Muslim mosque in 1992, and then was put aside by Mani Dixit, a notoriously hard-line Indian foreign secretary.

In addition, alone among strategic issues, the Indian army has had second thoughts on the solution that was almost reached. Today it is the only dispute that I know of where the Indian army has publicly opposed any change in the status quo, while the Pakistan army has publicly supported some kind of agreement.

India's reluctance to agree to the earlier settlement is due to Siachen's relationship to larger geopolitical issues. In the words of one senior retired Indian army general with extensive service in this region, the Saltoro Ridge and the Siachen Glacier are of no strategic significance in themselves.[52] Siachen has no practical connection to Chinese-controlled areas of the territory that Pakistan ceded to China in 1963. Nor is there a link between Siachen/Saltoro and Chinese forces in Tibet—they are already in Gilgit (in Northern Areas) in strength. However, India believes the Karakoram Pass is critical to its security—in a future scenario Pakistan and China might expand their presence in this area via the Karakoram, flanking those Indian forces that defend Jammu and Kashmir proper. As long as Kashmir is unsettled, and as long as India and China are strategic rivals (India threatens China's position in Tibet, just as China, with Pakistan, can threaten India in Kashmir), India will remain obsessed with Pakistan-China collaboration in the northern territories. Add to this the growing Chinese economic presence in other parts of Pakistan, and there are good military-related reasons for India to refuse to settle on the glacier question.

Does the nuclearization of South Asia change this calculation? Not in the minds of the respective armies (nor the Chinese), as their preparations for a conventional clash proceed. Both understand that a nuclear umbrella may not deter meddling should the Indian-dominated political order in Kashmir break down (or, for that matter, the Chinese-dominated political order in Tibet, or Pakistan's control over rebellious Baluchistan).

How can both armies be persuaded that the risks of a settlement are minimal and the gains tangible? A large problem, as Pakistani minister of defense Ahmed Mukhtar has observed, is that army egos are at stake on both sides of the line.[53] Despite the possibility of reduced casualties and the cleanup of the world's most polluted battlefield (some have called for the creation of a peace park in the Siachen region that could be devoted to research on high-altitude environmental and ecological concerns as well as transformed into a novel if stressful tourist destination), the soldiers are adamant and in India's case have a veto over policy.

The lack of progress on the issue is a frustration to well-informed observers such as television and print journalist Jyoti Malhotra, who suggests the problem could be resolved if Manmohan Singh were to order the military and the bureaucracy to agree to a negotiated settlement.[54] Her conversations in Islamabad persuaded her that the Pakistanis are now ready for a solution of Siachen, but others remain deeply skeptical as to whether Pakistan would in fact agree to a settlement and might not be playing for time, or whether Manmohan Singh could overrule the dark suspicions of his own army.

Suggestions that Siachen be traded for less sensitive territory (such as Sir Creek, as discussed in the conclusion to this chapter) skirt the issue as far as India is concerned. The Chinese play no role in Sir Creek; they could play an important role in territory in the Siachen region. China's concern about Indian support for Tibetans, which goes back to the 1950s, suggests a different kind of trade-off. Some disputes may be easier to resolve, or compromise, if they are made bigger rather than smaller, as their roots may be located in higher geopolitics rather than the topography of a glacier or a dry creek. It is not enough, as the defense minister has said, to sit at the table and discuss the matter. From an Indian perspective, China—which the Pakistanis regard as their best friend—will be an invisible presence.

If this does not suggest a solution, it does offer a methodology, which is to expand, not shrink, the context. Merely asserting, as did the minister, that India is a big country, and Pakistan expects that it would demonstrate magnanimity by making the first move, reiterates the classic Pakistani view, that as the bigger of two brothers, India has the obligation to make concessions. This evades the role of China in India's northern areas and suggests that the India-Pakistan conundrum must, in certain respects, draw in, rather than exclude, China.

New Developments

The India-Pakistan rivalry is indeed a textbook case of intractable conflict, one of the 5 percent that are highly destructive, never ending, and apparently impossible to solve.[55] It seems to have a power of its own, driving people and groups to act in ways that go against their best interests and sometimes their judgment, on occasion sowing the seeds of their own ruin.

Two developments suggest it is time for a reappraisal of the prospect of India-Pakistan relations. Although optimism is not in order, a glimmer of hope may be warranted by changes at the strategic level. These could provide the kind of political shock that may be necessary for the termination of an enduring rivalry. On the other hand, they could also ensure that this conflict will continue after 2047, or even end calamitously for one or both states. Together, they make high-level organized war unacceptably costly to both countries, and they provide a good reason to move toward normalization.

One of these developments is the nuclearization of South Asia, formally achieved in 1998 but well under way before that. A few months after coming to power, the coalition government in New Delhi led by the Bharatiya Janata Party (BJP) conducted five nuclear tests and declared India to be a nuclear weapons state. Pakistan then conducted its own tests. Today India and Pakistan are exactly in the same position as the United States and the Soviet Union used to be. Mutual and assured destruction is alive and well in South Asia.

Second, 9/11 had immediate and long-term consequences for India and Pakistan, and for the policies of major outside powers.[56] This event came at the flood tide of globalization in Pakistan (and to a lesser degree, India). It showed that Islamic solidarity had supplanted ethnicity and linguistic allegiances, replacing communism as a coherent rallying point for the discontented of the Islamic world.[57]

Islamic extremism, which advocates a transformed global paradigm, is highly disruptive to both states. Around 20 percent of the world's Muslims live in these two countries, and in each there are pockets of retrograde social and economic orders. For many Pakistanis and for some Indian Muslims, "justice" is a legitimate and effective rallying cry, and Pakistan in particular has been unable to generate the kind of economic growth and political institutions that provide a realistic answer to radical Islamist rhetoric. This jihadist narrative explicitly targets Indian Muslims; it also demonizes professedly Muslim states that do not meet hyper-radical expectations or that have ties to the West, notably Pakistan. India is threatened by the rise of Pakistani Islamic extremism; it might contaminate India's own population, and elements in Pakistan might expand their attempt to destabilize India.

Although nuclearization and Islamic extremism make India and Pakistan more vulnerable, they also provide them, as states, with a shared interest in maintaining a common political front. It is hard to predict whether these new developments will transform the India-Pakistan relationship. It could go one of two ways: either a catastrophic nuclear exchange "proves" that proliferation will have terrible consequences, or Islamic extremism will overcome Pakistan and further destabilize India.

What is the best case to be made for normalization? Since India and Pakistan share much in terms of history, climate, language, economies, and culture, it would seem that they should act upon these shared interests. They also share many strategic choke points. Rather than fight each other, they might want to cooperate, as other once-hostile pairs of states have done. The World Bank has sponsored numerous studies that describe the benefits accruing to both states if the obstacles to trade and economic cooperation were reduced. Others have suggested that they cooperate on water resources, or allow movement of their citizens between the countries, or "solve" the Kashmir issue—or at least put it aside.

Yet urging the two states to cooperate has become tiresome—only the World Bank doggedly pursues that goal. Most governments offer lip service to normalization but have long since given up on diplomatic initiatives that would see India and Pakistan working in the same direction. Indeed, the George W. Bush administration was praised for "dehyphenating" India and Pakistan, as if they were in different parts of the world.

Rich in Disputes, Poor in Solutions

Trade, water, Kashmir, and Siachen are just the four most important disputes between India and Pakistan. There are others. A small boundary dispute exists over the area around Sir Creek between Sindh and Rajasthan, which has some mineral deposits but is in no sense a strategic prize. It is related to another dispute, over the Rann of Kutch boundary between India and Pakistan, which was resolved by the three-member India–Pakistan Western Boundary Case Tribunal in Geneva in 1968 (see box 2-2). The tribunal's

Box 2-2. ***Rann of Kutch, A Questionable Success***

About the only territorial dispute that has been settled with outside help concerns the Rann of Kutch, a desolate area on the Sindh-Rajasthan border that had an ambiguous status, like Kashmir or Junagadh.[a] After being routed by China in 1962, India wanted to demonstrate firmness along its border. Meanwhile, Pakistan's president Ayub Khan was confident of his forces. The battle for control over the Rann was indecisive; neither army was very effective. The British high commissioner in Pakistan persuaded Ayub to agree to a ceasefire, with the final result to be mediated by Britain and the United Nations. The two countries agreed to abide by the judgment of a three-man commission. One member was appointed by India (a Yugoslav, presumably favorable to New Delhi), another by Pakistan (an Iranian, likewise favorable to Islamabad), and for the chair, the UN secretary-general stepped in and nominated a Swede. The final judgment was mixed: India kept some territory, Pakistan got the rest, but the political consequences were such that both countries were affected by more than a small loss of territory. Ayub was roundly criticized by Pakistanis, notably Zulfikar Ali Bhutto, his foreign minister, for vacillating, while the Indians were determined to never again submit their borders to the judgment of outsiders. Thus the one "successful" example of outside mediation had completely unpredictable results in both countries.

a. For one narrative, see Lubna Abid Ali, "The Rann of Kutch and Its Aftermath," *South Asian Studies* 24 (July–December 2009): 250–56.

award also demarcated the boundary on Sir Creek, which later became a bone of contention between India and Pakistan.

Other grievances include the regular attacks on innocent populations and religious symbols in both countries, and the harsh treatment each side metes out to the other's diplomats. These all refresh paranoia, which has become so deep and pervasive that it is now an independent factor.

Complicating matters, any agreement on river waters, Kashmir, and Siachen would have a Chinese dimension. The Chinese would now seem to be an unlikely facilitator of India-Pakistan normalization, but this cannot be ruled out in the future. Does Beijing want a normal Pakistan as much as it wants to exploit Pakistan and rely on it to balance India? This will be a test of China's claim that it is a responsible rising power, but even if it is interested in such a role, will it be acceptable to India? These questions have no clear answers.

Leaving aside the China factor, what are the odds that India and Pakistan can tackle some or all of these disputes? The significance of Pakistan's changed policy on trade and business cannot be exaggerated. Of the four central issues, it remains the one easiest to resolve, because both states would get tangible benefits. Trade is the most likely candidate for progress. It is in the interest of both countries, but it took economic desperation on the part of one side to break the logjam. The army turned to India only when it concluded that Pakistan's economic situation was truly desperate and the United States was turning hostile. Yet many opportunities may still arise to frustrate progress: there will have to be a trade-off of tangibles, such as the benefits and costs of trade, as well as the intangibles, such as status and political issues within each country. The process of expanding trade might create more opportunities for political obstruction, or a lobby that makes it easier to progressively expand trade, perhaps moving on to and influencing other issues, such as water and boundary settlement.

In the Indus water dispute, outsourcing proved an aid to problem solving. Success was achieved because the issue was treated positively as a technical question that did not necessitate politically problematic trade-offs. In the end both sides received assurances about a steady supply of water, even though it was not an optimal agreement. This has changed now, with the issue more politically charged in both countries, involving not only India-Pakistan relations but also disputes between different Pakistani provinces and between several Indian states, not to mention the still-unclear role of China. Further, the United States—which brokered the deal in partnership with the World Bank—was then seen as a benign friend in both countries, as both were heavily dependent on American and World Bank aid for their economic development.

The Kashmir issue exists largely in the realm of intangible costs and even more intangible gains that are very hard to measure. Any effort at a solution will require both countries to reassess not only the nature of their zero-sum game, but also the "game" each government plays with domestic constituencies, especially in Kashmir, as well as with Pakistanis and Indians of Kashmiri extraction and ethnicity. Some of these constituencies are also locked in a zero-sum competition.

Siachen, on its face the easiest issue to resolve, may be the most difficult if Indian and Pakistani strategic calculations (mostly by the respective armies) take into account China's role in the region. Thus because of the three-way calculation, it may actually be harder to resolve Siachen than any other dispute between India and Pakistan.

As the next three chapters make clear, these four areas of disagreement have deep causes that reflect profound differences between the two countries, so that even if the disputes were resolvable, the differences might remain. In view of the many unsuccessful attempts to resolve each of the four issues, there may be only two realistic policy options for India and Pakistan. One is the equivalent of a medical policy of hope in the case of a chronically sick patient: avoid doing harm, but take no risk in trying to do good. The second option is metaphoric bypass surgery: go around a problem—certainly Kashmir at the moment—strengthening other arteries, that is, focusing on the doable issues, not those that still are deeply embedded in the identities of both states. It would be naive to hope for a metaphoric heart transplant in each, wherein all attitudes and grievances of the past are removed, replaced by a new, functioning, and optimistic outlook toward each other.

CHAPTER THREE

INDIA

Indian attitudes toward normalization with Pakistan have always been complex—sometimes a euphemism for confused. Few other issues have generated as deep a conflict between Indian adherence to cherished ideals on the one hand, and hard military, economic, and political realities on the other.

Most Indian leaders opposed the creation of Pakistan on the grounds of principle—a Muslim, let alone an "Islamic," country flew in the face of the ideal of a unified, secular state. Prime Minister Jawaharlal Nehru, who steered India until his death in 1964, was the chief proponent of this view, and he was not shy about sharing his views publicly and with foreign leaders.

In a 1958 letter to President Dwight Eisenhower, he wrote that Kashmir, water issues, and other disputes between India and Pakistan were the result, and not the cause, of Pakistan's hostility. Others, implying the West, had exacerbated the problem; their military aid and willingness to enter into pacts with Pakistan allowed it to "think in terms of coercing India." This was unacceptable, and India was not only the aggrieved party, but Pakistan profited by its aggression. Unfortunately, observed Nehru, Pakistan was being encouraged by the UN Security Council and other powers to continue its policy of aggressive intransigence.

> How anxious we have been ever since Independence to have normal and friendly relations with Pakistan. We had hoped that the old conflicts and the policy of hatred and violence, pursued by the old Muslim League, which indeed had led to the Partition, would cease. It was obviously to the advantage of both countries to live in peace and friendship with each

> other and to devote themselves to their social and economic development which was so urgently needed to give a social content to our freedom and independence. Unfortunately for us and for Pakistan, our hopes were not realised and the Pakistan government continued to pursue that old policy of hatred and violence. Every government that comes to power in Pakistan bases itself on this policy of hatred against India.[1]

However, Pakistan was not on another continent; it was India's neighbor. It shared a water system, a climate, and cultural and trade links. It feared India more than it disliked alliances that made it dependent on outsiders. To add to India's consternation, Pakistan did not collapse as Nehru and others expected, and from an Indian perspective this was the worst possible outcome. The two states became mired in a strategic no-man's-land, neither truly peaceful neighbors nor at war. While over the decades some Indian leaders and a few private groups have tried to fix things, nothing has worked.

As discussed in chapter 4, Pakistan's internal cohesion is rapidly changing, with an increased likelihood of transformation or even collapse. However, the vivisection of Pakistan by India, as in 1971, has to be ruled out now that both countries have nuclear weapons.

Besides the advent of nuclear weapons and Pakistan's political incoherence, other new factors have arisen, notably the economic liberalization policies of the 1990s. These were spearheaded by Manmohan Singh, who became India's prime minister in 2004 and happened to be born in a small village in what is now Pakistan. Singh has organized yet another cautious peace effort, this one backed by Indian business and commerce. Given widespread doubts about Singh's normalization goals—which are shared by only a few Indian political leaders—it would be foolish to predict success. Yet the compulsions for normalization remain.

India's newfound capabilities and Pakistan's weaknesses add up to a paradox. As the Pakistani state weakens, normalization becomes all the more urgent, and the economic means to bring it about may be within India's capabilities. Yet the arguments against pursuing normalization with a fading country are also powerful: why act, when the fruit will fall from the tree on its own accord? There are other obstacles to normalization, including the structure of the normalization process. Bilateral normalization requires willingness on both sides, the neutralization of those who hold a veto, and at least the tacit consent of major third parties. Finally, there are important differences among and between Indians and Pakistanis in defining what "normal" might actually look like.

Indian uncertainty is evident in the history of efforts to reach agreements. Indian officials argue that they have taken the initiative on many occasions, but the record is very mixed, regardless of which party was in power. Nehru offered Pakistan a "no war" agreement, and a year before his death his foreign minister suggested formalizing the cease-fire line in Kashmir as an international boundary.

Nehru's successor, Lal Bahadur Shastri, met with President Ayub Khan at Tashkent, in a Soviet-brokered summit, formally ending the 1965 war. Nehru's daughter, Indira Gandhi, met with Zulfikar Ali Bhutto in Simla in 1972 to wrap up the 1971 war. She had moved decisively against Pakistan in 1971 and brought about the partition of the country by midwifing the birth of Bangladesh. However, Indira shied away from either a continuation of the military conflict in the west or major concessions that would have accommodated Pakistan's core concerns. She agreed with Bhutto to abstain from the use of force or from fostering subversive elements in each other's country; further disputes were to be settled bilaterally, not with the help of outsiders or at the United Nations. None of these pledges were kept. Although Indians assumed that the war was over and relations could return to normal, Pakistan was left with deep fear, which was exacerbated by the 1974 Indian nuclear test.

A new generation then had its opportunity. Indira's son (Nehru's grandson) Rajiv Gandhi reached several agreements with Benazir Bhutto (Zulfikar Ali Bhutto's daughter). One, in 1988, was an agreement *not* to attack nuclear installations. Rajiv also reached, but did not formally conclude, an agreement on the Siachen Glacier.

After two subsequent crises, a non-Congress government (all of the above were members of the Congress Party) reached an agreement in 1990 to set up hotlines, and one year later P. V. Narasimha Rao, who had been a foreign minister under Indira Gandhi, submitted six "non-papers" to Pakistan; these included a pledge not be the first to use nuclear weapons, which neither country had at the time.

Passionately interested in normalizing relations with Pakistan, India's prime minister Inder Gujral reinstituted the hotlines, met with Pakistan prime minister Nawaz Sharif four times, and sought to remove Kashmir as the central subject of India-Pakistan dialogue. In keeping with his "Gujral Doctrine," which advanced the principle that no South Asian country would allow its territory to be used against another, in 1997 he unilaterally shut down India's covert active operations in Pakistan—this brought considerable criticism in India and no apparent reciprocity from Pakistan.

The non-Congress streak continued with the coming to power of the Bharatiya Janata Party (BJP) in a coalition; the new administration not only set off a nuclear weapon in 1998, but Prime Minister Atal Bihari Vajpayee traveled to Pakistan (by bus) for the Lahore Summit in 1999, and in a first for an Indian prime minister, he said that a stable and prosperous Pakistan was in India's interest. He invited President Pervez Musharraf to India for a dialogue on nuclear issues, and his party colleague, L. K. Advani, suggested a confederation of South Asian states.

Congress returned to power in the form of Manmohan Singh, who in 2004 continued the Composite Dialogue process begun by Vajpayee. A secret effort in 2007 reportedly fell just short of an agreement on Kashmir. Singh talked about "making borders irrelevant" in South Asia and revived the dialogue with Pakistan after it was interrupted by the 2009 attacks on Mumbai.[2]

Of these efforts, the central concerns here are the attitudes and policies toward normalization with Pakistan and the factors that have shaped them (some other efforts are examined in chapter 5). It is certain that any normalization process will have to surmount at least three obstacles: (1) the lingering impact of the past, including Pakistan's impingement on India's own identity and domestic politics; (2) competing Indian "theories" of the nature of the Pakistani state; and (3) geomilitary and geopolitical calculations, such as Pakistan's military power and its relations with allies and others. At the same time, normalization might benefit from the fear of a nuclear war and the potential role of new economic and environmental developments. Together, these factors will shape (or defeat) any Indian effort at normalization with Pakistan, but they will not necessarily create conditions in Pakistan to reciprocate.

India's Pakistan Problems

Not surprisingly, given the complexity of domestic politics and the history of sixty plus years, much of India's Pakistan policy begins at home. While the relationship has a geomilitary element, the fact remains that partition still matters, as does the presence of a large Indian Muslim community.

Indian scholar-lawyer A. G. Noorani has termed the partition of the subcontinent one of the ten modern catastrophes.[3] While most Indians regard the division as unfortunate, few would want to now undo it. The events of 1947 are embedded in popular culture and mythology.

Some in India are busy rewriting history so as to instill in new generations a warped view of the past.[4] Past Muslim rulers are routinely portrayed as bigots, and this is often linked to Pakistan's current government. Emperor

Akbar's unique enlightened status is explained in terms of positive Hindu influences. While it happens more often in Pakistan, events that took place during India's pre-British years are given a communal twist, with some Indian texts portraying Pakistan as a medieval, antimodern state. These images are held across the political spectrum, from left to right, and are evenly distributed north and south. Yet the picture is not one of unalloyed hatred. Most national institutions in India are committed to teaching a secular view of history, even if the pressures to adopt a more communalist interpretation are strong, especially in Uttar Pradesh, Gujarat, Madhya Pradesh, and Maharashtra, where the Hindu nationalist movement is influential.

In an ironically positive way, partition is also important because it impinges on India's own identity and domestic politics. While Pakistan's experiment as a religiously inspired state is widely seen as a failure, it has reinforced India's secular identity—Indian secularists can point to Pakistan as an outcome of theocratic political leanings. Also, Pakistan's military-dominated politics strengthened the hand of Indian civilian politicians, who, after Pakistan's first military coup in 1958, tightened control over the Indian armed forces. Seeing Pakistan's recent mismanagement of its economy, Indian leaders are more confident that their own form of economic liberalization is the better one, and most Indians feel that "well, we are not yet up to China's economy, or Europe's levels of democracy, but we are certainly not like Pakistan."

Indians, like many others, remain confused over Pakistan's contemporary identity, both as a failed military and a struggling liberal democracy, all the while trying to give meaning to its Islamic identity. On all three counts, it is at variance with India. When told that Pakistan is a state where Muslims can live as a secure majority in their own homeland, most Indians respond that they would not change their own secular identity to accommodate a retrograde and "medieval" view of politics. This is not just a theoretical point: for all of its shortcomings, Indian secularism effectively accommodates very diverse religious and ethnic groups. Further, Indians resent the way in which Pakistan has mobilized international "Muslim" opinion against them on such issues as Kashmir, which they widely regard as a domestic issue.

In its raw form, this is what Samuel Huntington would have called a clash of civilizations, with a conflict between the cultural organizing principles of both states. In practice, Huntington's characterization of the India-Pakistan frontier as a border between civilizations is flat wrong. India's secularism makes concessions to religion, and Pakistan's Islamic state has many elements of their shared secular British Indian legacy. The two have much in common, and in many instances there is a degree of convergence because both states must respond as South Asian countries to similar global trends—notably new concerns about social equity, the environment, and climate change—not merely as an Islamist or a secular state. Indeed, the post-9/11 world gives them a new common enemy, one lacking in the past: namely, rising militant Islamists who would attack both the moderate Islam of Pakistan and India's secularism.

American support for Pakistan after 1950 and its subsequent entry into several Western-sponsored alliances used to be a major issue for Indians, who for forty years explained away their usually cool relations with Washington and scoffed at Pakistan's dependent relationship with it. Now that U.S.-Indian relations are closer than U.S.-Pakistan relations, "pactomania" is no longer an issue, although Pakistan's ties to China, discussed later, remain a factor.

At the same time, Pakistan's political order, with an establishment that draws from the armed services, large landowners, and an intellectual class that has accommodated itself to a militarized state, is regarded as a threat. As Shekhar Gupta, one of India's leading journalists, points out, after the cold war India remained Pakistan's permanent hostage: "The Pakistani establishment knows only one trick works—in fact, it always works. It is a provocation, and an escalation of tensions with India." The incoherence and irresponsibility of Pakistan's military-civil establishment worries Gupta, as it worries many others.[5]

India as a "Muslim Country"

Formally a secular country, India is also a state with one of the world's largest number of adherents to Islam. The latest available Indian census data (from 2001) put the number of Indians practicing the religion in the country at 138.2 million, or 13.4 percent of the total population.[6] A 2010 study by the Pew Forum on Religion and Public Life estimates India to be the homeland to 177.3 million Muslims, just a few hundred thousand less than the number of Muslims in Pakistan (178.1 million). This means that there are more Muslims in India than in Iran, Morocco, Afghanistan, and Saudi Arabia *combined.* Given the impressive growth rate of Islam in India (76 percent since 1990), India now may be home to the world's second largest Muslim community (it was fourth in 1990, behind Bangladesh).[7]

What is euphemistically called the communal factor grows out of the still-ambivalent position of India's by now nearly 200 million Muslims. Their presence, no less than Pakistan's survival as a declared Islamic state, is a reminder that India was once conquered and ruled by Muslims, and that there were mass conversions from Hinduism to Islam. Indian Muslims are otherwise intertwined with Pakistan. An unknown number of families have relatives on both sides of the border who travel back and forth for family occasions, for tourism, and for religious festivals.

Of the Muslims who stayed behind, some supported Pakistan, others did not, but almost all were considered suspect for years, if not decades, after partition. A few families subsequently migrated out of personal grievances, family ties, or economic disadvantage (one notable emigrant, Abdul Qadeer Khan, later became central to the Pakistani nuclear program).

Indian domestic politics are also linked to Pakistan because of regional variations in the status of Muslims. There is much less discrimination against Muslims and communal violence in the south, whereas in the northern and western states anti-Muslim riots have occurred regularly. These communal riots have a long and complicated history, but in almost every case they stem from the desire to raise the "Green threat" in order to rally Hindu votes. Indian Muslims often cannot retaliate effectively, especially if the police are controlled by unsympathetic state governments, and demagogues try to link them to Pakistan.[8] (How these communal riots figured in shaping Pakistani views toward India is taken up in chapter 4.)

Kashmir is another factor for Indian Muslims. Pan-Indian communal conflict is more closely linked to Jammu and Kashmir than most people imagine. On a visit to New Delhi, Sheikh Abdullah—a close friend of Nehru and the state's most prominent politician at the time of independence—noted that "there isn't a single Muslim in Kapurthala, Alwar, or Bharat Pur [three former princely states that went to India]. Some of these had been Muslim majority states. Try to . . . understand the Kashmir Muslims. They are afraid that the same fate lies ahead of them as well."[9]

Since the early 1990s the grievances of Muslims in India have shifted markedly, and their theoretical connection with a struggling Pakistan is less important to them than their self-awareness as one of India's poorest groups.[10] The travails of the Indian Muslim community that migrated to Pakistan (the Mohajirs), concentrated in Karachi and Hyderabad, are evidence that *not* leaving India may have been the better choice—although for millions of poor Indian Muslims, especially those located away from the borders, migration was not a practical option.

Some sections of India's Muslim community flaunt identification with Pakistan to assert their distinctiveness and provoke Hindu nationalists. Some even express resentment toward India openly by supporting Pakistani cricket and hockey teams, which prompts some Indians to question their loyalty. These and other symbolic gestures are used to increase their visibility and their claim to state-controlled resources. A few have resorted to terrorism to make their political points even clearer. As noted by Pakistani educator F. S. Aijazuddin, however, over the past sixty years the attitude of Indian Muslims toward Pakistan "has shifted perceptibly down-scale, from being a dream immediately after 1947, to disappointment after 1965, then disillusionment after 1971, and now derision after the Mumbai attack of 26/11. The grass may have been greener over the septic tank once, but to them Pakistan is now no better than simply a septic tank, infested by vermin-like terrorists."[11]

With their large presence, Muslims and their vote are a fact of Indian politics. Although they constitute a majority only in Jammu and Kashmir—a very special case—and Lakshadweep, they have sizable populations in Assam (31 percent), West Bengal (25 percent), Uttar Pradesh (18 percent), and Bihar (17 percent). Of the 403 (electoral) assembly positions in India's largest state, Uttar Pradesh, Muslims make up 25 percent of the electorate in at least 170 constituencies as of 2007. Of the 593 districts in India, 240 districts have a significant Muslim population of at least 10 percent or more and are home to nearly 82 percent of India's Muslim population, that is, nearly 113 million people.[12] Except in a few states, however, Muslims tend to be underrepresented in the Indian parliament. Paradoxically, Indian Muslims are both marginalized and courted. Their marginalization is well documented and was the subject of the 2005–06 Sachar Committee, which examined almost all aspects of Indian Muslim life.[13]

Muslims are courted because they often account for the swing vote that determines which coalition governs in a state, and even the nation. Indeed, the position of Muslims in the central government is a visible sign of their political importance: three Muslims have been president, one an acting president, and three have been vice president (including Hamid Ansari, the current incumbent). There are also usually five to ten Muslims on the Council of Ministers. Some states with vast Muslim populations, such as Uttar Pradesh, have large numbers of Muslim ministers. Members of their community behave very much the way other rising castes and linguistic groups function: they indirectly shape Indian foreign policy relating to a number of countries, especially in the Middle East, which is home to about 5 million overseas Indians, many of them Muslims. Policy toward Israel and Palestine clearly stems from a desire not to alienate Indian Muslim sentiments, as do policies toward Iran (India has the second largest Shia population in the world after Iran). In each case, however, there were and are also realpolitik reasons for the relationship: in the case of Israel, India studiously ignored that state until it discovered that Israel could be a good supplier of military technology (it is now India's second largest supplier by value), and in the Iranian case, besides having the Shia tie, it supplies India with more than

10 percent of its crude oil supplies, while India is the largest exporter to Iran of refined oil products. Ironically, the leadership of Indian Muslims is in many ways more conservative than their Pakistani counterparts. Indian law caters to Muslim sensitivities in ways than Pakistan's does not. The outright pandering to the Muslim vote plus anti-India cheers by a few Muslims at sporting events have led to discussions about the degree to which Indian foreign policy should be steered by an ethnic or religious minority. Opponents of this approach have accused several Indian governments of being craven in the face of "minority" opinion, or of being "Pak lovers" or anti-Hindu. This complaint commonly arises during debates over special quotas or treatment for Muslims, even though they are underrepresented and segregated by caste, socioeconomic status, ideology, and regional distribution.

The actions of groups, quite apart from those Kashmiris who openly advocate independence, tend to cast even greater suspicion on India's Muslims. These include extremist groups with ties to Pakistan's intelligence services, notably the Students Islamic Movement of India (SIMI), founded in the 1970s, and the Indian Mujahiddin (IM), possibly a spinoff. Muslim extremism in India is clearly linked to the rise of Hindu extremism and tends to draw its followers from the lower middle classes.[14] Both groups are comprised of Indian Muslims, and the rhetoric of both supports the global jihad proclaimed by al Qaeda, although their actions are so far limited to India.

As far as public reputation goes, an important countervailing factor is the prominent role that Muslims play in Indian popular culture. Much of this culture is rooted in the courts of the Mughals and the nizam of Hyderabad. It is hard to state an exact number, but many of the top-tier film actors (Yusuf Khan/Dilip Kumar, Shah Rukh Khan, Aamir Khan, Salman Khan, Saif Ali Khan) are Muslim. Several front-line directors (in the past Mehboob Khan, K. A. Abbas, Kamal Amrohi, K. Asif) are also Muslims, and several Pakistani stars have worked in India, where they have achieved great fame, notably the glamorous Veena Malik, who denies she posed nude with a mock tattoo labeled "ISI" [Inter-Services Intelligence] on her shoulder.

Echoes of the Raj

Much of India's policy toward Pakistan flows from geopolitical and strategic considerations, often derived from the Raj's geopolitics, although now two states contest the choke points that the Raj fought to protect. Partition established a geographically unnatural boundary between them. The new western border ran through the populous Punjab, and several major Pakistani rivers rise in India; in the east, partition severed an economically integrated Bengal along religious lines.

The British expected that Pakistan would continue to serve as India's northwest bulwark. Its location was considered important to the goal of containing Soviet ambitions, a strategy reinforced by Pakistan's membership in several cold war pacts. India rejected this idea. Led by Nehru, New Delhi was guided by a vision of India—and only India—as the great South Asian power, one of the globe's five cultural-strategic regions, and in cooperation with the others would manage world order. The view mirrored that of several American presidents (from Theodore Roosevelt to Franklin Delano Roosevelt, including Woodrow Wilson), the idea being that a coalition of the world's powerful states would ensure global order and prosperity. In response, Pakistan not only disputed India's status as South Asia's leader, but it brought the cold war into the region through its alliances, challenging India's self-perception as the legitimate—and sole—inheritor of the Raj's strategic legacy.

The end of the cold war and the disappearance of the Soviet Union in 1991 radically altered strategic assumptions about Pakistan's importance in the West's containment strategy and weakened outside support for Islamabad. This led to a regional paradox. Pakistan—ostensibly on the winning side and a formal U.S. ally—was placed under U.S. sanctions resulting from its nuclear weapons program. India—seemingly the cold war loser—gave up its experiment in socialism and began to liberalize its economy, reaping rich dividends.

Yet after September 11, 2001, the old view of the northwestern quadrant of the subcontinent as a bulwark against Islamic extremism reemerged; India found itself uncomfortably on the same side as Pakistan in the badly named "global war on terror." Both became quasi allies of the United States and as such were invited to cooperate with America, although not directly with each other. With U.S. pressure on Pakistan to cooperate in Afghanistan, the threat to India began to shift from one of Kashmiri separatism to Islamist terrorism. After 9/11 Pakistan's role changed, and it was now part of the solution since its cooperation was necessary to dampen down and contain terror attacks.

The focus on Kashmir was replaced by two contradictory developments. On the one hand, more Indians came to see Pakistan as a barrier to large-scale Islamic militancy that might flood India, in exactly the same way that the British saw Afghanistan and the Frontier Provinces of undivided India. Second, Pakistan's preoccupation with its western border led to a change in its overall security calculus, to be examined in the next chapter.

After becoming surrogate partners, the two states held meetings on terror threats and issued a promise of cooperation between their intelligence agencies. This process was interrupted when, in late November 2008, a terror attack on Mumbai was launched from Pakistan itself, with evidence of ISI tolerance if not collaboration. Later the two navies participated in Persian Gulf antipiracy operations (but not with each other). India did not give up its counterbalancing strategy regarding Pakistan and put pressure on it via Afghanistan, but the chosen instrument was aid and police and military training. Because these were supportive of the goal of normalizing Afghanistan, they were half-heartedly accepted by Washington. The missed opportunity, a chance to strengthen the larger normalization process by addressing mutual Indian and Pakistani interests in Afghanistan, is discussed in chapter 6, and the dysfunctional structure of the United States government for developing a strategic policy toward South Asia is discussed in chapter 7.

Three recent developments have the potential to transform India-Pakistan relations. One, alluded to earlier, is the qualitatively different nature of the "Islamic" threat facing India. It is not only Indian Muslims that are a political factor, but also their relationship to a Pakistan under challenge from violent Islamic ideologues. The other two new factors are the post-1998 nuclearization of the subcontinent and the prospect of rapid economic growth for India, and perhaps for the entire subcontinent.

Nuclearization put India and Pakistan on the same side of a foreign policy dilemma, as did 9/11. When the Raj faced threats from the communist Soviet Union, Nazi Germany, and Imperial Japan, its British managers decided to accommodate the Soviet bloc in the face of greater threats from Germany and Japan. Since 1962 the dual threats of Pakistan and China have presented India with a similar sequencing problem. Should it normalize with Pakistan or with China, with neither, or with both? Indian opinion has differed radically on these choices, but technology has intervened, practically ruling out some options for India, for better or for worse.

For decades, Pakistan was a constant running sore, a distraction from the task of economic growth and a burden that retarded India's march to regional and global greatness. The default option for India for years was "masterly inactivity," which led Indian officials to routinely claim that *India* was the one seeking normalization, while a recalcitrant *Pakistan*, supported by allies, meant no good to its neighbor. Between them, Pakistan, China, and the United States, each for its own reasons, wanted to contain India, the new, independent, and rising power. This was the dominant Indian strategic outlook in the decades of the 1970s and 1980s, up to the end of the cold war.

India was able to pursue a policy of inaction for several reasons.[15] First, it was the preferred policy most of the time—the default policy, and the guiding philosophy of one of India's least-heralded prime ministers, P. V. Narasimha Rao. He used to tell associates that in time most problems would take care of themselves. Rao demonstrated this by forwarding no significant initiatives toward Islamabad during his tenures as foreign minister and prime minister. At the same time, India has often been unable to act because of deadlock among its bureaucracies and the lack of national consensus on Pakistan-related issues.

Second, after 1998 India apparently ruled out the use of nuclear weapons other than in retaliation against a nuclear attack. This "forceful option" has been "organized out" of the process because the use of such weapons is widely believed to be unthinkable or impossible. This was the view of India's most eminent strategist, Krishnaswamy Subrahmanyam, who saw these devices as political and symbolic, not practical military weapons:

> Deterrence can be exercised with very modest arsenals. The survivability of the retaliatory force can be ensured by making it mobile on land or under water. Once the idea of war fighting is given up as infeasible then the command and control over a modest retaliatory arsenal will not be as costly as those meant for war fighting. The mutual deterrence generated by possession of nuclear weapons is now-a-days called existentialist deterrence. It is hard to imagine today disputes in which nations will have such high stakes as to risk the use of a nuclear weapon which will invite certain retaliation.[16]

As India seems to have ruled out large-scale war with Pakistan, certainly the use of nuclear weapons, it also seems to have ruled out the idea of full normalization with Pakistan. How was the nuclear option ruled out?

Before simple nuclear devices were introduced into the arsenals of both countries some time after 1992, India deterred Pakistan by a substantial defense; if that failed it could always launch a calibrated, retaliatory strike to redress the problem and deter future attacks. This was how the wars of 1948 and 1965 were fought (and the war with China in 1962 was lost). When India decided to produce nuclear weapons, it had to reconcile discrepancies in its position. For one thing, almost all Indians had been opposed in principle to nuclear weapons; only a few sought a nuclear program, and even they were uncertain about what kind of nuclear state India should become. For another, the existing defensive military doctrine was developed entirely in the context of conventional weapons that included a component of deterrence, both by denial and by punishment. The nuclear weapon was a deterrent weapon *par excellence*, but it could not be used for defensive purposes, except in a first strike, which Indians rejected.

After 1998 Indian military strategy with respect to Pakistan was thus turned on its head. India would prepare for a nuclear war, but it would not fight one. Moral qualms made India the first Gandhian nuclear weapons state: having them would make it unnecessary to use them. Although this was the wise thing to do, it did not lead to normalization. What followed instead was subconventional war by intelligence services, competition in third countries, heightened state-sponsored propaganda, and a great deal of wishful thinking.

The early Indian hope that nuclear weapons would make war impossible turned out to be false, exemplified by Kargil, the first limited war between the two countries fought under the nuclear umbrella. It was a spectacular failure of Indian intelligence and strategy and set off a scramble to deal with Pakistan's subnuclear threat. Kargil was also an ironic war: India claimed victory although it suffered serious casualties, while Pakistan claimed victory because of India's losses. It may be that both sides tacitly understood that this was the way in which their wars would now end.

After Kargil Indians came to the conclusion that they had an ineffective low-level response and a high-level response that was not credible. Defense by punishment did not work—because India could not attack Pakistani high-value targets without risking a Pakistani nuclear response that might amount to a total, nuclear war. India is now moving to a version of limited war doctrine, trying to retain a façade of victory in a situation where compromise and blurred results are inherent. The politicians and nuclear absolutists, who argued that nuclear weapons would ensure India's security, do not want to give the military more of a role in decisionmaking, as this would move India closer to the actual use of nuclear weapons, as would Pakistan's first-use doctrine. Thus the possible use of large-scale force against Pakistan (and China) has been relegated to India's security process—and India is attempting to perfect military doctrines to cover this. Limited war is the direction in which the region is moving, although that has obvious risks. One is that one or both sides will not understand that limited wars between nuclear weapons states do not resolve deep conflicts; the other is, of course, that a limited war can get out of hand and become a total war. The likely default, for India as well as Pakistan, is the expanded use of intelligence services and unofficial surrogates in the face of extreme provocations.

With the growing difficulty of managing a conventional war with Pakistan, and with nuclear war ruled out for moral and political reasons, Indians are now turning to economics and business, where they have a real advantage over Pakistan. This could become the most important factor in shaping India's policy toward Pakistan, and it could have two dimensions—a socioeconomic one and an environmental/energy one.

As for India's supposed economic superiority, it is not entirely accurate to assume that economically the country is in another league than Pakistan.

Although the Indian economy ranks 136th in terms of GDP per capita (2010) and 73rd on the *Economist*'s Quality of Life Index while Pakistan's ranks 147th and 93rd, some data show that poverty is more widespread in India than in Pakistan, and there are regional disparities in India, with over half of the world's poorest living there. Indeed, the overall socioeconomic profile is similar, with only a surprisingly small advantage for India in some of the indexes.

Yet by all of the gross measures (except the production of nuclear weapons), India is outperforming Pakistan by large margins, an especially important change from the past four decades. Economically, India came from behind and is now edging into the lead. This economic growth has led Indians to some contradictory conclusions. On the one hand, many believe that because India has gone so far and so fast, relations with Pakistan are no longer very important. This obviously supports the "do-nothing" school regarding Pakistan. On the other hand, some see the possibility of transforming Pakistan by economic means, replacing the long-standing military competition with economic integration. Somewhere in between are the economic opportunists, who are eager to do business with Pakistan but who do not regard this as strategically significant, just good business strategy.

As for energy and environmental issues, they have the potential to play a major role in shaping bilateral relations. Disputes over water are already having a detrimental effect on the relationship. Opportunities for better (or worse) relations could also arise out of shared natural gas pipelines as both countries' energy requirements mount. I return to these specific concerns in chapter 6.

Alternatives

What are India's options, and who advocates them? Theoretically, many policy alternatives are open to India, but they will be constrained by the pull of domestic politics, by Pakistan's ambiguous role in India's own identity, and by the existence of a Pakistani nuclear arsenal. Abstract calculations of strategy and realpolitik are necessarily compromised by these factors.

There are at least five major schools of thought regarding Pakistan. Although their ideas overlap to a certain extent, and range from the most accommodating to the most hard-line, all contain a mixture of the pragmatic and the idealistic, and each raises a special implementation problem. What, then, are their core assumptions regarding relations with Pakistan, what kind of engagement with Pakistan do they favor, what are the bases for cooperation, and what role should outsiders have in India-Pakistan relations?

Accommodate Pakistan

A small group of Indian politicians, scholars, and journalists would try to *accommodate* Pakistan. For years they have advocated or have tried to launch serious initiatives. This is not an organized group—its members differ as to background, generation, and political party. The most prominent individuals include Inder Gujral, who was prime minister (1997–98) in the left-center coalition government headed by the Bharatiya Janata Party, and who had served earlier as foreign minister. (Gujral passed away in November 2012.) A Congress politician, Mani Shankar Aiyar—a long-standing Nehruvian, a foreign service officer for many years, and India's first consul-general in Karachi in 1978—is a leading advocate of normalization.[17] So is the legendary Kuldip Nayar, an eminent journalist, former Indian high commissioner to Great Britain (1990) in the government of V. P. Singh, and nominated to the Rajya Sabha in 1997 by President K. R. Narayanan.[18] Members of this group included many on the left, along with members of India's small peace groups. They are, in some ways, a precursor to the next group, which focuses on specific issues that India and Pakistan have in common. One former Indian official with extensive UN experience, Shashi Tharoor, also sees an opportunity for serious India-Pakistan normalization, especially on Kashmir.[19]

The uniting feature of this group is a strong belief in the possibility of India-Pakistan cooperation. Its members do not challenge the legitimacy of the Pakistani state and see great opportunities for the two countries if they were to work more closely together on a range of issues, including economics (the dominant theme of the new pragmatists), cultural and water projects, trade, and even terrorism. Some (Nayar and Gujral) were Punjabi Hindus with deep cultural ties to Pakistan. In a meeting with senior Pakistanis, Gujral once made the case that Indians and Pakistanis are brothers, and that their differences could be readily managed if there was an effort on both sides to bridge the gap. (The nervous reaction of the Pakistanis who were present is described in chapter 4.) Gujral pursued some of these policies as foreign minister and prime minister, including the termination of covert Indian operations in Pakistan. He also promulgated the first version of India's "look East" policy, as a way of tempering Indian obsessions with Pakistan. In Inder Gujral's view, it was India's responsibility to ease Pakistani concerns. He did not quite appreciate the need for Pakistanis and Indians to grow apart and achieve their own identities before they could come together in peace.

As an indefatigable lecturer and writer, as well as parliamentarian, Aiyar has argued that India and Pakistan should work together in combating terrorism. Whether the problem comes from India or Pakistan, it has common roots, and it is in India's interests to help Pakistan address its social and political dysfunctionality so that it does not face the terror threat itself or export it to India.

Nayar, Gujral, and Aiyar have all recognized the problems of dealing with a Pakistani establishment dominated by the military. All have been scornful of India's hawks, concentrated in the intelligence services and the Ministry of External Affairs (MEA). Aiyar has spoken derisively of his "former colleagues" in the MEA, and Nayar has singled out hawks in India's intelligence services for blocking normalization with Pakistan, specifying M. K. Narayanan, who became national security adviser (NSA) upon the death of Foreign Secretary J. N. Dixit.[20] He also doubts that Narayanan's NSA successor, Shiv Shankar Menon, is a real friend of normalization, as he "may come to the conclusion one day, as some fanatics in Pakistan are realizing now, that there is no alternative to Peace." Nayar praises former Pakistani president Musharraf, who started with a policy of fire and brimstone, but whose plan for normalization may still be somewhere in Pakistan's foreign office, "accumulating dust."

Mani Shankar Aiyar has argued that with the departure of most Hindus from Pakistan, Pakistanis are no longer as anti-Hindu as were other states, such as Poland, which had "lost" their minorities but still demonize them. In Pakistan's case, anti-Hinduism may not resonate, but anti-Indianism does, and this has come to include Indian Muslims, who are regarded as traitorous to the Muslim cause, or somehow oppressed, and are evidence of Hindus' antipathy toward Muslims. Aiyar has also argued that Pakistan's antipathy toward Hindus has been redirected against other Muslims, Shia and Sunni, and above all the Ahmadis, who were declared non-Muslims during the oppressive regime of Zulfikar Ali Bhutto in 1974, hardly a promising development for relations with the still-secular India.

As for the role of outside powers, everyone in this group held the United States partly responsible for past bad India-Pakistan relations. They are, collectively, in favor of nonalignment for both India and Pakistan and believe in cooperative relations between the two, not formal alliances. They are strong supporters of the South Asian Association for Regional Cooperation (SAARC). Indians who advocate accommodation with Pakistan and helping it become a liberal democratic state are difficult to find now. Nevertheless, this perspective will return; the press coverage given to "Track II" diplomacy during the entire Kargil crisis and afterward indicates a continuing Indian interest in establishing ties with the people of Pakistan, even as the Pakistan army is demonized.

One other viewpoint might fall into the accommodationist category, but it comes from a realist perspective. When looking at the military realities of a nuclear stalemate between India and Pakistan, as well as the difficulty of governing Kashmir, one retired Indian army chief, Krishnaswamy Sundarji, publicly argued for a change in Kashmir's status and the acceptance of the fact that India and Pakistan could never have a serious war with each other. Sundarji was in every way a remarkable soldier—he was one of the masterminds of Exercise Brasstacks, which was probably intended to provoke a definitive war between India and Pakistan before the latter went nuclear. After he retired, however, Sundarji was very clear that the introduction of nuclear weapons into South Asia had introduced fundamental changes.[21] He publicly suggested a new autonomous status for Kashmir, as part of a South Asian confederation.[22]

Business and Trade Can Transform Pakistan

In the wake of the 1990 reforms, a new generation of Indian leaders, notably from the business community, have built a new argument in favor of normalization, singling out economics. There has always been some support for step-by-step cooperation in other areas, notably water issues and environmental concerns, and even nuclear security, but they have lacked political heft. The new approach, which seems to have the backing of the Indian government, takes the position that carrots, not just sticks, can facilitate the moderation of Pakistan, and the biggest carrot would be economic trade and investment, and nothing else would have a greater impact on Pakistan.

The core idea of this position is that India should cooperate with Pakistan when it is in *India's* interests, regardless of the kind of regime that governs in Pakistan and regardless of outside strategic alliances. The lead in pragmatic cooperation is being taken by Indian business organizations, and recent efforts have been strongly supported by Prime Minister Manmohan Singh and the Congress-led coalition.

This view is held by a range of Indians, from retired officials and businessmen to scholars and even the realist thinker Nitin Pai.[23] This approach is laid out in "Nonalignment 2.0, A Foreign and Strategic Policy for India in the 21st Century," signed and issued by eight individuals, with indirect government support.[24]

"Nonalignment 2.0" singles out China as India's major strategic challenge, noting that the world will soon be characterized by two "superpowers," the United States and China, but that Pakistan will be India's greatest *regional* problem. Therefore India needs to maintain a number of "negative levers," a deterrent and defense capability that will keep Pakistan from future provocations. But the document's real emphasis is on positive measures: besides economic ties, they urge movement in other areas of common interest, such as energy and water.

Like the first group, this one assumes that India's culture and society, and now its expanding economy, will have a positive impact on those Pakistanis who are exposed to it. They want to create a constituency in Pakistan that has a stake in peaceful and friendly relations with India, an argument that parallel's Nitin Pai's point that "far more than civil society, trade—more than culture—will benefit Pakistan's elite society. To the extent that it does, and further, to the extent that this creates vested interests among Pakistan's rich and powerful to prefer stable bilateral relations, better trading relations will be good for India." Pai would eventually like to see Pakistan's military-jihadi complex destroyed, but since this cannot be done directly, it would be strategically sensible to enlist the Pakistani civilian elite in this project. The failure of a trade initiative with Pakistan would not, in any case, hurt the Indian economy.[25]

Many in the business community support this strategy. With economic liberalization and rapid growth, they now operate from the center of the Indian establishment, not on its fringe.[26] Rajiv Kumar, one of the signatories of "Nonalignment 2.0" and the author of two books on the subject, was until 2012 director of the Federation of Indian Chambers of Commerce and Industry (FICCI) and, with the support of the Ministry of External Affairs, assembled a plan for India's strategic future that breaks with many clichés of the past, except in its title.[27]

A case has also been made for economic cooperation with Pakistan along subregional lines. The "PHD" grouping—the chambers of commerce of Indian Punjab, Haryana, and Delhi—has tried to establish ties with counterparts in Pakistan, and one scholar at an Indian think tank has highlighted the importance of subregional cooperation between India and Pakistan, bypassing the cumbersome national bureaucracies. Tridivesh Singh Maini, of the business-funded Observer Research Foundation, has urged Prime Minister Singh to visit Pakistan—no Indian prime minister has gone there since Vajpayee's visit in 1999—and to take with him the chief ministers of Haryana, Punjab, and Delhi. They could deal with common problems, such as water and agricultural issues, not merely the improvement of bus and rail travel. "Including the state governments in the dialogue with Pakistan," says Maini, "may also help establish common ground over such contentious issues as water, as both Punjabs face similar problems. Such dialogues might also help undermine the propaganda that plagues both sides."[28] As noted in chapter 6, India's Ministry of External Affairs went on public record in 2012 as opposing such a visit.

By and large, the economic pragmatists are not focused on Pakistan's form of government. They tend to overlook or dismiss Pakistan's covert actions, arguing that the benefits of trade will encourage it to cease or reduce such operations. While they find their strongest allies in Pakistan's business community, their core assumption is that trade and economic normalization will gradually broaden the government, and that the military can be included in the process, especially since there is a large Pakistani military-led industrial and production complex.

Alliances are not a central issue for this group, as long as these alliances do not obstruct Pakistan's normalizing with India and its integration into the South Asian community. Unlike Indian liberals such as Aiyar and Gujral, the economic pragmatists are not anti-American; indeed, many of them are the leading advocates of economic and strategic cooperation with the United States, but none would want it deeply involved in any India-Pakistan normalization process.

How should this pragmatic normalization proceed? Cautiously, but steadily is the pragmatists' advice. This perspective will grow in importance as the Indian economy becomes more market-driven, and as business interests play a greater role in influencing politics and foreign policy decisions. The pragmatists believe that the Indian strategic debate has for too long been obsessed with Pakistan, and that a balanced assessment would reorder the Pakistan threat, especially since China is a growing rival to India along many dimensions—military, economic, and strategic—throughout Asia.

Deter Pakistan until It Changes

The dominant position in India's strategic community is that India-Pakistan cooperation is a good thing, and economics and trade might ultimately lead to normalization, *but* that in the short and medium term India must be prepared to meet Pakistan's threatening actions at all levels until Pakistan changes its overall thrust. This view is widely held in the intelligence community, the armed forces, and by many in the nationalist-conservative Bharatiya Janata Party (BJP). The view is analogous to that held of the Soviet Union by many Americans, who patiently waited for the evolution of Stalin's Soviet Union into something less threatening. B. R. Raman, one of India's leading Pakistan specialists and a former official in the foreign intelligence organization, the Research and Analysis Wing (RAW), thinks it is very unlikely that Pakistan and India will enjoy good, neighborly relations in the short and medium term. Although normalization may be opposed by Pakistan's army, "this doesn't mean the two countries should not try for a more benign, friendlier approach to each other. There is a need for a common vision. The leaders of both countries need to meet more frequently to get to know each other, and like each other, and work painstakingly without undue expectations toward a common goal of peace."[29] There is room, Raman adds, for case-by-case cooperation not just in business, but also in sports, entertainment, science, agriculture, and operations to counter smuggling.

Raman even praised Pakistan army chief Ashfaq Kayani for his prompt release of the personnel of an Indian military helicopter that had strayed into Pakistani air space. He felt India should not hesitate to "highlight and hail the positive traits and reflexes of the Pakistani military leadership," adding, however, that negative traits and reflexes in matters relating to India did warrant criticism. Raman also hoped that this could be the starting point for more substantial relations between the armies of the two countries as a distrust-reducing measure and even suggested that India consider inviting General Kayani for a visit.

At the same time, members of this group favor a security capability that will deter Pakistan. It was the BJP that brought the nuclear program to its public culmination through a series of nuclear tests in 1998, and that stands for as large and as powerful a military as possible. It also supports an Indian capacity for covert operations against Pakistan. In the view of the BJP leadership, diplomacy alone will not be enough with Pakistan—or China, for that matter. India needs a covert coercive capability like Israel's; only a demonstrated ability to retaliate in kind will deter Pakistan from its own covert operations.

The political heavyweights that subscribe to this view of Pakistan do not regard it as hopelessly mired in its history: both L. K. Advani and Jaswant Singh, distinguished members of the BJP and former cabinet members, have written favorably of "Jinnah's Pakistan," in the hope that Pakistan might once again evolve toward the views of the relatively moderate Jinnah. Also, it was from the ranks of the BJP that some of the most forward-looking proposals have come on the Indian side. Atal Bihari Vajpayee, Jaswant Singh, and to some degree L. K. Advani have all been ahead of the rest of the party, notably its Rashtriya Swayamsevak Sangh (RSS) elements, in their desire to normalize with Pakistan.

Perhaps the best expression of its skeptical but not rejectionist view was that offered by a former finance minister, Yashwant Sinha, who has also served as foreign minister after a career in the Indian Administrative Service. At a Brookings Institution talk in May 2012, he commented on Prime Minister Manmohan Singh's use of the phrase "trust and verify," suggesting that the BJP would prefer to say "verify and then trust."[30] Although Sinha did not oppose the normalization process measures being attempted in mid-2012, he was skeptical of the government's approach. The difference between the two positions of course is not very wide—the BJP having taken the lead toward normalization with Pakistan under Atal Bihari Vajpayee.

Finally, many in this group believe that while Pakistan is threatening, it is China that is the greater long-term problem. In this skeptical view, Pakistan ranks low on India's threat hierarchy as its hostility to India is really due to domestic weakness that cannot be remedied much by India. Because great states require great enemies, many of those once obsessed with Pakistan are turning their gaze to China as the real threat to India. This group has a newfound respect for the United States and the belief that both America and India have a common interest in containing an expansionist and dangerous China. The journalist Bharat Karnad and others place China at the top of their threat hierarchy. Like many Indian strategists, Karnad is more concerned about China as a threat than Pakistan, which he rather pities.[31] Pakistan has missed the opportunity to become another India—a diverse and tolerant state, well suited to South Asia's religious, ethnic, and linguistic complexities. Instead, it has rejected a cosmopolitan model, unraveling a handful of threads at a time, destroying the rich fabric of its society, and losing its social and democratic ballast.

Balance a Dangerous Pakistan

A fourth Indian position, held by many in the military and the ranks of retired diplomats, sees Pakistan as it was, not as it might be, and regards it as an essentially threatening phenomenon. Its proponents see no basis for cooperation with Pakistan, which remains a dangerous state, and outsiders are part of the problem—the West for having pumped up and tolerated Pakistan to begin with, China for its continuing support for Pakistan.

What distinguishes this group is the conviction that there is something intrinsic about Pakistan that makes it a mortal threat. A large number of senior retired Indian government officials hold this view, notably those who served in Islamabad (such as Gopalaswami Parthasarathy) or who had a bad personal experience with Pakistan's security services. They are scornful of attempts to normalize or befriend Pakistan. One retired official, Kanwal Sibal, exasperatingly writes: "How should India deal with a Pakistan in turmoil? The romantics in India never lose faith in the possibility of friendship with Pakistan. To that end they will advocate the proposition of an uninterrupted and uninterruptible dialogue with Pakistan, one that removes any pretence of a link between dialogue and terrorism and therefore suits Pakistan." Moreover, "what diplomatic purpose is served by praising the prime minister of a country most hostile to us as a man of peace, particularly as he is in no position to deliver peace to us?"[32]

For many Indians, especially former officials, the very nature of the Pakistani state threatens India. In a 1982–83 survey of India's security problems, U. S. Bajpai, an eminent retired diplomat, treated the "Pakistan factor" almost as an indictment of Pakistan's many shortcomings.[33] Pakistan's limited cultural and civilizational inheritance; its military dictatorship, theocratic identity, unworkable unitary system of government (as opposed to India's flexible federalism), imposition of Urdu on an unwilling population, alienation of its rulers from their people, support of "reactionary" regimes in West Asia (India identified its interests with the "progressive" segments of Arab nationalism, such as Saddam's Iraq), dependency on foreign aid, and failure to develop a strong economic base were Pakistan's embarrassment. This perspective has enjoyed a renaissance in the ten years since Pakistan began open support for the separatist and terrorist movements that emerged in Indian-administered Kashmir.[34] The recent steps toward normal trade led one former director of Indian intelligence, Vikram Sood, to derisively write, "Hope is a policy."[35]

Why should India fear such a state? Pakistan is a threat because it still maintains that partition was imperfectly carried out, because some Pakistanis harbor revanchist notions toward India's Muslim population, and because it falsely accuses India of wanting to undo Pakistan itself. Thus Pakistan still makes a claim on Kashmir and has deeper designs against the unity of India.[36] In adhering to the theory that brought it into existence—the notion that the subcontinent was divided between two nations, one Hindu, one Muslim—and in purporting to speak on behalf of Indian Muslims, Pakistan in its very identity is "a threat to India's integrity."[37] More recently, Pakistan has served as the base for Islamic "jihadists" who not only seek the liberation of Kashmir but also the liberation of all of India's Muslims.

Pakistan's DNA, says Lalit Mansingh, is such that it cannot and will not normalize with India. Pakistan has been a threat to India since independence: it was a conventional military threat, then an unconventional one through its support for Kashmiri separatists and Islamic terrorists, and now it is a nuclear threat. India must avoid a confrontation with Pakistan. However, it needs at least fifteen years of steady growth before it can proclaim itself to be a great power, and diplomacy must shield it during that period, especially diplomacy of the kind that worked on Pakistan's allies, notably the United States. The diplomatic strategy of some in this group is to sever the

Pakistan-America tie, using India's new economic power to do so, and not succumb to American attempts to normalize with a still-dangerous Pakistan.

K. Natwar Singh, a former close associate of Indira Gandhi and foreign secretary, has written that the nature of the relationship—complex and accident-prone because Pakistan is too changeable, too unpredictable—makes normalcy impossible.[38] Pakistan's fate is of no concern to proponents of this view, who say that even its collapse would not affect India, which is far more stable and could withstand the shock. India cannot expect a peaceful transformation of Pakistan from within, so must focus on containment, maintaining a robust military capacity to defend against Pakistani incursions and relying on active diplomacy to counter Pakistan in the outside world.

> Indian diplomacy should take the form of balancing Pakistani in third countries, notably Afghanistan, and provide limited support for Pakistani dissidents in dissident provinces such as Balochistan, or Gilgit-Baltistan, since Pakistan has been doing this to India for some time. In case of a serious provocation, many Indians still talk about a limited war against Pakistan in Rajasthan and Punjab.[39]

In Singh's opinion, Pakistan is motivated by pique, is weak internally, and is rooted in the past, notably in the Kashmir dispute. He dismisses attempts to deal with Pakistan, especially by Prime Minister Manmohan Singh, who "should by now know that genuine and sustained cordiality between the two countries is a pipe dream," and who is too weak politically. The do-nothing philosophy degenerates into a series of clichés: "At this moment we have limited options. Wait and watch. Maintain status quo. Practice masterly inactivity. Bottom line: do not lower our guard, and keep your powder dry!"[40]

Break Up Pakistan

Many on the Hindu right and its supporters would go further: they would seek to break up or transform Pakistan, through force if necessary. This view is particularly popular among the more extremist wings of the Hindu nationalists, many of whom are part of the RSS and Hindu-centered organization Vishva Hindu Parishad (VHP), and often appears in *The Organiser*, the official newspaper of the RSS. It also circulates in military circles, especially among former generals, but has little effect on policy. Although rarely stated in public, such views are widespread on the Internet.[41]

This would seem to be a risky approach in the nuclear era, yet its proponents see absolutely no basis for cooperation with Pakistan. Instead, they would urge India to use military force in conjunction with support for separatists to bring about the transformation of Pakistan and believe some outside powers might even join in this endeavor.

Calls for such a transformation are even louder in the U.S. Congress—but then Americans do not have a border with Pakistan. A few hard-liner elements in the BJP and the military routinely argue that Pakistan remains an artificial country, that a newly partitioned Pakistan would leave behind a viable Sindh and Punjab, the Mohajirs could create a "Jinnahstan" in Karachi, and Baluchistan could become a weak state or revert to Iran. Some in the Indian military even talk about bringing Pakistan to its knees, defeating it militarily, disgracing the Pakistan army once and for all. Others would use covert means to exploit ethnic, linguistic, and sectarian differences in Pakistan, creating wedges between the dominant Punjabis and the rest of the country.

Yet few in India today would seriously advocate a fight to the finish against Pakistan. Most who do so belong to the generation of strategists who were turned into hawks by the 1962 war with China and were strong supporters of the 1971 war with Pakistan, or those who see Pakistan as an obstacle to India's emergence as a major power. Some were also strong advocates of nuclear weapons, although the introduction of nuclear weapons into South Asia now makes this position untenable.

The uber-hawk tactics fall into three categories: lure Pakistan into a military confrontation, leading to a final triumph over the Pakistan army (the aborted 1987 Brasstacks model); merely give Pakistan a push in the form of increased support for separatist forces in Sindh, North-West Frontier Province, and Baluchistan, which would lead to a civil war and the breakup of Pakistan (the 1971 model); or let India's greater economic potential naturally dominate Pakistan and persuade its outside supporters that it is a failed state (the Soviet model). These positions derive from two common assumptions: that Pakistan is a fundamental threat to India and that it is inherently vulnerable. They differ only in their estimate of the risk and cost of an overt military initiative.

This proactive position has not displaced the flexible realism of the BJP's recent policies toward Pakistan. The party's combined pragmatism and optimism eventually led India back to the negotiating table. While the Bajpai-Jaswant team publicly abandoned this position—insisting upon evidence of good behavior from Pakistan before resuming negotiations—the policy was followed by its successor, Manmohan Singh, who absorbed the attack on Mumbai and after much patience restored the Composite Dialogue with Pakistan on a wide range of issues.

Ambiguity: Modi, Sonia, and Rahul

Finally, several important political figures in India appear ambivalent in their position on Pakistan. Three of these are Narendra Modi, Sonia Gandhi, and her son and heir-apparent to the prime ministership, Rahul Gandhi. All three are pursuing a cautious approach and a balancing of interests.

Narendra Modi, the chief minister of Gujarat and a rising star in the BJP, epitomizes a certain ambivalence toward Pakistan. Ideologically hawkish, but economically opportunistic, Modi was associated with several communal atrocities, yet he is one of the most effective of India's politicians, at least in his home state, which borders Pakistan. On the one hand, he regularly excoriates it for supporting terrorism and has been vehement regarding other states, notably America, for the lack of clarity on their stand on Pakistan-based terrorism. His strong views here may reflect America's refusal to give him a visa, but his attacks on Pakistan please the RSS component of the BJP establishment.[42] During a trip to China—seeking Chinese investment—Modi took an appropriately hard line on the role of Chinese troops in "Pakistan-occupied Kashmir."[43] But undoubtedly the Chinese told Modi that they favored good India-Pakistan relations, and Gujarat, bordering Pakistan, would benefit enormously from trade with that country. His requests for Chinese investment balance out his concern for Pakistani-based extremism, so he has not come out directly or strongly on the India-Pakistan normalization process, except to criticize the Congress and Manmohan Singh for softness.

The views of Sonia Gandhi are conspicuous for their blandness. While publicly supporting the initiatives of Prime Minister Singh, she does not seem to hold very strong views on Pakistan one way or another. Sonia speaks publicly of giving a "fitting reply" to any Pakistani aggression, but that is conventional Indian obfuscation.

Meanwhile, Rahul seems to hold standard Indian liberal views toward Pakistan. In August 2012 he publicly accepted an invitation to visit Pakistan from Bilawal Bhutto, the Pakistani president's son and co-leader of the Pakistan People's Party. Both Rahul and Sonia are largely focused on domestic Indian politics, and for them, as for Modi, calculations of the impact of normalization on India's Muslim community may be decisive, especially in Uttar Pradesh, which has long been the bastion of Congress politics and where Rahul is most likely to again seek a parliamentary constituency.

The Sixty-Five-Year Short-Term Problem

Pakistan was the first significant Asian power that India had to deal with. India's strategic puzzle is to cope with a smaller state that has challenged it for sixty-five years by merely existing and that maintains a significant military capability. Much of the latter derives from its borrowing power: Pakistani resources are limited, but outside states have been eager to help it.

India cannot apply Raj geopolitics to Pakistan as it can to other, weaker, smaller (and nonnuclear) South Asian states. Pakistan is neither a princely state to be tolerated or absorbed nor a major power to be accommodated, and for some Indians its relationship to domestic politics in India amounts to "interference." Its very existence is thus a problem.

As should be evident by now, Indians see Pakistan in many ways: as a retrograde Muslim state, an irredentist state, a militarily dominated state, a member of hostile alliances, a state that strays from a workable past identity, and a potential South Asian partner. There is no consensus either on Pakistan's identity or on the best Indian policy toward this troubled and troublesome neighbor. These divergent perspectives have yielded a pattern of intermittent conflict and uncertain reconciliation. In the current atmosphere of rancid views, a new kind of skepticism, bureaucratic inertia, political division, and the rise of China—there are many reasons to do nothing, or to oppose normalization, or to set the barrier so high that nothing will ever be done. Recent Indian polls confirm this skepticism: in a 2012 *Hindustan Times* poll of urban Indians, younger respondents were generally more hawkish toward Pakistan than were older generations.[44] They also had a dramatically more positive view of the United States and more negative views of both Pakistan and China.

One of India's great problems has been that Pakistan is more than a regional rival—it is tied forever to India's persona. Thus until recently New Delhi has felt the need to accommodate or balance Pakistan, primarily by judicious use of intelligence services, great cultural power, and a competitive diplomacy. India's practical challenge was to deal with those states (America, China, the Arab powers) that had built up Pakistan as a serious rival. Now that this competition is practically over and that some outside states, notably America, seem to have chosen India over Pakistan (symbolized by the civilian nuclear energy agreement), will India pursue a policy of strategic accommodation with a failing Pakistan, or will it try to give it a final push? It takes two hands to clap: Pakistan must be a willing partner in the first case, but a defiant Pakistan that pursues hard-line policies in Afghanistan might provoke the latter response. The Indian debate has not yet reached the point at which these alternatives are clearly thought out. India still does not know what it wants to do, and its policy will likely remain one of drift, unless events compel a decision.

Policy is complicated by an operational reality: the level of distrust between the two countries is always so high that serious negotiations can only be conducted at the most senior political level, and if that happens, then both sides run the risk of opposition from unconsulted actors. As one senior Indian diplomat has noted, no secret talks are under way, and Track II dialogues are not taken seriously by the core political leadership. Indian leaders are wary of arrangements with a Pakistani leadership that seems to be double-dealing or unable to sell an agreement at home. Some Indians recall Pakistan's transparently insincere response to Morarji Desai's attempts to control regional nuclear proliferation and his highly publicized (and quite convincing) unilateral renunciation of nuclear weapons. These statements (and Morarji) were greeted warmly in Islamabad. Only later did India and the rest of the world come to know of the scope of the Pakistani nuclear program, and of Pakistani intentions to move toward a weapon regardless of what India did. Similarly, Gujral's disclosure of Indian covert operations in Pakistan reaped no rewards. An even stronger sense of betrayal arose in the aftermath of the Kargil crisis of 1999. In that case the civilian government headed by Nawaz Sharif appeared to be both deceptive and weak.

Looking only at the Indian side of the equation, one finds room for cautious optimism. Many see that for the first time India is not a primary factor in Pakistani domestic politics. Many also realize that normalizing relations with Pakistan will speed up India's ascent to major power status. While no Indian wants a strong Pakistan, most (excepting some hawks) do not want to see it fail either. India could do more than any other state to stabilize Pakistan and help it pass through its current political, economic, societal, and identity crises. If the worst should happen and Pakistan should truly fail, India would also be central to any damage-control effort.

Many Indians would like to see Pakistan become their Canada, but instead it is becoming their nuclear Cuba. How such a state might be transformed into a friendly neighbor is India's greatest strategic challenge, greater than choosing a strategy to contain, balance, or accommodate a rising China. Indeed, India-China relations are held to be better than relations with Pakistan—at least India and China have entered into full-scale trade with each other. As C. Raja Mohan has written, the national leadership of India's two major political parties, the Congress and the BJP, are not in the lead when it comes to normalization with Pakistan. As he also points out, neither party has picked up the ideas once forwarded by Atal Bihari Vajpayee and Manmohan Singh regarding normalization. Their place has been taken by the new "ambassadors" to Pakistan, regional Indian leaders such as Chief Ministers Nitish Kumar (Bihar) and Sukhbir Singh Badal (Punjab), while such Congress stalwarts as Defense Minister A. K. Antony allegedly blocked Manmohan Singh's initiatives regarding visiting Pakistan in 2012.[45]

From an Indian vantage point, relations with Pakistan are not necessarily written in stone. The present may not be the future. India has been able to transform its policies in several domestic and foreign spheres, and there is nothing inevitable about India-Pakistan hostility. While generation after generation of Indian leaders have tried to normalize relations with Pakistan, only to be stymied by what many see as Pakistani recalcitrance, its structure, or its political and cultural "DNA," this is not a satisfactory explanation of past events or a predictor of future ones. The future is never path dependent, and humans are capable of inventing new ideas and propounding new theories that lead to real changes in perception and policy.

The test of a normalization process will be whether it can withstand deliberate attempts to sabotage it, by individuals and groups on either side. That is to say, while it may be in India's strategic interest to normalize relations with Pakistan, and while India may now have the economic heft to make the process work, is Pakistan also in a position to move forward in this regard?

CHAPTER FOUR

PAKISTAN

The question of whether Pakistan will ever be willing to forge closer ties with its neighbor revolves in large part around its views about regional conflict. Pakistani thinking in this regard differs from Indian attitudes in three important ways. First, Pakistan takes a more "ideological" approach, in the sense that it justifies its existence and policies on the grounds of the need for an Islamic state and a homeland for an oppressed minority—Indian Muslims.[1] Many minorities seek rights and independence without the umbrella of an ideology but base their actions on the Wilsonian principle of self-determination. Furthermore, many states promulgate ideologies but never act seriously on them or cease doing so when they become dysfunctional, as was the case with most communist parties. Since its founding, when some Indian Muslims pressed for minority rights, Pakistan has toyed with the idea of self-determination for other oppressed Muslims. Yet it has been wary of these claims by its own citizens, particularly after the catastrophic separation of East Pakistan from the state.

Second, Pakistan is socially more skewed than India. Although both are examples of South Asia's astonishing diversity, Pakistan's social structure has always been more hierarchical than that of India and its ethnic and linguistic diversity less complex, especially after the loss of almost the entire Bengali population. Today, Punjab (at 56 percent) constitutes more than half of the population, Sindh makes up 23 percent, with much smaller numbers for the other provinces: 6 percent for the Khyber-Pakhtunwa and 5 percent for Baluchistan, with only 2 percent for the Federally Administered Tribal Areas (FATA), although they are geographically the largest. Plans to carve up the populous Punjab by creating a separate province out of the Saraiki-speaking areas of South Punjab will alleviate some of the anti-Punjabi feeling; this is politically important since most of the army is also recruited from the Punjab. In India the largest Indian states do not provide the bulk of military manpower, and India's Punjab, which provides the greatest proportionate military share of recruits, ranks only fifteenth of thirty-five states in overall population.[2]

Third, the ideology of Pakistan has come under official state sponsorship—it is a project directed at defining the Pakistani state and nation and specifying what good Pakistanis should believe in. This takes two forms: it contrasts Pakistan with India (always portraying the negative features of the latter), and it contrasts a unified, purposeful Islamic Pakistan with the negative tendencies of regionalism and separatism. This project, encapsulated in the constructed discipline of Pakistan studies, at its best inculcates patriotism, at its worst promotes stereotypical images of an evil and corrupt Indian state, a permanent threat to the purer "Islamic" Pakistan. The ideological component of Pakistan studies also denigrates regional and subnational loyalties. Often it links the two, blaming all separatist movements and dissents on Indian manipulation. That this did actually occur in part is another example of how a paranoid state can actually have real enemies.

All states foster this kind of we/them outlook to one degree or another, but in Pakistan's case conservative elements of society early on gained control over the development and promulgation of ideology.[3] India forms a major component of the ideology of Pakistan, of what Pakistanis are taught about themselves and about threats to Pakistan. As Ayaz Amir, a popular columnist and former army officer, has written, "In our journey towards nationhood we eschewed the rational and chose instead to play with the semantics of religion. What Pakistan has become today, a fortress not so much of Islam as of bigotry and intolerance, is fruit of these sustained endeavors."[4] Pakistan plays an important but much smaller role in India's national identity.

Pakistan's India Problem

When in an optimistic frame of mind, the Pakistani establishment feels even more threatened than its Indian counterparts but is better able to withstand the challenge than the much larger and more powerful India. Its leaders have a profound distrust of New Delhi, and the latter's reassurances that India "accepts" Pakistan's existence are not taken seriously. In the past few years this anxiety over India has been joined by pessimism about Pakistan itself. Mohammed Zia ul-Haq's colleague and army commander, General K. M. Arif, has written scathingly of India, but Pakistan, he says, "is a wounded nation, hurt by both friends and foes. Her national body is riddled with injuries of insult, neglect and arrogance inflicted by dictators and democrats; judges and generals, the bureaucrats and media. None of them are blame-free."[5]

The long-standing Pakistani explanation of regional conflict is that from the first day of independence India has made a concerted attempt to crush the Pakistan state. The original trauma was refreshed and deepened by the loss of East Pakistan in 1971, an impact that was never fully appreciated by Indians. Many Pakistanis still think their state is threatened by an increasingly extremist India, motivated by a desire for Hindu religious revenge and a missionary-like zeal to extend Indian influence to the furthest reaches of South Asia and beyond. Thus anti-Indian passions are often united with classical geopolitics, as both India and Pakistan compete in the same spaces for influence.

Like Israel, Pakistan was founded by a people who felt a sense of persecution when living as a minority, and even though they now possess their own states based on a religious identity, both remain under threat from powerful enemies. In both cases, an original partition demonstrated the hostility of neighbors, and subsequent wars showed that this remains the case. Pakistan and Israel have also followed parallel strategic policies. Both sought an entangling alliance with various outside powers (at various times, Britain, France, China, and the United States); both ultimately concluded that outsiders could not be trusted in a moment of extreme crisis, leading them to develop nuclear weapons; and both see themselves as defenders of minority grievances, even grievances that belong to another era.

Pakistani hostility to India has sources other than the tortured relationship between the two countries. According to Indians, Pakistan needs the India threat to maintain its own unity. There is an element of truth in this—distrust of India and the Kashmir conflict do serve as a national rallying cry for Pakistanis, and thus as a way to smooth over differences between Punjab and the less populous provinces. India-as-an-enemy is also useful to distract the Pakistani public from other concerns, such as social inequality, sectarian (Sunni-Shia) conflict, and the distinct absence of social progress in many sectors of Pakistani society. These factors do explain Pakistan's fear of India in part—but there remain real conflicts between the two states, led but not confined to Kashmir.

In the dominant Pakistani narrative, the state, along with Muslims in India, is the victim of Hindu domination. This has led to the grandest of all trust deficits, but it is a deficit that cannot be eliminated because it stems from the very identity of Indians as dominating, insincere, and untrustworthy neighbors; Pakistan can do nothing to change this essential threat. In some eyes, the state is still advancing a separatist movement as far as India and its "captive" minorities are concerned. A typical statement, by a distinguished Pakistani economist, Parvez Hasan, summarizes the issue clearly:

> I feel strongly that my generation and I owe a deep debt to the creation of Pakistan. I do want to tell the younger audience—that is almost everybody here—that you cannot imagine the opportunities that the creation of Pakistan—and the large transfer of populations across the borders—opened up for Muslims especially persons like me that were just beginning their college education at partition.[6]

While there are negatives in the Pakistani enterprise, Hasan notes that the Pakistani elite and diaspora have very high living standards, which would not have been possible "without the efforts of millions upon millions of honest, hardworking, resourceful, and committed Pakistanis."[7]

All new nations devote considerable attention to creating a viable narrative of their origins and their rationale for existence. Pakistan is no different, but it has made a more concerted and usually successful attempt to create a narrative that roughly follows Hasan's portrayal and to introduce it to successive generations of Pakistanis. Thus propping up the "ideology of Pakistan" has been a central preoccupation of the state, a policy disseminated through the educational curriculum.[8]

What is taught in Pakistan's schools, notably those controlled by the state, is not tempered by objective historiography.[9] Partition is portrayed as a victory in spite of the Hindu mission to keep Muslims in a subordinate position. Indian Muslims are widely thought to be persecuted. This is what is taught and commonly believed in Pakistan. As noted in chapter 2, this is not accurate. Admittedly, some Indian Muslim communities, for example, the Dawoodi Bohras, are routinely attacked by Hindu mobs during communal riots because they are instantly identifiable as Muslims, but this quiescent Shia sect prefers India to either Pakistan or Bangladesh, where they are persecuted more violently and with less state protection than in India. This Pakistani view eerily mirrors the Hindu communalist interpretation of history, as it also treats history as a struggle between Muslims and Hindus (and Christians).

If Pakistanis have defined themselves as a separatist movement, they have in theory extended this claim to all Indian Muslims, particularly to those who live in Jammu and Kashmir. The Kashmiri "dispute," which I discuss in chapter 5, resonates with most Pakistanis because it correlates with their own narrative of an unjust persecution of a minority. Needless to say, New Delhi provides enough evidence of persecution to make it easy for the Pakistani media, not just state-controlled organs, to replay the threatened minority motif over and over.

The Army

Unlike India, Pakistan has made the army a central force in politics and strategic policy.[10] Those who have dealt with both armies point out that Pakistanis take a more ideological approach to the function of the military than their Indian counterparts.[11] The Pakistan army is also trying to turn Pakistan into a state that would be worthy of its own high standards, but it finds it difficult to find—or groom—politicians that meet such standards. Conversely, those civilians who have taken the reins find that they need the army to govern; those who thought of challenging the army (Nawaz Sharif and Benazir Bhutto) found themselves exiled or (like Zulfikar Ali Bhutto) swinging from a noose. Even generals who came to power were not immune: General Iskander Mirza was sent packing by Ayub Khan, and both Ayub and Pervez Musharraf were sidelined or exiled by their successors. Pakistan is one part military autocracy and one part aspiring civilian government; outsiders cannot always tell which Pakistan they are dealing with.

From the very beginning, the army held strong views on normalization with India. Received wisdom in the army is that India made a concerted attempt to cripple Pakistan. Army messes still overflow with third-generation memories of the partition, how the Indians stole the library, or the silver, and then how India stabbed Pakistan in the back economically and militarily, and broke its promises on Kashmir. As one retired senior officer has written in his own study of India-Pakistan relations, Jinnah was perceptive in that he "saw through the Machiavellian machinations of Hindu extremists. They planned to enslave Muslims after the end of the British empire."[12] No other Pakistani institution has institutionalized distrust of India to such an extent; it forms part of the curriculum at every training level. As a result, Pakistani officers have few opportunities to test the stereotypes of their Indian counterparts. One of their beliefs is that "close to the time of their retirement from military service many senior Indian army officers create situations that raise regional tensions." General Arif gives five implausible examples.[13] But these negative views of India are joined by increasing contempt for their own politicians and officials. Although parallel images are found in the Indian military, it has only a tiny fraction of the influence of the Pakistan army. Well-intentioned recommendations that peace might be advanced by military-to-military dialogues miss the point: Pakistan's army shapes policy and the destiny of the entire country; India's army does not. A recent joint article by a former Pakistan army chief (Jehangir Karamat) and a retired Indian air force chief (Shashi Tyagi) is cited by American columnist David Ignatius as a "welcome bit of good news" from South Asia. It is certainly welcome, but somewhat inaccurate. The air force in both countries is politically unimportant, while the army is politically unimportant in India but central in Pakistan.[14] Within the Pakistan army, the Inter-Service Intelligence Agency plays an especially important role. It does more than gather intelligence—it spreads "official" views throughout Pakistani society, maintaining close ties to many in the press and shaping Pakistani opinion both in the army and civilian society.[15]

The army has dominated India-Pakistan relations since the mid-1950s, after Ayub Khan carried out the first of a series of army coups. Yet the army is not a monolith. While armies are bureaucracies, and thus slow to change, the good ones are also learning machines that respond to powerful events; the role of the officer corps, the "brains" of an army, has been critical in this regard. In their response to major events over time, "generations" of officers form an age and attitudinal cadre. Elsewhere, I have described the British and American generations of officers whose worldviews and approach to war were shaped by extensive contact with these two countries; in Pakistan, there was a "Zia" generation, men who came into the army after the 1971 East Pakistan–India war and who served under the Islamicizing Zia, who was both more intelligent and more fanatic than anyone suspected.

A liberalizing trend set in after the 1991 departure of Aslam Beg, Zia's successor as army chief. Beg had energetically battled the Americans and supported Islamic extremists in Kashmir and elsewhere—in retirement he remains a well-funded uber-hawk. This trend (under army chiefs Asif Nawaz, Abdul Waheed, and Jehangir Karamat) was set back by the American decision in 1990 to sanction Pakistan because it violated its nuclear commitments. Senior officers begged American officials not to cut off training in U.S. institutions, training that was only restored in the first administration of President George W. Bush. By then anti-Americanism had grown in the army, strengthened by the American invasion and occupation of Iraq and Afghanistan and giving rise to the belief that the United States intended its next target to be Pakistan. This view was also strengthened in the army and among civilians by the second Bush administration's move to enter a nuclear agreement with India. This seemed to be proof of a new U.S.-Indian-Israel alignment directed against Islamabad.

By 2004, however, the Pakistan army, through no fault of the Americans, found itself under attack from the Pakistan Taliban (Tehrik-i-Taliban,

TTP), the soul mates of the Afghan Taliban supported by Pakistan. Pakistani forces took heavy casualties in fighting against their own countrymen who had seized parts of the North-West Frontier Province and Swat. This has led to a major shift in army opinion: while India remains the main enemy, and the United States is not a friend, the attacks by the TTP, al Qaeda, and other groups became, by 2010, the immediate problem. Although they are being carried out by Pakistanis, conspiratists claim that India, Israel, and the United States are behind them.

> Let there be no doubt that external manipulation exploiting and aggravating skillfully internal dissensions has pushed Pakistan to the brink. The debacle of East Pakistan is a classical example of external orchestration of the inner political unrest. A similar situation is taking place again, particularly in Balochistan. . . . Ever since the US/ISAF [International Security Assistance Force] forces ousted the pro-Pakistan Taliban government from Afghanistan, and the pro-Indian Northern Alliance dominated the government, India's notorious intelligence agency, the RAW, has become fully entrenched in the war-torn country. Backed by the Afghan Intelligence Agency and allegedly supported by the Mossad, CIA and others, it is aiding and abetting insurgency in Balochistan, FATA [Federally Administered Tribal Areas] and our urban centers. Their common goal seems to be to internally destabilize Pakistan to its ultimate disintegration. Already, various U.S. think-tanks are discussing the post-disintegration scenario. Lately, a joint U.S.-India study has been initiated for that very purpose.[16]

This view of the matter is considered inaccurate by most army officers, especially those who were in savage combat with the homegrown militants after 2010. The Pakistan Taliban pose a direct threat to the very kind of Pakistan that an officer would favor, as is abundantly clear from direct contact with members of the officer corps, their writings, and also their middle-class nature. Army Chief Ashfaq Kayani, for example, is the son of a noncommissioned officer and like other officers abides by middle-class values. These men do not condone revolution in their own country, although their support for Islamic revolutionaries in Afghanistan and India is another matter. The army is more flexible than many civilians when it comes to the nature of Pakistan's Islamic identity. It does not discriminate between Sunni and Shia, and even takes in the occasional non-Muslim. These generalizations must be tempered by the observation that Pakistan's middle classes are becoming increasingly intolerant. The Constitution of Pakistan sanctions discrimination against some Muslim sects (the Ahmadis are defined as non-Muslims), and increasingly Pakistan's middle class is defined by sympathy to extremist Islam and anti-Americanism.[17]

The Pakistan army remains central to relations with India. It is distracted by the need to cope with the Pakistan Taliban and by cross-border conflict with American forces in Afghanistan. Its own credibility was badly damaged by the American attack in Abbotabad in May 2011, which killed Osama bin Laden. The incident left most Pakistanis wondering whether their revered military was incompetent or negligent. Although the extended tenure of General Kayani as army chief stabilized the role of the army, it is strapped to an improbable civilian government headed by President Asif Ali Zardari. The army does not want to govern, but it is unhappy with the way Zardari and the Pakistani judiciary have asserted their authority. On one critical issue, India, the army seems to have sided with the Zardari view that India can be managed, and that normal relations are possible—this is epitomized by the offer of most-favored-nation status to India, agreed to by the army and thus implying a major shift in army policies, if not in its judgment about India.

Geostrategy

Pakistan's long-standing identity crisis is also linked to its geostrategic position. From the beginning Pakistan's leaders felt its sought-after Islamic identity stemmed in part from the geopolitical compulsions instilled by the British Raj. In the view of Jinnah and other Pakistani leaders, West Pakistan had inherited the tasks of British India's northwest as the guardian of the world's strategic frontier, standing in the pathway of an aggressive communist Soviet Union. Jinnah and other pro-Pakistani Indians had supported the allies in the war against Nazi Germany and Imperial Japan, whereas the Indian National Congress Party made its first great statement of nonalignment by sitting out the war.

Pakistan thus made a plausible case that it was the more reliable ally for the West than the untrustworthy Congress Party, that Muslims were "naturally" more allied to the West than Hindus by the organic connection between the two monotheisms, Islam and Christianity. Margaret Bourke-White recounted a conversation with Mohammed Ali Jinnah, where in response to a question about Pakistan's development Jinnah replied: "America needs Pakistan more than Pakistan needs America," adding that Pakistan is the pivot of the world.[18] If America had awakened to the Soviet threat, bolstering Greece and Turkey, "she should be much more interested in pouring money and arms into Pakistan." If Russia were to walk in, he said, "the whole world is menaced." Only a deeply religious and monotheistic people—namely, Islamic Pakistanis—could resist an existential communist or Soviet threat, as the Indians were untrustworthy and sympathetic to both the Soviet Union and communism. Bourke-White recalls this argument being repeated by government officials throughout Pakistan. "Surely America will build up our army," they would say to her. "Surely America will give us loans to keep Russia from walking in." Presciently, she noted that "this hope of tapping the U. S. Treasury was voiced so persistently that one wondered whether the purpose was to bolster the world against Bolshevism or to bolster Pakistan's own uncertain position as a new political entity."[19]

Pakistanis presented themselves to America as a Muslim Israel: loyal to Western values, committed to the same God as Christians and Jews (although their position was vehemently anti-Israeli in the context of the Palestinian conflict).[20] Pakistan was also portrayed as the Muslim David facing a Hindu Goliath—perhaps a smaller state, but one that was much tougher. Pakistani leaders used this argument with considerable success until the fall of the Soviet Union.

All states tend to have bipolar views of the world, dividing it into friends and enemies, but from its very beginning Pakistan took this to extremes. As one Pakistani professor has written, "Since its inception, the state has inculcated highly polarized and totalizing conceptions of 'friends' and 'enemies' in the Pakistani mind. These conceptions of the 'other' have parallels in the conceptions of 'patriots' and 'traitors' within our own borders."[21] One can hardly blame Pakistanis for this creative fiction—it was widely accepted in the West, especially in the United States, but the price is now being paid for it.

Thus Pakistan's position in the Western alliance system was bolstered by its bipolar worldview and geostrategic location as much as its religious identity. With the fall of the Soviet Union, one-third of the argument vanished. With the 9/11 attacks and the rise of Islamic militancy in Pakistan—some of it supported and encouraged by the government of Pakistan itself—another third disappeared. What remains is state-sponsored paranoia. Pakistan is a paranoid state with real enemies—but the frame of mind is detrimental to figuring out Pakistan's interests as well as its threats in a transformed world. As one Pakistani journalist observed in 2012, "An ordinary Pakistani is still unlikely to be exposed to informed public debate about 'friends' and 'enemies' of the state":

> These simplistic notions have provided a fillip to xenophobic politics and to conflicted understandings of the world more generally. So until two decades ago, Americans were "ahl-i-kitaab" and great friends in the fight against godless communism. Now the same Americans are the biggest kafirs of them all, and principled resistance to their hegemonic

> designs is now incumbent upon all of us. Needless to say, a distinction between Americans as people and the American state as an imperialist power is glossed over.[22]

This is not just history. Pakistan sustained itself for sixty years by a conjunction of its Islamic identity and geographical location; when the geopolitics were transformed and the Islamic identity began to backfire, it seriously lost its way. This would not have been critical had its leadership fostered the kinds of domestic political and economic reforms that were characteristic of other American allies (notably Taiwan, South Korea, and Japan), but Pakistan retained a pseudofeudal society and evolved a ruling elite—the so-called establishment, really an oligarchy—that has resisted reform and change up to the present day. This establishment was and remains composed of senior military leaders, civilian bureaucrats, and coopted political and business leaders, along with large landholders. Pakistan never developed a left political movement, or more specifically, the left was hounded out of relevance by the state, with the approval of the United States and other Western allies. By the 1970s the middle class and even peasant resentments were channeled through the Islamic parties and regional separatists.

Pakistan's ninth prime minister (and fourth president), Zulfikar Ali Bhutto, embraced the idea of an Islamic state after he took power from the generals following the loss of East Pakistan. This was as insincere as it was portentous. He was deposed in 1977 by General Zia ul-Haq, who took conservative Islam more seriously, perhaps irreversibly putting Pakistan on the path of religious extremism.

New Challenges and New Opportunities

While the foregoing are the perceptions of many Pakistanis, especially the security and foreign policy apparatus, some important recent developments raise new prospects and opportunities, as well as new or unaccustomed dangers. Following are some of the concerns:

—Pakistan is a nuclear weapons state with a very bad record of proliferation.

—It has, as a matter of state policy, actively supported jihadists and militants in its neighbors and has either turned a blind eye or professes incapacity when it comes to opposing militants abroad.

—Pakistan's economy is stagnating, complicated by the massive damage due to recent earthquakes (2005) and floods (August 2011). Long gone are the days when Pakistan was knocking on the door of middle-income status.

—Demographic indicators are not improving: the population is unofficially estimated to be closing on 200 million in 2012; social tensions are exacerbated by the weak economy.

—Separatist forces remain active in several provinces, as do truly revolutionary forces that want not merely to secede from Pakistan—the historic threat—but to transform it into a genuinely revolutionary Islamic state.

The integrity of the Pakistani state and the growing incoherence of Pakistani society will negatively affect the India-Pakistan relationship. Some recent assessments of their possible impact on Pakistan's future find that Pakistan actually has greater internal coherence than outsiders give it credit for, and that the country will muddle through. Indeed, most serious writings on Pakistan argue that the country will survive, more or less in its present form.[23] Books by Maleeha Lodhi and Anatol Lieven make this case, Lodhi in particular being optimistic that once the present crisis is surmounted, Pakistan's early promise as a secular, economically prosperous but Islamic state can be fulfilled.[24] Lieven emphasizes the durability of Pakistan's patron-client relationships, a web of obligations and commitments that provide the state with its social backbone.

There is also a more pessimistic view of Pakistan, call it muddling-through minus, which points to a single factor, the rise of Islamic extremism, and makes a persuasive case that Pakistan may come to a dangerous end, overtaken by radical Muslim groups. Books by Ahmed Rashid, John Schmidt, and Pamela Constable fall into this category.[25] All are worried, if not deeply pessimistic, about Pakistan's survival as a normal state.

There are too many variables to make a firm judgment about Pakistan's stability beyond a few years, let alone the next thirty: everything is important and everything is uncertain. The other factors that will shape Pakistan fall into four clusters. One such cluster includes its youth bulge and demography, high rate of urbanization, stagnant economy, and abysmal educational system. These are all closely related and are very hard to modify. The exception might be the economy, which is theoretically subject to new policies and outside assistance. A second cluster consists of the collective identity of Pakistan's people, as they identify with and act on the basis of their national, regional, and ethnic identities. A third cluster of factors includes the ability of Pakistanis to work with each other—to cooperate in governance at the national, provincial, and district levels. All of these are shaped by the new, expanding role of Pakistan's media, with their 100 plus national and regional television stations and half-dozen mobile phone networks. A fourth cluster includes the policies and attitudes of important foreign states and the processes of globalization, which penetrate Pakistan in many ways: globalization has heightened Islamic extremism, but it has also brought Pakistanis in touch with developments around the world. Flooding into Pakistan on a media wave of high and medium technology, globalization has influenced the ambitions and identities of Pakistanis, which in turn have both aided and undercut the workings of the state. As General Kayani told me in 2011, "We can't just order things to happen; people have a voice and we have to listen to it now."

It is not difficult to see that Pakistan's future will depend not only on its relations with India and other powers but also on forces at work within itself, forces that cannot easily be influenced by outsiders. India's influence could be considerable, however, not only because of its growing economic power and its geographical and environmental ties with Pakistan, but also because it figures so powerfully in Pakistan's national identity.

Pakistan's Uncertain Future

A heavy angst has settled over Pakistan like a grey fog. Pervez Musharraf gave false hope of a restoration of values and a functional policy, leading many Pakistanis and foreigners to believe that good intentions, plus the backing of the army, were enough. The trouble was, the intentions sprang from a desire to remain on both sides of every issue, and the backing of the military was illusory. Moreover, Musharraf was not held in high respect by his former colleagues, who removed him when he overreached at home and contrived an invasion across the Line of Control into Indian-held territory, triggering a major crisis.

His civilian successors are trying to undo the damage, but the ennui remains, as reflected in Hamza Usman's lament, "At Home Nowhere." A Mohajir, Usman was part of the community that migrated from India after Pakistan was established and that was very much responsible both for the breakup of the old India and for the failure of the new Pakistan.

> An inevitable question Pakistanis always ask me is, "what are you?" Often, I've wondered the same question. Besides "Pakistani," I don't know what else to say. I'm not Balochi or Sindhi. I can't speak Punjabi. In my house, besides English, Urdu is the only other language spoken. When people ask me what language my parents speak, that's what I tell them. Unlike many of my acquaintances, I don't come from a town or village in interior Pakistan. Like millions in Pakistan, my family migrated from India . . . believing Jinnah's ideal, searching for a homeland that was ours, for all Muslims, with freedom, tolerance

and dignity. . . . I struggled with the bitter taste of irony, that I, privileged, educated, capable of helping this country through the miasma of failure, extremism, violence and stagnation, was powerless because I couldn't speak the language properly. . . . Today, my Urdu is mishmashed with English incorporating more colloquial slang than literal Urdu. Like my Urdu, I find myself a mix of different peoples and personalities, Pakistani at heart, but at home nowhere.[26]

One development during four years of more or less democratic government has been a series of exposés revealing the excesses of the past, and at times, the present. It comes as no surprise that the state itself was used as a personal bank by whoever was in power. Many of these scandals—such as Mehrangate, named after the Mehran bank that provided funding for bribes of politicians—featured collusion between the military and civilians. Pakistan's chaotic political order and unsettled social and economic structures will affect relations with India in many ways, not least because the ensuing unpredictability makes it difficult to engage in and stick to the kinds of agreements that the two countries must have to avoid future conflicts.[27]

Although much of Pakistan's turmoil is blamed on the military, or on the dysfunctional civil-military relationship, at least one of the deeper causes of this pathology is Pakistan's historic willingness to challenge India. This has, since the 1950s, placed India policy at the top of the state's agenda and thereby planted the army at the core of those who formulate Pakistan's overall policies. That is why time and time again military leaders have been able to resist—or in some cases remove—those civilians who seem to be too soft on India. Ironically, this has made some civilians even more hawkish on India than the military—a prime example being Benazir Bhutto. Many Pakistani civilian leaders are rhetorically more aggressive toward India than army leaders—even if they don't take the India threat that seriously, they feel that they must take a hard line to placate the supposed (but sometimes real) ultras in the army leadership. This, of course, persuades many Indians that *all* Pakistanis are hawkish and anti-Indian.

Recent Developments

Given Pakistan's troubled history, and a twenty-year spell of continuous political and social chaos, the record of the current government is credible, and one hopes that its successor will be even better. President Asif Ali Zardari, in power since 2008 and with two separate prime ministers, is on paper the most reform-minded leader in Pakistan's history. His agenda has been the same as that of Benazir Bhutto, with a systematic attempt to undue past distortions. Democracy, of sorts, is working, and one of its most remarkable aspects is that India is not demonized, as it was during parts of the "decade of democracy" when Benazir Bhutto and Nawaz Sharif vied for power and competed in vilifying India. Zardari's government has completed the first-ever full term in office by a civilian leader, and a new national election is due in mid-2013.

The Zardari presidency, plus the revived Supreme Court of Pakistan, with the tacit cooperation of the military, came up with a string of reforms that provide the framework for the positive transformation of Pakistan. There remains the question of whether Pakistan's long list of liabilities will outweigh the weak impulse to reform, but they deserve to be listed, so historic is the break with the past.

The centerpiece is the Eighteenth Amendment to the Constitution of Pakistan passed in April 2010 and then signed by Zardari. It was the first time a president had reduced the powers of the office. The amendment renamed the North-West Frontier Province, restored a provision that allowed the president to dissolve parliament, and prohibited judges from endorsing the suspension of the constitution (the so-called Doctrine of Necessity, which was used by all military dictators from Ayub Khan onward to justify their coups). Finally, it prohibited the president from unilaterally declaring emergency rule in any province and took away the power to appoint the election commission, which is now nonpartisan and modeled after the Indian election commission. The president has in effect become a ceremonial head of state, although in practice he remains an active politician.

The newly emboldened courts have also confirmed that the Doctrine of Necessity was illegal, held the army and the intelligence services accountable for human rights violations, and pushed the prime minister to accountability in a case involving bribes to a Swiss company. The government is slowly, very slowly, working with India to examine what happened in Mumbai when terrorists attacked several Indian hotels and facilities, and it conducted a serious examination into Mehrangate charges of bribery and corruption involving the Inter-Services Intelligence (ISI) Directorate, and charges that the ambassador to the United States had somehow conspired with an American citizen to circumvent an army coup, which of course would be banned by law in any case. The courts are trying to align Pakistan's judicial system to some kind of international democratic norm.

In 2012 the Pakistani parliament, once an object of derision, undertook a serious examination of Pakistan's foreign and security policy and followed up with a report in March of that year that called for comprehensive reforms in relations with America. This was a far more responsible effort than that of the

U.S. Congress in hearings of February 2012, when several members of Congress and witnesses supported the breakup of Pakistan. Pakistani politicians are beginning to cooperate at the national and provincial levels—in fact, all governments in the provinces and the center are coalition governments—and as in India, they are learning to work together under these circumstances.

None of this would have happened had the army itself not shifted its attitude toward civilians. Although the army is currently doing its best to keep out of politics, it will not stand aside indefinitely if it feels that civilians are seriously mismanaging governance. This applies above all to foreign relations—the armed forces believe that they are the only true professionals in dealing with India, as their entire lives and careers have been spent studying Indian aggressiveness—but they are also concerned about the decay of the Pakistani state. Their interventions have backfired. Pakistanis did not appreciate army officers sitting in tax offices, airports, and media studios—nor did the army itself, realizing that this only opened up huge areas for temptation and corruption of the services. The army's dilemma, noted above, is that it cannot run Pakistan, but it won't let others do it either. Nor will it be easy to return to power as in the past, when the army could control crowds and streets through a display of force, could readily seize TV stations and important bridges, and announce that a particular event was blessed by a contrived legal document. Now there are too many sensitive points to block, and even if the Internet comes down, there are too many TV channels and radio stations plus the phone system to stand in the way. Seizing all of these is difficult, if not impossible, and there would be resistance from the Pakistani population, as well as foreign governments.

Since the time of Aristotle, political scientists have spoken of "mixed constitutions" that pull the state in several directions at once. Pakistan is a good example: it is part military autocracy, part aspiring democracy, while also a self-proclaimed Islamic state. In Pakistan's hybrid politics the armed forces use democracy to legitimate their rule, and civilians depend upon the military to stay in power. Add the Islamic element—and Pakistan's identity and future become even more complicated. As Reeta Chowdary Tremblay and Julian Schofield also point out, this situation makes it hard to normalize with India.[28]

In the hierarchy of elite concerns, Kashmir has slipped; the economy, sectarian violence, and outright insurrection by radical Islamists all take precedence. An astute observer of Pakistani society, Khaled Ahmed, fears that in becoming less obsessed with Kashmir, Pakistanis will also become less capable of formulating a coherent domestic policy, let alone reformulating relations with India.

Crises and the Nuclear Factor

Wherever nuclear weapons are involved, war in the form of an organized battle between industrialized states employing the latest and most destructive weapons is hardly imaginable. Incorporating these weapons into a state's strategy so their advantages are achieved but their disadvantages are minimized is always a challenge, particularly so for Pakistan with its history of paranoia and bad strategic decisions.

Pakistan was born in crisis, and it has remained embroiled in crises since 1947. This pattern did not change after Pakistan became a nuclear weapons state. Furthermore, the way it became a nuclear state led to a series of crises with India, earning the region the title of the most dangerous place in the world.[29]

Theoretically, Pakistan's possession of nuclear weapons should have advanced the possibility of normalization with India, strengthening Pakistan so that India could not militarily overcome it, no matter how big its conventional forces were. The two could have engaged in a leisurely but stable arms race. As early as 1981, however, Pakistani officers suggested to me that once they got a nuclear weapon they could again open up the Kashmir issue, as well as protect themselves against India's larger conventional force. Thus nuclear weapons were not merely another way of countering Indian power; they could also give Pakistan a decisive strategic advantage in the struggle over Kashmir. This emboldened Pakistan to probe across the border, demonstrating to India that it is indeed a threatening and dangerous state and contributing to a string of crises, some the result of calculation, others the result of misjudgment, but all involving a series of intelligence failures of one sort or another.

Although nuclear weapons have not brought about a genuine peace, their destructive consequences ensure that no rational leader will ever employ them. As a result, they have in effect ended classic, large-scale industrialized war in South Asia. There still remain four threats: (1) a conflict between India and Pakistan might *escalate* to nuclear use, (2) nuclear weapons might be used *accidentally* or in an irrational moment by either side, (3) *inside theft* could occur (with the possible transfer to some terror group), and (4) nuclear technology, or even complete weapons, could be *transferred outside* for political reasons or sheer greed.

Nuclear weapons are as valuable to Pakistan as they are to North Korea—they constitute survival insurance for both. As Samar Mubarakmand, one of the leaders of the Pakistani weapons design team, reminded the world recently, Pakistan, like North Korea, is too nuclear to fail. He noted, probably correctly, that if it were not for Pakistan's nuclear deterrent, "Pakistan would have not survived after Kargil, Indian parliament and Mumbai incident episodes."[30] One might ask, of course, if Pakistan had *not* possessed nuclear weapons, would it have pursued the provocative strategies that led India to contemplate a military response?

It is hard to predict future military and nuclear behavior, but this much is known. Pakistan has been remorseless in using its military forces and intelligence assists to take advantage of Indian weakness. It sent armed raiders across the border between Pakistan and Kashmir in 1947, precipitated a war with India in 1965 by fabricating an uprising in the Kashmir Valley, supported Sikh separatists in the 1980s, and worked with the United States in Afghanistan in backing the Mujahiddin against the Soviet invaders in the 1980s. Afterward it supported Afghan Taliban against the warlords and continued to back them after a new pro-Western government was established in Kabul—also supporting them against Americans based in Afghanistan. It supported Kashmiri separatists in India in the 1990s and trained radical groups for operations in India afterward; when these groups attacked the Indian parliament and a series of hotels and other targets in Mumbai in 2008, each time precipitating a crisis, it never disbanded them.

Further, Pakistan has looked the other way in many instances, often complaining that it lacks the resources to monitor violent groups that use its territory—pleading for mercy like the orphan who has just killed his mother and father.[31] It is hard to predict how Pakistan will behave in another crisis, whether or not it initiates the event, which is a paradoxical strength of Pakistani diplomacy. For example, in 1999 it implemented the classic "under-the-threshold" strategy when it pushed light infantry across the Line of Control in Indian-controlled Kashmir, calling them Kashmiri freedom fighters. This led to a serious but limited war with India, not to mention great humiliation when the fiction was uncovered, but Islamabad cautiously avoided a wider confrontation.

Is a more normal relationship with India a necessary condition for Pakistan to avoid further deterioration? Although India does not want to see an assertive Pakistan, a failing Pakistan has the capacity to do India considerable damage. The nuclearization of their sixty-year conflict makes the stakes even higher. Further crises, deliberate or inadvertent, will distract Pakistan from the rebuilding task. Pakistani opinion on normalization with India suggests a variety of answers to these questions.

Pakistan was the state trying to change the status quo in Kashmir after India's initial support for a plebiscite evaporated. Pakistan concluded that there was no harm, and a lot of public relations advantage, in making one offer after another. This also led Pakistan to support the use of force, a strategy that has consistently failed to produce a change in Kashmir. Pakistan also plays to an international audience, trying to appear reasonable, willing, and even eager to involve others in disputes with India, and thus make New Delhi look stubborn when it refuses to allow a third-party role. This also strengthens the case that it is India, not Pakistan, that makes the region the most dangerous place on earth.

The record of Pakistani proposals is richer than India's, but also highly repetitive. I once described it to General Zia ul-Haq as resembling two playmates chasing each other around a tree, when suddenly they turn and run after each other in the opposite direction. India and Pakistan have occasionally offered the other side exactly what they had earlier rejected. This mixture of force and diplomacy can backfire, allowing India to portray Pakistan as the military aggressor, as in the 1999 Kargil adventure.

Pakistan's pursuit of normalization with India has almost always involved wringing concessions on Kashmir that India has been unwilling or unable to make. But the range of disputes has grown, and with it the frequency of Pakistani proposals, most of them rejected by New Delhi. However, the two sides have reached agreement on a few issues where their common interest is clear. The details are taken up in chapter 5, while the following paragraphs examine the process from a Pakistani perspective.

Pakistan's normalization offers began with Mohammed Ali Jinnah, the man who single-handedly created Pakistan and became the country's first governor-general. Although Jinnah did not trust the British, he retained more British generals for a longer period of time than India did, partly because Pakistan needed their expertise and partly because many of them supported his vision of Pakistan becoming a military partner of the West. Jinnah did not believe that India and Pakistan would enter into open conflict. Rather, he assumed that he would be able to keep his house in Bombay after the partition; similarly, other Pakistanis (and some Indian Muslims) thought that they would be able to move freely between the two new Commonwealth states.

In 1947 Jinnah proposed that all disputes be brought before the international community and settled in the United Nations, and that it administer the Indian-occupied princely state of Junagadh. This proposal went nowhere. Jinnah's successor, Prime Minister Liaquat Ali Khan, met with Nehru for talks in Delhi and Karachi (then still Pakistan's capital) and proposed that the Commonwealth issue a collective guarantee of territorial integrity of Pakistan and India and oversee a plebiscite in Kashmir.

Khawaja Nazimuddin, Pakistan's next prime minister, reiterated the offer to settle disputes through conciliation, mediation, and arbitration. In 1954 Pakistan's last civilian leaders before the first coup explored the possibility of formalizing the cease-fire line in Jammu and Kashmir as an international boundary. Nehru rejected the proposal.

In 1960 General Ayub Khan proposed a joint defense agreement, focusing especially on Ladakh, which was vulnerable to a Chinese incursion, and offering to send Pakistani troops. Nehru dismissed this with the phrase, "Defense against who?" One retired Pakistani ambassador has written that when India rejected Ayub's offer, this ensured that never again would such an offer be contemplated, let alone made.[32] Ayub also offered a no-war pact to India, just before the 1965 war; and immediately afterward proposed to Indian prime minister Lal Bahadur Shastri a plan for a proportionate reduction of defense spending. On the eve of the 1970 secessionist uprising in East Pakistan, Ayub's successor, General Yahya Khan, proposed the demilitarization of Kashmir.

With Yahya's disgrace and departure in 1971, civilian rule returned to Pakistan. In 1972 President Zulfikar Ali Bhutto stated that Pakistan would leave the Central Treaty Organization (CENTO) and South East Asia Treaty Organization (SEATO) if India renounced its defense agreement with the Soviet Union. He also firmed up Pakistan's relations with China and initiated work on a nuclear weapon. Both the China connection and the bomb program flourished; the offer to jointly leave the cold war pacts was rejected by an India that had grown dependent on the Soviet Union for military technology and equipment.

Zulfikar Ali Bhutto was deposed by General Zia ul-Haq, and the country returned to military rule. Zia, educated partly at Delhi's elite St. Stephens College, brought with him a busy agenda regarding India. In 1981 he proposed a no-war pact, a cap on the armed forces of both sides, and a schedule for resolving remaining disputes. He first supported and then ended assistance to Indian Sikh separatists and in 1985 proposed the mutual inspection of Indian and Pakistani nuclear facilities. As for the latter, Zia was responding to American pressures on his own program, and he also proposed simultaneous India-Pakistan entry into the Nonproliferation Treaty regime with mutual inspection, a South Asia nuclear-free zone, and a declaration renouncing the acquisition of nuclear weapons. At the same time, Pakistan secretly indicated to America that it would cease its own nuclear weapons program in exchange for a U.S. security guarantee against an Indian attack. The United States declined, and the nuclear program continued unabated while the arms control proposals were revived during and after the period when India and Pakistan went nuclear.

In 1986 Zia proposed a joint monitoring mechanism to investigate India's claims of Pakistani cross-border terrorism, and in the following year, after an India-initiated crisis (Exercise Brasstacks), Zia visited Jaipur and proposed informal, backstage consultations ("Cricket diplomacy"), as well as talks on the disposition of the frozen wastelands of Siachen, where India had preemptively seized the glacier's heights.

Civilian rule returned with Zia's mysterious death, and Prime Minister Benazir Bhutto and Rajiv Gandhi had several rounds of talks on arms control, a reduction in defense expenditure, and joint actions to prevent nuclear proliferation on a nondiscriminatory basis. Benazir also proposed third-party mediation to defuse border tensions and, while in opposition (1991), called for the convening of a Camp David summit between India and Pakistan to work out regional security arrangements, leading to arms-reduction talks.

Benazir's successor, Nawaz Sharif, proposed a five-nation conference (for the United States, Soviet Union, China, India, and Pakistan) to discuss South Asian nuclear proliferation. In Benazir's second term as prime minister she had asked President Farooq Leghari to support trade between the Indian and Pakistani private sectors, saying this would be in Pakistan's national interests. Then during Sharif's second tenure as prime minister, the idea of a nonaggression pact was resurrected in his address to the UN General Assembly. In 1999 Sharif (who was a businessman and a believer in closer relations with India) invited Indian prime minister Atal Bihari Vajpayee to come to Pakistan. Vajpayee accepted, traveling by bus, and the two signed the Lahore Declaration. When it was later revealed that Pakistan was planning an attack across the Line of Control in Kargil during that visit, Vajpayee and the Indian leadership were furious.

Pakistan's decade of democracy ended when Nawaz was deposed by General Pervez Musharraf, the man behind the Kargil adventure. In 2000 Musharraf offered several times to meet anyone, anytime, and anywhere for a full dialogue that would bring about normal India-Pakistan relations; he also proposed a no-war pact and a mutual reduction in forces. His most significant move came in 2004 when he stated that Kashmir was *not* a central issue and that a referendum there was not then feasible. Several new proposals followed: India and Pakistan could accept a softened Line of Control as a permanent border, there could also be a phased withdrawal of troops and implementation of self-governance for Kashmiris, and a joint supervision mechanism would supervise the process.

While Musharraf had talked about these ideas with me and others just after he seized power, they were now public statements and gestures. They led to the Composite Dialogue, which was broken off after the 2008 terror attacks in Mumbai but partly restored under a new name in 2011.

The incoming Zardari government was interested in promoting dialogue and normalization with India, but the Mumbai attacks occurred shortly after it came to power, forcing India to break off talks for several years. Despite no direct evidence of an ulterior motive, the attacks may well have been designed to break up the normalization process, a lesson for those now in charge of the process.

Another step toward normalization came in 2008 when, in New Delhi, Zardari indicated that Pakistan would not use nuclear weapons first (he was forced to recant this suggestion), and he offered to have an ISI official travel to India to assist in the investigations into the Mumbai attacks (he was forced to withdraw this proposal as well). His most startling act came in 2011 when the cabinet announced that it would grant most-favored-nation trading status to India, reciprocating a similar move from New Delhi in 1996. Zardari says normalization must be achieved through business and commerce (see chapter 6).

Alternatives

As one might expect, Pakistani thinking about normalizing with India is splayed across the spectrum, ranging from eager suitor to bitter opponent, with the curve tending toward the latter but potentially moving toward the center. A few Pakistani politicians like cricketer Imran Khan remain ambivalent, which points up the importance of normalization if the two are ever to reconcile on critical issues. Imran went to college with and befriended several Indians who are today important figures in India. As a world-class cricketer he both lost to and defeated Indians teams. And as a politician he declined to go to an event in India where Salman Rushdie was to be honored. He is also critical of the army, and his political agenda says little about India but a great deal about removing corruption from Pakistani politics. On Kashmir, he has confined himself to general remarks about restoring Kashmiri freedoms and has criticized the Indian occupation.[33] His policy views were further defined in a talk outside Pakistan, where he argued for good relations with India and the United States, and went somewhat beyond the establishment's consensus when he stated he was willing to rule out "military means of militancy," to ease Indian concerns about Pakistani support for cross-border terrorism.[34]

On balance, Pakistan has been far more proactive than India in making offers to normalize relations, and there is a wide range of elite and public opinion. At the same time, actual changes in policy have been few and very limited, often brought about because of tactical necessity.

Yield to India

Few Pakistanis have publicly and openly stated that their country should yield to India on important issues, such as Kashmir, trade, the distribution of water, and boundary conflicts in Siachen and elsewhere. To do so would skirt treason's boundaries. Yet many Pakistanis privately acknowledge that the partition of India was a mistake, that Muslims did not need a separate homeland to protect their rights. A number of Pakistani families, especially those that had positions in the Congress Party in undivided India or were not Muslim League members and involved in various regional coalition governments at that time, have no deep love for the state they now live in. Yet even many in this group now regard India as a threat and think that partition has so embittered both sides that undoing it legally or politically would be impossible. As Pakistanis, they are also critical of their own government for supporting terrorist attacks, and of the army's dominance at home. They look with envy at India's more normal democracy, although they have little interest in migrating to India.

They are now Pakistanis and want to make the best of it, which means normalizing with India. This view can be heard among some of Pakistan's minority religious sects: notably the Ahmadis, who since a constitutional amendment in 1984 are technically no longer Muslims; Pakistani Christians, also the systematic victims of Muslim bigots; and some in Pakistan's Hindu community.[35] The latter is sheltered by the state. Although largely apolitical, the Hindus, along with other minorities in a state created to protect them, often vote with their feet, leaving Pakistan for foreign lands.

Accommodate

In a major shift of elite and public opinion, more and more Pakistanis now talk openly of accommodating India on a range of issues as long as Pakistan's interests are safeguarded. There are new proposals, official and unofficial, for discussions on trade, the disposition of such hoary disputes as Kashmir and Siachen, and more regional cooperation, notably in areas such as visa policies and people-to-people exchanges as well as education. The locus classicus for this viewpoint can be found in a short book published in 2000 by a wise and influential retired Pakistani general, Mahmud Ali Durrani, whose study reflects the views of a then-unique Track II India-Pakistan group called Balusa.[36] General Durrani, who was briefly Pakistan's national security adviser and ambassador to the United States, sets forth a strong case for normalization, with each side making adjustments in their long-standing positions on Kashmir, trade, Siachen, and other issues. The costs of conflict are burdensome to both states, he argues, besides which the two states have many shared cultural and other interests. While his own professional training in the Pakistan army taught that "the only good Indian is a dead Indian" and in several wars he tried to create more "good" Indians, he recalls his first encounters with Indians (at an American military school) with a mixture of nostalgia and remembered anxiety. Durrani notes that many of his countrymen (and many Indians) regard such contacts as misguided if not threatening, but several believe these meetings between soldiers are important for both sides.

This kind of thinking was rare until the early 2000s, when Pervez Musharraf launched several peace offenses toward India. These had not come out of the blue; as already mentioned, he had talked to me about normalizing relations with India over Kashmir right after his coup, although at that meeting he was quickly brought back to the "official" Pakistani position by an aide and reverted to the then standard policy of "plebiscite and accession" for the Kashmiris.

Musharraf's proposals divided elite opinion, sparking vicious attacks from Pakistan's Islamists who saw a potential for surrender when he went to India to negotiate at Agra. Many in the army greeted his ideas with skepticism. One senior general told me that Musharraf could make all the proposals he wanted, but Indians were not likely to yield on big issues such as Kashmir and could not be trusted in any case. Still, it was worth the effort: Musharraf's gambit was acceptable as long as it did not raise false expectations in Pakistan. Subsequent conversations indicate that Musharraf's own standing in the army was shaky after his coup, and that an officer with a different background (he was a non-Punjabi born in India and raised partly in Turkey) might have had more support among his colleagues.

The desire for a normal relationship with India has also spread to younger Pakistanis. They admire India's economic progress and its (relative) political freedoms, while often being appalled at Pakistan's increasing violence and instability. Many college-age Pakistanis are looking elsewhere for careers, although such opportunities are rare. An informed view of this generation comes from perceptive scholar Moeed Yusuf, who, like many of his peers, favors normalization not because it will be doing India a favor, but because it will improve the lot of Pakistanis.[37] He finds Zardari's expectations of a settlement of Kashmir and other disputes more realistic than the heady optimism of the government in 2007. Yusuf accepts that Pakistan will have to meet India more than halfway given the fact that no military solution is available and India is satisfied with the status quo. In this instance, as in others in the past, "the weaker, revisionist power has to concede more to break the logjam," and Pakistan does not have the luxury of waiting to start the process of normalization.

The difference between the accommodationists just mentioned (including, at times, Pervez Musharraf) and other Pakistanis is that they believe India can be moderated by Pakistani actions, whether by accommodation or negotiation, and that a deal must be done sooner rather than later. However, the center of the Pakistani establishment does not now believe this is possible.

Defend and Wait

Some Pakistani elites might, like Generals Durrani and Talat Masood, support negotiations with India but do not expect them to yield results. Instead, senior military and civilian officials tend to favor two strategies that have been part of Pakistan's approach for decades. The first is to seek the help of outsiders in putting pressure on New Delhi; the second is to get outsiders to help build up Pakistan. Many would now also push for domestic reform so that Pakistan will be stronger in the future. Those who hold this position often reiterate the empty cliché "Pakistan must negotiate from a position of strength" to ensure that it is not at a disadvantage in working through critical issues. The group's general pessimism about the possible outcome of negotiations stems from the notion that India is basically unwilling to negotiate seriously with Pakistan, and that in any case its inherent weaknesses will make a Pakistan buildup pay off—in which case negotiations might prove to be fruitful. However, neither this group nor the accomdationists have studied Indian negotiating behavior very carefully or looked closely at past instances of India-Pakistan negotiations. Such studies are rare or nonexistent, especially in the Pakistan military.

None of these are new arguments; they merely restate the ideology that propelled the original Pakistan movement. There are many examples of the view that Pakistan needs to bring in outsiders to balance India and also needs to reform itself. An eminent retired diplomat, Ambassador Munir Akram, writes that the United States—working together with China, Europe, and Russia—is in a position to create a security and political paradigm in South Asia that can promote sustainable peace and improve the prospects for prosperity. Skeptical about the possibility of reducing hostility, Akram believes India-Pakistan relations can be "managed" in directions that are "constructive and stabilizing." Such measures would include a conventional military balance; joint restraints on "certain destabilizing weapons systems, e.g., anti-ballistic missiles"; and formal acknowledgement of India's and Pakistan's nuclear weapons status and application of a nondiscriminatory nuclear regime to both, plus an agreement to "restrain the expansion of their nuclear and strategic capabilities." A "genuine" dialogue on Kashmir is essential, as well as on issues such as the water dispute, a South Asia free trade zone, and transit agreements, all expressly supported and encouraged by the international community through the United Nations or some other collective forum. All of this would be a new South Asian paradigm that "could transform South Asia from an area of instability and danger into the latest Asian miracle."[38]

In contrast to earlier years, writes Akram, "India's objective is no longer to undo Partition and absorb the territories of Pakistan. The cost would far outweigh the benefit." He takes a dig at those Pakistanis who would subscribe to a South Asian confederation led by India and reiterates a theme that has been a constant for Pakistanis for sixty or more years: that India's ambition, propelled by its self-perception and Western encouragement, is to weaken Pakistan and emerge as the supreme regional power and eventually a global power to rival China.

> Pakistan stands in the way of this ambition. It resists Indian presumption of South Asian dominion. It blocks India's geopolitical access to Central and West Asia. It reminds the world of Indian oppression of Muslim-majority Kashmir and exposes the fallacy of Indian secularism. It neutralizes a large part of India's military power. It gnaws at India's Achilles heel—Kashmir. It diminishes India's nuclear weapons status by demanding nuclear parity.[39]

It is hard to imagine this kind of India as a negotiating partner except to impose its own terms on a weak and prostrate Pakistan. Akram's agenda is so vast that no outside power has assumed, or is likely to assume, it. Past international efforts at mediation or at putting India and Pakistan in the same context have for the most part failed. This position is difficult to take seriously—its view of India is so negative that any Pakistani who thought that an agreement with India was actually possible would, in this perception, be on a fool's errand. Would trade be an exception? This and other specific issues, such as Kashmir and water, are explored in chapter 5.

Balance India

Some would remove the "defer" element of the above position and focus just on balancing and countering India in a never-ending struggle between two deeply antagonistic states. Many in both the military and civilian population approve of this course of action, despite Pakistan's weaknesses. Indeed, it is a growing sentiment, as reflected in Jinnah's displacement by Mohammed

Iqbal as the guiding star of political thought. As one Pakistani scholar has observed, "Despite his centrality to nationalist discourse and in 'Pakistan Studies' curriculum in schools, for many Pakistanis Jinnah has receded into the mists of history, belonging to a time that is irrelevant to the realities of modern Pakistan. Iqbal, on the other hand, as a religious and nationalist poet as well as an ardent advocate of pan-Islamism, is as relevant today as ever."[40]

The strongest advocates of a balancing policy are to be found in the military. The core assumptions of many in the military—what they are taught from an early age, after all—is that India is an implacable enemy, and while it may have international support now, this is temporary. It is also handicapped by structural weaknesses stemming largely from its multiethnic and predominantly Hindu identity. Meanwhile, Pakistan is the sturdier of the two states, even if it is smaller, because of its religious unity and strong international friends. Thus over the long term India will be the first to crack.

These assumptions justify discrete pressure by Pakistan in order to keep India off balance and persuade New Delhi to make concessions to Pakistan, respect Pakistan's integrity, and take more seriously the rights of the oppressed people "held" by India. The oppressed, in this view, include not only Kashmiris but *all* Indian Muslims. Pressuring India will also help Indian Muslims preserve their perilous position against an aggressive Hindu majority, as well as force India to negotiate more seriously or even to make concessions. This position contains a logical fallacy, comparable to that found in the Indian position that demonizes Pakistan. If India really is the assertive Hindu state, as it is often portrayed, why should it ever negotiate? Adherents to the position would answer: it would do so because it is fundamentally weak. Hence over the long run Pakistan's position is bound to be strengthened because of its ideological purity and unity.

Some hard-liners would go so far as to argue that India's weaknesses are typical of a multiethnic and chaotic democracy, that India's resulting loose federalism is not a viable system. India can be intimidated by force, which means that Pakistan's nuclear arsenal not only allows low-level probes but will also awe India by its sheer size.

Hard-liners would also see important policy lessons here indicating that compromise is truly misguided, even traitorous. They would say the same is true of looser provinces, or provincial autonomy, which would only lead them to break away, abetted by outside powers as in 1970. Of the outside powers, they point out, the United States has actually faded from consideration because of its ties to India and its strategy of building India up to balance China, which is Pakistan's only real and substantial ally. Further, those who adhere to this view believe that China will soon match the United States in military power and surpass it economically. Hence Pakistan, not India or the United States, is on the side of the future.

Go on the Attack

A fifth Pakistani position on normalization is even more hard-line. It is not quite the counterpart of Indian views about breaking up Pakistan. While it also regards the other state as unnatural (a conglomeration of soft Hindus and Sikhs, without any core principles), it differs in one respect. Indians who would destroy Pakistan do not want to incorporate it in a larger India—they would not want to add 200 million Muslims to an Indian political order, which already houses as many Muslims as are in all of Pakistan. This might change the already precarious Hindu-Muslim political balance and would complicate the already exasperating process of coalition-building in such states as Uttar Pradesh, Bihar, and West Bengal. Rather, Pakistanis who would see India broken up want to restore a larger Muslim political order, by force if necessary, along the lines of the Mughal Empire. India was grand then; it could again be grand if martial Muslims assumed their rightful place in the vanguard of an Indian revolution that would unite all Muslims of the subcontinent. Indians—Hindus—are naturally subservient and will consent to living in a Muslim-dominated political order that provided good government, protection for minorities (including Hindus and Sikhs), and adhered to the high moral principles of Islam.

For those who hold this view, Pakistan is analogous to Trotsky's Soviet Union: the base of a large revolution that would spread throughout Asia and wherever large Muslim populations dwell. The view is not dissimilar to that of al Qaeda and is identical to the view of the founder of the Jamaat-i-Islami, Maulana Maudoodi, who opposed the creation of Pakistan on the grounds that the Muslim revolution should target all South Asian Muslims, not just a few.

The Future of Pakistan

My first excursion into Pakistani futurology was in 1984.[41] At that time the country had India on one side and an expanding Soviet Union—in Afghanistan—on the other. It was unclear where its future lay. One possibility, envisioned by many in the army, was that Pakistan would emerge as an Asian Prussia, backed by the United States and China, with Saudi and Gulf support, strong enough to challenge India, and able to dominate its region as a mini-power. Alternatively, I wrote, it could become a latter-day nineteenth-century

Poland, partitioned out of existence by its powerful neighbors. Or it could become a modern Finland, a state that subordinated itself to an India allied to Moscow, independent but not challenging the regional hegemon or its superpower patron. It is inconceivable now that Pakistan will ever become a modern Prussia, although it could disappear, Poland-like, or subordinate itself to a thriving India.

Three other countries should now be added to my 1980s list. Brazil and Indonesia are two former military dictatorships that have turned themselves around; the former is one of the BRIC countries (Brazil, Russia, India, and China) and Latin America's most important power. Indonesia, like Pakistan, is predominantly Muslim. In both states the army found better things to do than to rule incompetently. The third country on my new list is more cautionary: Yugoslavia. Established just three years before Pakistan, it was composed of six nominally independent republics, plus two autonomous provinces (analogous to Pakistan's FATA). The structure disintegrated after the death of its charismatic leader, Josip Broz Tito, just as Pakistan weakened after Jinnah's death. In both ethnoreligious tensions and economic disparities surfaced, and in both a single province (Punjab and Serbia) was militarily and economically dominant. In each the army asserted the principle that the interests of its home province could be conflated with that of the federation. In both states a victim psychology arose after the loss of key provinces (East Pakistan in one case, and Slovenia, Croatia, and Kosovo in the other). In both air strikes deepened a sense of victimhood (these were carried out by NATO in Yugoslavia and in Pakistan by U.S. and NATO forces based in Afghanistan). For many Pakistanis, China is what Russia is to the Serbs, the ultimate guarantor of military and diplomatic support for a historically important but declining state that survives in a hostile region and that refuses to cope with its decreasing global regional importance. Pakistan did get one thing right. Unlike Tito, it went for a nuclear weapon. As one of the founders of that program once told me, the provocation came from India and the Soviet Union, direct assistance came from China, and the Reagan administration saw but did not try to stop the program.

The ironies are abundant: Poland is back, the Soviet Union is gone, and Pakistan may or may not follow the promising paths blazed by Brazil and Indonesia. India is in the position of being a neighbor that can influence Pakistan more than any other state, but it seems paralyzed as to whether it wants to see Pakistan struggle, give it a final push, or attempt normalization. With the existence of a nuclear arsenal that is probably bigger than its own, the second option is not very attractive, but there was little public support for normalization after the 2008 televised horrors of Mumbai.

Guns, Brothers, and States

For years I have heard variations of the following theme from many Pakistani officers and civilians: *Indians and Pakistanis are brothers, but when my brother has a gun, and I do not, I will feel a bit uneasy. As the bigger of the two countries shouldn't India be more generous and make concessions?*[42]

The views of many Pakistanis reflect the original theories that powered the Muslim League's opposition to a united India. They resemble strongly the recalcitrance of Iqbal rather than the compromising attitude of Jinnah, who in the end settled for what he could get, not for what he may have wanted—ironically, some say, he got more (an independent Pakistan) than he really expected.

The Pakistani establishment, especially the army, is desperately afraid that any concessions to the larger India would put it on a slippery slope, heading toward surrender, from which there would be no return. It is the fear, the anxiety, and the prospect of something unacceptable that drives much of Pakistani thinking.[43] The hard-core Islamists give a cultural and civilizational twist to this view. They fear the loss of what is special about Pakistan, its Islamic identity, as the first state to be formed as a homeland for Muslims. They also fear losing what they have fought so hard and so long for, and even moderate Pakistanis cannot imagine "giving up" the struggle for Kashmir. This and other issues are at the heart of Pakistani anxiety and permeate policy not just in relations with India, but also with the rest of the world. Pakistan is fundamentally trying to keep or regain something that rightfully belongs to it. Much social science research demonstrates that people and states fight harder to possess something of their own than to seize something that belongs to someone else. In this regard, the Indian and Pakistani claims are similar, as is their stubbornness to hang on.

Yet Pakistan clings to this anxiety at a time of increasing concern about the state's very existence. While the government still tries to indoctrinate its citizenry, the process is being challenged by globalization. The government has lost control over the public space in Pakistan, but the deeply middle-class and conservative army is reluctant to resort to totalitarian methods, preferring to leave "politics" to a civilian government that can be monitored from the outside.

Note, too, that although opinion toward relations with India remains distributed across the spectrum, more dovish views are being articulated now than at any time in Pakistan's history. One reason is that the positive aspects of globalization are diminishing the insularity of the Pakistani elites.

However, its hard-line Islamists have also hooked into their own global networks as Pakistan has become a stop on the international jihadist tourist trail.[44] Age and generation seem to make a big difference in civilian society, which is less so but still evident in the military; younger people, including officers and jawans, are exposed to far more information—good and bad—than previous generations.[45]

Despite its obvious failings, the relative success of the Zardari presidency must also be acknowledged. It is the best government that Pakistan has ever had, but it also faces problems greater than any of its predecessors. Future governments could strengthen and expand its reform efforts or just as easily revert to a risky India policy.

Finally, despite the growth of parliament and the parties, the military remains the core institution in Pakistan, yet it is not monolithic. While tending to hold conservative views on all issues, it is still open to some social and ideological diversity; in this it resembles Pakistan's civil society as a whole. Neither is dominated by the jihadists, and both army and society seek a definition of Pakistan that is compatible with the tenets of Islam and the realities of Pakistan's neighborhood. Normalization with India will be greatly affected by the outcome of this dialectic.

CHAPTER FIVE

EXPLANATIONS

As may be clear by now, the complexities of attitudes on the subcontinent make it very difficult to pinpoint the causes of the India-Pakistan rivalry. From the huge literature on Kashmir, it seems a prime source, but that line of thinking is like arguing that the Israeli-Palestinian dispute is primarily a struggle over Jerusalem—it is, but it is not. Also, factors that may have contributed to the origins of the rivalry can be muted, transformed, or displaced, and subsequently different explanations may fit better. For example, the vivid memories of partition that affected two generations of Indians and Pakistanis are fading, and other factors, notably the subcontinent's nuclearization, have grown in importance.

Numerous studies have also examined the historical and cultural roots of the dispute, the regional wars and crises, possible solutions, or ways to promote normal relations through diplomacy or Track II activities.[1] One large conclusion such analyses point to, as noted in a recent comprehensive overview, is that the rivalry is both enduring and asymmetric. Pakistan is clearly the smaller and theoretically weaker state, but it has been able to compensate by a number of military, strategic, and diplomatic means.[2] Why and how Pakistan has managed this, and the impact of its resistance on India, is one axis of their complex relationship.

Today the relationship is influenced by important "Westphalian" issues: concerns of both states that the other is violating Westphalian norms by their behavior, notably the use of terrorism, subversion, and propaganda and the reluctance to negotiate. The overlap between the two makes it hard for them to treat each other as unitary entities, or like political billiard balls. The overlap also makes it easier to meddle. It is these issues that have come to dominate recent dialogues.

Six Accounts of the India-Pakistan Rivalry

The India-Pakistan rivalry has been explained in at least six ways: as a civilizational clash, a competition of state types, a group of specific territorial disputes, a power politics rivalry, enmity based on the psychological abnormalities of the other side, and antagonism abetted by the nefarious role of outside powers. Some of these explanations overlap. A few can be falsified, and all are affected by important recent events, notably the nuclearization of the subcontinent, the rise of Islamic extremism, and U.S. intervention in Afghanistan, as well as America's search for a friendly, good, or strategic relationship with both India and Pakistan.

Culture and Civilization

When Samuel P. Huntington wrote *Clash of Civilizations,* he contributed to the world's stock of misinformation about India and Pakistan. For Huntington, the critical boundary in South Asia was that between Muslim and Hindu civilizations, the India-Pakistan border.[3] This is not a new argument. It goes back at least a thousand or more years and still carries weight in both countries, especially in Islamic and Hindu nationalist narratives.[4] These narratives were central to the Pakistan movement and also influential among those who saw Hinduism as a proper organizing principle for the new India, including many Indians who were secular.

Civilizational differences—which can be defined as culturally distinct ways of organizing the state and viewing the world—are of course real, but the argument is easily refuted by examples drawn from subcontinental history. There have been important cases in which Muslim rulers presided peacefully over largely Hindu populations (Hyderabad state), or in which Muslim populations lived peacefully under Hindu rulers (Kashmir and some other princely states). Both Islam and Hinduism encompass accommodative, conciliatory traditions. Sikhism, which was a Punjabi movement, incorporates elements of both, and all three religions have shrines and historic monuments on both sides of the border.

Brought to the region by conquerors and missionaries, Islam spread throughout South Asia both violently and peacefully. To be this successful—it reached what is now Bangladesh and Northeast India—it had to absorb much of Hinduism's accommodativeness. The Islamic Sufi tradition was especially attractive to South Asian Hindus, and many Hindus and Muslims traditionally prayed in each other's mosques and temples.

Huntington did not appreciate the commonalities that often transcend what he called "civilizations." These qualities include deep and widespread patterns of political organization and social intercourse that appear in both countries, although not distributed equally in either—Pakistan shares much with North India, but less with the latter's southern states. The common culture is particularly strong in Sindh and Punjab, and among Pakistani migrants from India. In some instances commonality generates conflict: notably the rivalry over Kashmir, regarded as a sacred space in both countries and among migrants who were forcibly evicted from their ancestral homes. Another common factor is cuisine, different but related and expressed perfectly in the popular television reality show "Foodistan," in which Indian and Pakistani chefs compete.[5] The show's motto is "Make food, not war," and to alleviate religious sensibilities each show is preceded by a notice that neither beef nor pork products were used in its production. Cuisine is also a barrier, as a group of university students discovered when they tried to organize a beef and pork festival designed to challenge limits on the right of individuals to eat their food of choice.[6]

Other regional traditions are Western-derived, sometimes hundreds of years ago, notably in sports (especially cricket), upper-class dress, and the modern professions. British-style uniforms, organizational patterns, and modes of thought are prevalent in the Indian and Pakistani civil services, armies, and police forces. More recently, pop culture and film and TV unite specific generations in India and Pakistan. New music bands like Indian Ocean have a strong following among both Indian and Pakistani urban middle- and upper-class youth and regularly perform on both sides of the border. Their style is known as South Asian fusion, a popular mix of traditional subcontinental music with Western pop. A Pakistani equivalent is showcased by the live musical television show *Coke Studio,* which includes Pakistani classical, folk, qawwalis, bhangra, Sufi, and contemporary hip-hop, rock, and pop music styles. Bollywood movies and Indian television shows are widely popular in Pakistan, so much so that even at the height of the Kargil War in 1999, and even when Islamabad canceled licenses and banned Indian TV channels, their audience ratings in Pakistan were unaffected.[7] Lollywood, as the Lahore-based Pakistani movie industry is known, is also making inroads into Indian audiences, especially with popular actors Waheed Murad and Shabnam. Indian and Pakistani literary intelligentsia also meet regularly for various festivals, including major events in Jaipur and Karachi. The sharing may be less important than the differences common *within* each state. For example, Islamist groups in Pakistan—and to some degree orthodox Hindus in India—are hostile to Bollywood culture. While popular in Pakistan, its films are publicly condemned by orthodox Islamists in both countries and the more prudish elements of India's Hindu right.

Some Hindu and Islamic traditions suggest ways of reducing differences and ameliorating conflict, such as the many Quranic statements about seeking peace and compromise, searching for the truth and knowledge: "The ink of the scholar is more holy than the blood of the martyr." Elements of each also contribute to the idea of what Elias Canetti terms a war-crowd.[8] Indians and Pakistanis draw selectively from these traditions and point to those aspects of each other's traditions that seem to "prove" that the other intends to conquer and dominate. Pakistani strategists like to cite the *Arthashastra* and its *Mandala* (circle of states) as evidence of an Indian or Hindu approach to statecraft that emphasizes subversion, espionage, and deceit.[9] For their part, Indian strategists, especially on the Hindu nationalist end of the spectrum, emphasize those aspects of Islamic teachings that portray a world divided between believers and unbelievers, and they set forth the obligation of the former to convert the latter, by jihad if necessary.

While Pakistani ideologues see the spread of Islam to South Asia as having purged and reformed the unbelievers, Indians see this history as part of a comprehensive civilizational and cultural threat to India. Before the Muslims arrived, India was temporally weaker, but morally greater. India's riches and treasures lured outside predators, who despite their momentary technical or military superiority lacked the deeper moral qualities of an old and established civilization. The first predators were the Islamic invaders; these in turn betrayed India and failed to protect it from the subsequent wave of Western conquerors. In the history of Islam and Christianity in India, Hindus were the odd men out according to the Hindu hagiography.

In the view of many Indians, Pakistan is also facilitating the civilizational West's attempt to reestablish an imperial presence in South Asia. Both Nehru and the Hindu nationalists believed that India's natural dominance of the region was undercut by Pakistan's alliance with foreign civilizational powers, first those in the West, then more recently the Chinese. Pakistan is seen as an essential element in a shifting alliance between the West, Islam, China, and other hostile states directed against New Delhi.

In recent years the emphasis has expanded to include the sea of extremist Islamic forces led by Pakistan, with China as a conspirator. Huntington's thesis of a grand alliance between Islamic and "Confucian" civilizations was greeted warmly by a portion of the Indian strategic community. The ring of states around India provides ready-made images of encirclement and threat. There are threats from the north, the east, the west, and over the horizon, as naval theoreticians eagerly point out the threat from the sea, whence both the Arabs and the Europeans came, and—thirty years ago—the USS *Enterprise,* sent by President Richard Nixon in an attempt to browbeat India with a nuclear-armed carrier. Cultural and civilizational overlap both strengthens and weakens the India-Pakistan conflict.

When examining civilizational and cultural differences, one needs to keep two points in mind. First, tiny differences can become inflated, what Freud called the "narcissism of small differences," or what Jonathan Swift characterized as the difference between the Lilliputian Big Enders and Small Enders in *Gulliver's Travels*.[10] In some cases, Pakistanis and Indians are fearful because the differences between them are not that great, but the desire to have a separate identity is. Thus they seize upon what to outsiders would appear to be minor differences in food, culture, or lifestyle. Second, it is important not to confuse the differences between Indians and Pakistanis with differences between India and Pakistan. While the former may be very small, the latter are quite large with respect to adherence to constitutional norms and some political values. The two nations are alike in many ways, as I have noted, but they are not the same kind of state.

State Identity

Some would attribute state-to-state conflict to the propensity for war created by certain kinds of political systems. For example, military dictatorships are said to be prone to conflict with their neighbors, while others, notably democracies, are generally peaceful, especially toward other democracies.

In this framework, the Indian view has it that democratic, secular India is battling dictatorial nondemocratic Pakistan. Yet as seen from Pakistan, India's democracy is a sham, and egalitarian, Islamic Pakistan has more democratic potential. It is in conflict with India's revisionist faux-democracy, which is also inherently expansionist. Another criticism is that India represses its Muslim minority: it cannot deal fairly with Muslim states; it is so insecure that it must dominate all of its neighbors. This is the zone where religious identity and state identity overlap. As the American scholar Vali Nasr has observed, both India and Pakistan have become far more reliant on religious identity than was the case at independence.[11] Indeed, India's vaunted liberalism toward religion is under siege: one Indian religious leader, Mufti Muhammad Bashiruddin, who is recognized by both the state government and the center as grand mufti of Jammu and Kashmir, demanded that India's Ahmadis also be declared non-Muslims, a practice that was enshrined in the Pakistani constitution in the 1970s.[12]

At its crudest level, this kind of state-difference argument can be easily disproved. The Indian state is neither entirely democratic nor entirely secular, while Pakistan retains many of the secular foundations of the British Indian political and judicial system and aspires to democracy, even if it is not always able to achieve it. At times India has found it very easy to deal with Pakistan's military dictators, some of whom have been more interested in normalization with New Delhi than are civilians. Both states remain in the Commonwealth and have more in common with each other than, say, with China.

As noted throughout this book, another kind of state difference pertains to identity. India and Pakistan were defined by opposed ideas. They have grown apart even though their societies have much in common. India is becoming increasingly secure in its identity and mature in its economic and political orders; Pakistan is struggling on both counts.

At best, state type, whether democracy versus military rule or Islamist versus secular, is an intermittent explanation of state rivalry. Democratic, secular, dictatorial, authoritarian, or Westphalia-abiding versus terrorist are often euphemisms for the claim that the two countries are destined for conflict because of their cultural and civilizational differences, or because of moral differences. There are notable paradoxes here. Some would argue that India cannot do business with a military dictatorship, yet it manages to have good relations with worse regimes, including Iran, which is truly a radical Islamic system, or Saudi Arabia. Or they might say that Pakistan cannot countenance close ties with India's phony democracy, although it manages close ties to Islamist Saudi Arabia and communist China and North Korea.

The existence of a struggling democratic movement in Pakistan might make it easier for political leaders in both countries to bring about normalization in the context of a set of shared values. This might also be one part of the solution to the Kashmir puzzle; "democracy" is an ideal that all parties subscribe to. Indians still debate whether it would be easier to deal with the military than with insecure and politically dependent civilian leaders, but in the end they know that the armed forces of Pakistan will have to be part of any comprehensive peace agreement, so the question does not matter very much. Indeed, in recent years the awareness that the Pakistan army is deeply implicated in the failing Pakistani economy opens up a new reason for practical steps that would contribute to normalization, such as increased trade. India could normalize with a now civilian government in Pakistan but direct some of its economic investments toward the demonized military.

Kashmir

Popular with government and foundation officials and journalists, "Kashmir" is a term often used to refer to the main cause of India-Pakistan rivalry. As a *cause* that comprehensively explains the rivalry, however, "Kashmir" is, at best, inconclusive. Although it touches upon many dimensions of the

Box 5-1. *Academic Peacemaking*

Stanley Wolpert, a renowned historian of India and Pakistan, organized a conference at his university, inviting several hundred Kashmiri Muslims, Pandits, and other India-Pakistan scholars.[a] The goal was to formulate resolutions to be submitted to the United Nations, Washington, New Delhi, and London. When one Britisher of Pakistani origin (Lord Ahmed) gave an inflammatory speech about the rape of Kashmiri women by Indian troops, violence nearly broke out, and the organizer contemplated calling the police, despite pleas of reasoned debate. Wolpert then wrote a short book urging reason and restraint on both countries and acceptance of the Line of Control. While widely regarded as the only feasible outcome for Kashmir, it is still formally unacceptable to India, Pakistan, and some Kashmiris.

a. See the account in Stanley Wolpert, *India and Pakistan: Continued Conflict or Cooperation* (University of California Press, 2010). Most scholars shy away from the dispute because of a lack of expertise or concern that they might damage their research access, especially in India.

India-Pakistan rivalry, it is not the whole story—if resolved, there would still be important differences, even pathologies, to address (see box 5-1).[13]

Kashmir is a specific place, and as John Vasquez observes, there is a natural tendency to infuse territory with ideological, religious, and cultural rationales. When a territory comes to symbolize these notions and they are combined with ethnic differences that center on the control of that territory, hard-line constituencies emerge that make it difficult to engage in territorial division or partition.[14] This is true: Kashmir is important as a territory, but its interaction with other factors is what is critical.

There are many such factors. The territory's internal makeup creates political problems in both India and Pakistan; it remains strategically "vital" at least in the eyes of the two armies, and it is a centerpiece of the shared water and ecosystems. Moreover, it raises deep questions about justice and equity that go to the heart of governance problems in both India and Pakistan.

To complicate matters, Kashmir's ethnic and social diversity links it to the politics of both India and Pakistan, as well as of foreign countries, especially the United Kingdom. Some important Indian political families are of Kashmir extraction (the Nehru-Gandhi dynasty), and many of Jawaharlal Nehru's biographers note the special place that the state held for him, and the influence that his love for the mountains and Kashmir had on his policies. Likewise, many migrants from the Mirpur district live in Lahore and other Pakistani cities, and they are prominent in the Pakistan-British community in the United Kingdom.

Minority rights and simple justice are also embedded in the Kashmir issue. In Pakistan and India, respectively, the fate of Kashmiri Muslims and Kashmiri Hindus (especially the Pandit community, many of whom have fled the Valley) is a popular and emotional issue. At the same time, the Valley is home to a Kashmiri (Muslim) *independence* movement that seeks greater state autonomy. For both Indians and Pakistanis the question of minority rights is intimately linked to the fate of Kashmir—those of Muslims for Pakistanis and of Hindus for Indians, replicating the original struggle for Pakistan. The Pakistan army's claims to Kashmir are part and parcel of the larger Pakistani lament over the "lost" Muslim brethren held captive by India, an argument that implies that Pakistan has irredentist concerns about *all* Indian Muslims.

The struggle for minority rights extends to the small and often ignored Buddhist community in the Ladakh district of Jammu and Kashmir. The Buddhists want to remain in India at all costs. They reject an independent Kashmir because they are afraid of Muslim domination. Ironically, "minority rights" is the rallying cry for Kashmir's Hindus *and* Buddhists seeking self-determination as much as for Kashmiri Muslims calling for accession to Pakistan or an independent state.

Technology has also perpetuated and expanded the conflict. For decades Kashmir was largely inaccessible, but advances in road building, mountain-climbing technology, and the use of air forces have opened all parts of the state—including the distant Siachen Glacier—to both armies.

The Indian air force was the first to make headway there when in 1947 troops entered Srinagar to stop raiders that had crossed over into the state from Pakistan's North West Frontier Province (NWFP). In 1959 China easily occupied large parts of the Leh region once it conquered Tibet, and India and Pakistan turned the Siachen Glacier into a battlefield in April 1984 because both had expanded their use of modern mountaineering techniques, enabling them to fight a war over useless terrain at heights of more than 15,000 feet.[15]

Both armies now insist that control over Kashmir is critical to the defense of their respective countries, as well as necessary to the fulfillment of national identities. While some Indian military officers would settle the Siachen issue with a compromise, others have come to view it as part of the consolidation of the Indian nation.[16] Politically, Kashmir has been badly mismanaged by both countries. In the absence of democracy in Pakistan, the territory under its control was effectively run by the army in cooperation with approved and

Box 5-2. *Simla*

After India defeated Pakistan in 1971, India kept outsiders at a distance as it sought to reach a bilateral understanding with Pakistan. Indira Gandhi and Zulfiqar Ali Bhutto met in the Indian hill station of Simla in late June and early July 1972. There, after a long and complicated negotiation, they committed their countries to a bilateral settlement of all outstanding disputes. Presumably, this included Kashmir (which was mentioned only in the last paragraph of the text). The Simla Agreement did not rule out mediation or multilateral diplomacy, if both sides agreed.

Ironically, divergent interpretations of Simla added another layer of India-Pakistan distrust. While there is a formal text, there may have been verbal agreements between the two leaders that have never been made public. According to most Indian accounts, Zulfiqar Ali Bhutto told Mrs. Gandhi that he was willing to settle the Kashmir dispute along the Line of Control, but couldn't do so for a while because he was still weak politically. Pakistani accounts claim that Bhutto did no such thing, and that in any case the written agreement is what matters.[a] For India, Simla had supplanted the UN resolutions as a point of reference for resolving the Kashmir dispute. After all, Indian leaders reasoned, the two parties had pledged to work directly with one another, implicitly abandoning extraregional diplomacy. For Pakistan, Simla supplemented but did not replace the operative UN resolutions on Kashmir.

a. According to Abdul Sattar, a senior Pakistani foreign office official who was with Bhutto at Simla.

politically reliable political parties. India's record in Kashmir is one of long, dismal, and well-documented military occupation, human rights abuses, and the detention and arrest of Kashmiri leaders. Its links to rival national identities make compromise virtually impossible, even though an agreement was tentatively reached on a method to resolve the entire Kashmir issue at Simla in 1972 (see box 5-2) and regarding Siachen in 1989.

As for the strategic value of Kashmir, both armies make the same argument: because Kashmir was once under unified strategic control by the British, both have an equal right to be concerned about who controls Kashmir, which gives rise to a new zero-sum conflict. Pakistan strategists point out that historically the main route to Kashmir lay through what is now Pakistan. This proximity makes Pakistan's capital, Islamabad, vulnerable to an Indian offensive along the Jhelum River. Pakistanis also bizarrely argue that the inclusion of Kashmir would give it a strategic depth that Pakistan otherwise lacks.[17]

In an unusual move, the Indian army has made Kashmir—especially the Siachen Glacier—the *only* foreign policy issue on which it has publicly refused to even entertain compromise or yield territory. This is ironic since the commander who seized Siachen originally regrets his actions, and the army suffered terribly in trying to maintain positions above those of the Pakistani forces.[18]

Adding yet another dimension to the Kashmir issue is the dispute over water control. Many vital South Asian rivers have their source in the territory, including the Indus and the five rivers that flow into both Punjabs: the Jhelum, Chenab, Ravi, Beas, and Sutlej. The 1960 Indus Waters Treaty divided the water through a series of dams and canals, but the system is long overdue for reexamination, if only because China may divert the waters even before they reach India and Pakistan.

In sum, it is practically useless to talk about solving *the* Kashmir problem when there are many Kashmir problems, most of which are not amenable to any solution over the long or short term. The failure of diplomacy is impressive here. Between 1972 and 1994 India and Pakistan held forty-five bilateral meetings, only one of which was fully devoted to Kashmir, the oldest conflict inscribed in the body of UN resolutions.[19] Further, Kashmir is not, as it is widely assumed, only an India-Pakistan problem, since China has claimed and occupied a good chunk of it for many decades—and has been granted de facto sovereignty over part of the state by Pakistan. China is, in fact, a real component of South Asia's hard-core security conundrum.

Realist Explanations

In the "realist" explanation, India and Pakistan are said to have become rivals and competitors by virtue of their separate and joint pursuit of power. According to realist assumptions, insecure leaders will increase their power by either building up their armed forces or pursuing alliances, or both. Of course, as John Vasquez has written, "this gives rise to a security dilemma in that taking these actions makes one's opponent insecure and encourages them to do the same thing."[20] Realists tend to look closely at alliances and wars to explain India-Pakistan rivalries, and in some cases to establish new "facts on the ground."

Alliances may precede or follow a military buildup, or, as in the case of Pakistan, the alliance may provide the means for the buildup—but the results are the same in that mutual actions lead to an arms-race psychology. That is, no one will ever know how much is enough.

Seeking outside allies against each other has been a consistent Indian and Pakistani policy for over sixty years and one of the most important ways in which they have constructed their own relationship. At times these allies have been willing to take sides, but usually they have been reluctant. Pakistan has enlisted several Arab states, Iran, the United States, China, and North Korea in its attempt to balance Indian power. Washington usually felt uncomfortable in this role, resisting Pakistan's efforts to extend the security umbrella to include an attack by India. The Reagan administration drew the line at calling India a communist state, which would have invoked the 1959 agreement to take measures to defend Pakistan against communist aggression. The Chinese have been less restrained, and although no known treaty binds Pakistan and China together, Beijing has provided more military assistance to Pakistan than it has to any other state. Between 2007 and 2011 Pakistan accounted for 64 percent of the total volume of Chinese defense exports.[21] Beijing believed its support for Pakistan would serve double-duty, since a stronger Pakistan could counter the Soviet Union and resist Indian pressure. Yet China has moderated its support for Pakistan's claims to Kashmir and gradually normalized its relationship with India. In turn, New Delhi saw an opportunity after 1988 to weaken the Beijing-Islamabad tie by moving closer to China and has been circumspect in its criticism of Chinese policies in Tibet and elsewhere.

For its part, India saw the Soviet Union as a major ally in its competition with Pakistan. Soviet support included a veto in the United Nations, massive arms supplies, and general sympathy for New Delhi. However, it was directed not so much against Pakistan as against China; when the Gorbachev government began to normalize relations with Beijing, Soviet support for India gradually declined.

On a number of occasions, one or both sides used force to change their relationship. No war succeeded in doing so. Instead, all of their conflicts contributed to the steady hardening of attitudes while damaging prospects for economic growth and cooperation. This was especially noticeable in Pakistan after the 1971 loss of East Pakistan, and in India after both the Kargil miniwar (1999) and the attacks on Mumbai in 2008. In other words, war has not worked, and now that they are both nuclear weapons states, war on a large scale is almost unimaginable.

The closest the two have come to a decisive turning point was in 1971, when the Indian army achieved the surrender of the Pakistan army in East Pakistan. However, rather than pressing on to a decisive victory in the west—which would have been very costly and might have brought other states into the contest—India settled for a negotiated peace and the Simla Agreement.[22] A second opportunity came in 1987 during the Brasstacks crisis, when India had conventional superiority and Pakistan had not yet acquired a nuclear weapon, but Rajiv Gandhi recoiled from the prospects of a general war.[23]

The India-Pakistan wars fall into two categories. The first were probes, to see if one side could gain an advantage by initiating conflict (or to avoid suffering a disadvantage if it did not take the initiative). The other type of war was "inadvertent" conflict: a war or a conflict triggered by some third party or by the escalation process itself.

Their first war was purposeful: Pushtun raiders sent by the NWFP government invaded Kashmir. The incursion was met with an innovative Indian response, resulting in a military stalemate and a series of unsuccessful attempts to negotiate peace. India's encroachment on territory held by the People's Liberation Army (PLA) in 1962 was also purposeful, as was Pakistan's probe in Kutch and in Kashmir in 1965, and its 1999 Kargil gambit. Several near-wars were also purposeful: India's Brasstacks exercise was intended to provoke a Pakistani response, which in turn was to have led to a decisive Indian counterattack. One could add to this list India's seizure of the heights of the Siachen Glacier.

Most of these operations ended in defeat or disaster. The initial 1947 attack by raiders made Kashmir the centerpiece of the India-Pakistan conflict for fifty years. It did not result in more liberty for the Kashmiris but merely intensified their enduring misery. The 1965 war, also initiated by Pakistan, led to a major Indian response across the international border and contributed directly to the growth of separatism in East Pakistan; Pakistan's clampdown against the Bangladeshi separatists provided the opportunity for Indian military intervention on a large scale. Indians grossly underestimated the impact of this on Pakistani thinking, both military and civilian. The 1987 Brasstacks operation was aborted for fear of a Pakistani counterinvasion against Punjab and persuaded both India and Pakistan to proceed with the development of nuclear weapons. India's Siachen Glacier initiative led to a very costly war of attrition and cemented the Pakistan army's desire for revenge. The small war in Kargil was precipitated by a Pakistani infiltration that was countered by a strong Indian response. Both sides claimed victory: Pakistan because India now had to defend more areas of the Line of Control, India because it was able to roll back Pakistani forces, albeit at great cost. The deeper results of this event, widely publicized and televised in India, were not in the realm of realpolitik, but they seared many Indian minds with the vision of a treacherous Pakistani attack, one that had been planned at the very moment that the Indian prime minister was in Lahore on a high-profile peace mission.

Sixty-five years of conflict support realist theories in that both countries now seek to maximize their military power by acquiring more and better nuclear weapons. After three wars and several crises, they covertly exercised their nuclear options by about 1990—creating still more crises and in 1999 a low-level war in Kargil. Kargil happened because Pakistan judged that it could probe and eventually dominate India through small-scale operations under the nuclear umbrella—the explanation I heard from senior Pakistani officers in 1981, and they subsequently behaved as if they believed it, by increasing covert activity in Kashmir and crossing the Line of Control in Kargil in 1999.

Kargil was a strategic failure, as was India's contemplation of escalation after the 2008 Mumbai terror attacks, and while both still brandish their missiles and boast about their nuclear prowess, the presence of about a hundred or more nuclear weapons in each arsenal has transformed the military-strategic relationship.

Nuclearization has not, however, ended the contest. Nuclear weapons serve several purposes; they can be used as a last resort to deter an enemy from attacking, and theoretically they can be used to play "chicken games of nuclear diplomacy that might be a way of making gains on the territorial issue."[24] As many have warned, just because America and the Soviet Union did not go to all-out war or use their nuclear weapons against each other, this does not ensure that this will be the case in the India-Pakistan situation. Scholar Scott Sagan, in particular, has made a strong case for worrying about the operational inadequacies of the Indian and Pakistani deterrents, and a book by the strategically well-informed Indian military analyst Admiral Verghese Koithara describes in considerable detail the steps needed for India to turn what is a declaratory policy into a secure operational nuclear force.[25] John A. Vasquez is pessimistic: the India-Pakistan case fits his "steps to war" explanation, and with the exception of the 1947 war, all the steps are present: territory is the factor driving the dispute; alliances and a military buildup follow, first with one side and then the other, and lead to an arms race. For Vasquez, the territorial dispute and the relative equality of capability lead the issue to fester, and therefore only overwhelming preponderance can prevent war, but one side being merely larger does not.[26]

Of course, it is impossible to know when nuclear deterrence will fail until it does. There is considerable evidence that both Indian and Pakistani leaders understand Kenneth Waltz's central argument that nuclear weapons will reinforce stability because of the devastating consequences of a nuclear war.

Sagan, who has studied India and Pakistan closely, is not as sanguine, noting the importance of doctrine in establishing a stable relationship, and the happenstance of accident, miscalculation, and intelligence failures in estimating the stability of a particular nuclear pair. Further, the situation in the South Asian case is one of a dyad-plus, with India having to calculate the risks, costs, and gains of a nuclear exchange with two serious nuclear weapons powers that, theoretically, might act in concert against it.

Emulating the "great" powers, believing they have inherited the Raj's mantle, India and Pakistan pursue the great power game against each other more than against real threats to South Asia. They learn from others, strengthening their own realpolitik perspective without either the resources of the truly major powers or the understanding that they are fighting a foe with pretty much the same strategic interests as themselves. This may be realpolitik, but it is not realistic. Thus it is not surprising that few of their wars have turned out well (whether against each other or against other countries—Pakistan in the case of Afghanistan, India in the cases of China and Sri Lanka). Realism may "explain" much of Indian and Pakistani relations, but it is a dead-end theory when it comes to being a guide to what they *should* be doing, as opposed to what they have been doing.

Identity and Creating an "Other"

A fifth explanation of the India-Pakistan conflict is that the psychological abnormalities found in one or both states prevent a normal relationship between the two. This is a variant of the idea promoted by the United Nations Educational, Scientific and Cultural Organization that the origins of war are found in the minds of men. If you change how people think and perceive each other, then you change how war and conflict will end. Kenneth Waltz calls this the "first image" of conflict, based on a liberal, optimistic view that humans can be taught not to hate (or the pessimistic view that such conflicts are inevitable and can only be marginally managed).[27] In the case of Pakistan and India, the systematic creation of identities in conflict with each other began *before* independence but really took off after 1948. Both countries were unsure of their purpose and identity—Pakistan especially had been created in opposition to the idea of India—and it is there that the educational systems are most aberrant. This is the central argument of several important studies of India-Pakistan relations, although they vary considerably in their understanding of how easily such images might change.[28]

First, Pakistan and India defined each other as "enemy" states through legislation regarding the properties left behind after the 1947 partition.

Initially, it was assumed that even if new states were created, individuals would be able to move back and forth; but after 1965 both treated their former citizens like enemies vanquished in war—literally seizing "enemy" property. India introduced an Enemy Property Act in 1968, while Pakistan had begun the process even earlier. Relatives of those who had fled had a hard time claiming the property of their own fathers, brothers, sisters, uncles, aunts, and even children, who were now "enemies" of the state. Most of the cases involved Mohajirs who had fled Uttar Pradesh and other Indian states for Pakistan after 1947, and in Pakistan much of the Sikh community and hundreds of thousands of fleeing Hindus. In East Pakistan the migrants were entirely Hindu.

The process began even earlier in Pakistan, notably in East Pakistan, where "enemy" property—that is, property owned by Hindus who fled East Pakistan for India—was seized after 1949. New acts were passed in Bangladesh after the 1972 war, permitting the state to declare as enemies Bangladeshi citizens who were Hindu. In a prolonged and contentious process everywhere, the state redistributed some of these properties to migrants who came from the other country.

Liberals attacked these laws arguing that they further communalized relations between India and Pakistan.[29] The acts imply that all Pakistanis are enemies of India. As the "enemy properties" were left behind by migrants to Pakistan, not during a war but owing to the exigencies of partition, there was never any justification for calling them that. Conservative Hindu-oriented parties attacked them on the grounds of "minority appeasement."

Subsequently, these abnormalities were perpetuated by defective educational systems, advocated by ideologically narrow politicians, and cheered on by hypernationalist media. India and Pakistan have created dueling "war crowds," with their populations taught to hate each other. The pathologies are seen even in sports—for example, in cricket nationalism. Some have argued that the prospects of peace are complicated by a culture of mistrust expressed in India's characterization of the "Pakistani other" as a "religious fanatic" and Pakistan's perception of the "Indian other" as a "bully" that then renders peace complicated.[30]

Three scholars have written that from an academic-theoretic perspective "the competition is deeply engrained in each society, both in the public psyche and in military and government planning." They pessimistically observe that a political shock alone, even if one were to occur, would not end the rivalry. Nor do they see the presence of other conditions associated with enduring rivalry termination, which remains "probably unlikely for the foreseeable future."[31]

The pathology of India-Pakistan relations is well documented. The works by Krishna Kumar on education in India and Pakistan, of K. K. Aziz on the abnormality of Pakistani historiography, and of social scientist Ashis Nandy on the sporting and cultural scenes are all relevant; so is the depressing record of attempts by outsiders to bring the two countries to the bargaining table, as well as India's and Pakistan's own feeble attempts over the years at normalization.

Some steps have been taken to make the academic curricula in both countries more accurate and thereby to deal with the problem of creating and maintaining hostility. Much effort has also been put into informal diplomacy, but most of those who have written about these perceptual pathologies rarely offer policymakers advice beyond the obvious pointers on how to manage the normalization process.

The obsession in creating an enemy is evident in how each country educates its youth about the history and society of the other. Both countries overhauled their national education systems to promote a strong national identity, often unified under the respective Hindu and Muslim faiths:[32]

> On both sides of the border Indian and Pakistani children are being educated in an exclusive, nationalistic and religiously inspired way which automatically puts them in conflict with each other. Their shared past has been distorted beyond recognition in some of the history textbooks. As children and their families generally believe what they are taught at school and what is written in state-sanctioned education materials, one can safely assume that a lot of the lies will be swallowed without question.[33]

School textbooks in Pakistan are state-controlled and written from an Islamic perspective, with four themes emerging from the bulk of the curricula of the three compulsory subjects (social studies and Pakistan studies, Urdu, and English): (1) "that Pakistan is for Muslims alone"; (2) "that *Islamia* is to be forcibly taught to all the students, whatever their faith, including a compulsory reading of Qur'an"; (3) "that Ideology of Pakistan is to be internalized as faith, and hate be created against Hindus and India"; and (4) that "students are to be urged to take the path of *Jehad* and *Shahadat.*"[34]

Pakistani education presents systematic negative portrayals of Hindus and Christians: "State-sponsored textbooks illustrate how history has been appropriated to reinforce a national philosophy or ideology. Historical interpretations are therefore predetermined, impregnable and concretized."[35] Official textbooks contain many examples of historical distortion, of Muslims portrayed as victims in religious clashes, whereas in fact they had also participated in the aggression.[36] Pakistan's Islamization, intensified under Zia ul-Haq after 1977, was meant to unify a country that he believed was suffering from regional divisions and conflict—instead he may have accelerated sectarian violence between Pakistan's Shias and Sunnis, and against the minority sects such as Ahmadiyya, further endangering Pakistan's Christian and Hindu communities.[37] Pakistani textbooks frequently link Hindus with adjectives such as "cunning," "scheming," or "deceptive."[38] Further, the texts often ignore the early Hindu and Buddhist civilizations in the region, "except to put the Hindu predecessors in a negative, sometimes racist light."[39]

Education "reform" in India was accelerated by and large under the Bharatiya Janata Party government between 1998 and 2004, during which time Hindu nationalists sought to install Hindutva thought as the educational norm.[40] This marked a sharp departure from the previous Nehruvian approach to education, which "envisaged India as a secular democracy."[41] In 2000, for example, a national curriculum issued under the slogan of "Indianize, nationalize, spiritualize" called for all foreign elements and histories to be purged from Indian curricula. It also instituted a "massive revision of textbooks for history and the social sciences which actively discriminated against the Muslim minority and set Pakistan in a bad light."[42] Muslims are now often represented as solely responsible for partition. Further, children are led to see Muslims in India as "fifth columnists" and not fully Indian.[43] The most important contrasting representations of history, and the one that may most greatly contribute to hatred toward India's Muslim neighbors was defined by one scholar as the 1947 partition; Indian textbooks depict it as a tragedy, whereas Pakistani textbooks celebrate it as a moment of birth.[44]

Kashmir remains the outstanding example of creating "an other," with Kashmiris on both sides of the Line of Control being induced—or forced—to become loyal national citizens of Pakistan or India. For Pakistan, which defined itself as a homeland for Indian Muslims, the existence of a Muslim-majority area under "Hindu" Indian rule was grating; the purpose of creating Pakistan was to free Muslims from the tyranny of majority rule (and hence of rule by the majority Hindu population). For Indians, their country had to include such predominantly Muslim regions to demonstrate the secular nature of the new Indian state; since neither India nor Pakistan, so defined, could be complete without Kashmir, this raised the stakes involved for both enormously.[45]

Pakistanis have long argued that the Kashmir problem stems from India's denial of justice to the Kashmiri people (by preventing them from joining Pakistan), and by not accepting Pakistan's own legitimacy. If New Delhi pursued a just policy, then a peaceful solution to the Kashmir problem could be found.[46] As a result, Kashmir remains the "unfinished business" of the

1947 partition. Pakistan, the self-professed homeland for an oppressed and threatened Muslim minority in the subcontinent, finds it difficult to leave a Muslim-majority region to a Hindu-majority state.

Indians argue, however, that Pakistan, a state defined and driven by its religion, is given to irredentist aspirations in Kashmir because it is unwilling to accept the reality of a secular India. As a formally secular state, India finds it difficult to turn over a Muslim-majority region to a Muslim neighbor *just because* it is Muslim. The presence of this minority belies the need for Pakistan to exist at all (giving rise to the Pakistani assertion that Indians have never reconciled themselves to Pakistan).[47] Indians also point to Bangladesh as proof that Jinnah's notion of a separate religion-based homeland for the subcontinent's Muslims was untenable. In contrast, India's secularism, strengthened by the presence of a Muslim-majority state of Kashmir within India, proves that religion alone does not make a nation. Indians maintain that Kashmir cannot be resolved until Pakistanis alter their views on secularism. Of course, this would also mean a change in the identity of Pakistan, a contentious subject in both states.

Kashmir is especially important in the identities of India and Pakistan because the same themes of dominance, hegemony, and identity are replicated within the state. The minority Buddhist Ladakhis would prefer to be governed directly from New Delhi and (like their Shia neighbors in Kargil) fear being ruled from a Sunni Muslim–dominated government in Srinagar. In Jammu, much of the majority Hindu population has long been discontented with the special status lavished upon the Valley by the Union government in New Delhi. And the few Kashmiri Pandit Brahmins left in the Valley are especially fearful. The Pandits lost their privileged position within the state's administration and much of their dominance in academia and the professions. After the onset of militant Islamic protests, most of the Pandit community fled the Valley for Jammu and several Indian cities (especially New Delhi), where they live in wretched exile. Some of their representatives have demanded *Panun Kashmir*, a homeland for the tiny Brahmin community within Kashmir.

As Sundeep Waslekar has wisely written, "The conflict is . . . about who we are and who we want to be as people. On the surface it appears to be a conflict about what we want to have—water, or land or whatever else. The reason why we are not able to reach a negotiated agreement on sharing what we want is because we confuse what we want to have with what we want to be."[48]

Outsiders

How have outsiders, notably the United States, tried to influence this dispute? The parallels to the Middle East are obvious, and several scholars have made them. However, some question the overall effectiveness of outsiders in such disputes: "At best, mediation might increase the length of the interval between militarized disputes in some rivalries, but does not influence the likelihood of subsequent war."[49] Outsiders have seldom been successful at promoting normalization. The World Bank role in the Indus Waters Treaty is frequently cited because it is virtually the only success story.

More realistically, outsiders have been critical in *sustaining* the dispute. Before Pakistan was created, the British forecast that it would barely be able to maintain internal law and order, and various experts that it would be as weak as Iran and Afghanistan, not in India's league. Until it became associated with the West's larger cold war strategy, Pakistan was regarded as a military cipher, but the alliance with the United States, and connections with other allied states, pumped it up with equipment, training, and diplomatic support to the point where it could plausibly claim to balance India.

At times outsiders may have made normalization more difficult if only by holding out the promise of support for one side or the other and thus reducing incentives to compromise. This was an argument that used to be made by Indians, who pointed to the U.S.-Pakistani cold war alliance, but is now being made by Pakistanis who are persuaded that the United States has sided with India.

Kashmir was linked to the cold war as well, but indirectly. The Kashmir issue was born at the same time the cold war got under way. Washington and Moscow armed India and Pakistan (sometimes both at the same time) and supported one side or the other in various international forums, while the Soviet Union wielded the veto threat on behalf of India in the UN Security Council. However, they ultimately reached an understanding that they would not let the Kashmir conflict (or India-Pakistan tensions) affect their own core strategic relationship. However, the process by which the cold war ended—with the forces of democracy and nationalism bringing down the Soviet Union and freeing Eastern Europe—was also at work in Kashmir.[50] Other revolutionary models that influenced the debate among Kashmiris were the liberation and revolutionary movements in the Islamic world—Iran, Afghanistan, and most strikingly (it was extensively covered by Indian and Pakistani television services) the Palestinian intifada.

Some Indians and Pakistanis argue that the superpowers deliberately kept the conflict going, although they disagree as to the motive. In the view of Indian Canadian Ashok Kapur, outside powers, especially China and the United States, intervened to keep India from growing.[51] Without massive U.S. and U.K. support for Pakistan and external pressure against India, he argues, "the Indo-Pakistan rivalry would not have been so prolonged." Kapur also echoes the widely held view that Pakistan's internal identity, shaped by the two-nation theory, "required continued differences with India to maintain Pakistan's Islamic identity and to manage the power asymmetry.[52] Otherwise Pakistan would be as insignificant as the British military leadership had predicted. For decades, the Indian answer to "why war" in South Asia was simple: persuade outsiders to end their support for Pakistan; it will then sink to its natural level of military capability, which is considerably inferior to that of India. Of course, the argument takes on a new twist with the introduction of nuclear weapons, the great equalizer between large and small, rich and poor. The solution to the "Pakistan problem" is no longer simply to cease outside support.

This is not so different from the classic Pakistani view that India was the one threatening the West, unlike the pro-West Pakistan, and that New Delhi had to be contained by an alliance that included Pakistan, then the West, and finally China. The Pakistani argument has some subtle aspects. Asserting that India is inherently expansionist and anti-West to boot, Pakistan says that it serves Western interests (and China's too), by being the only South Asian state willing to stand up to the machinations of New Delhi. Furthermore, the substantial outside military and economic help it has received has been put to good use because Pakistan has the capability to balance the larger and inherently expansionist (and aggressive) India.

The end of the cold war further enfeebled these arguments. Pakistan's claim to be balancing an aggressive India cuts no ice with the United States, although it figures in Pakistan's appeals for Chinese support, playing on Beijing's concerns about a rising India. Pakistan has found some mileage, however, in the argument that it is still an ally of the West, but this time against militant and extremist Islam, not India. By drawing upon its earlier but now tattered reputation as a "moderate" Muslim state, Pakistan levies a claim on the West and China, which at the same time is weakened by its substantial links with the very extremists that it professes to oppose—the price it pays for being on both sides of the so-called war on terror.

On the whole, outsiders played a decidedly greater role in "tilting" toward India or Pakistan than they did in promoting cooperation between the two. Instead, the great powers, including China, found it useful to include India and Pakistan in their larger strategies. At various times, Indians but especially Pakistanis found it expedient sign up with these alliances in order to acquire the military and economic strength to balance each other.

Indeed, the alliances helped New Delhi acquire technology and military expertise that were otherwise unavailable—preparing the Indian military for the modern world in general, even if the challengers were Pakistan or China.

In Pakistan the impact may have been more dramatic: while the Western alliances were transparently designed to build up capabilities against India, they also enabled the Western parties to pressure Islamabad after 9/11 to formally adhere to Western goals regarding Islamist terrorism. This has tentatively brought Pakistan into conformity with Indian (and Chinese) policies regarding terrorism and radical Islamic threats. Military alliances may be corrupting from a liberal perspective, but in this case they provided leverage over a state that had been toying with extremism as a matter of state policy.

Paired Minority Conflicts

Can these diverse explanations be consolidated into a single description?[53] They can, because the India-Pakistan conflict belongs to a class of disputes that I term "paired minority conflicts."[54]

The world's most intractable disputes fall into this category. Such conflicts are rooted in perceptions held by important groups on both sides that they are the threatened, weaker party, under attack from the other side. This is true even if the group is not a numerical minority. Paired minority conflicts are most often found *within* states, but a few occur at the state level, such as that between Israel and some of its Arab neighbors, or, for years, between Germany and France. Iraq and Iran would also qualify, especially before Saddam's downfall, in that Iraq feared the larger (and ideologically threatening) Iran, which in turn saw Iraq as the spear point of a hostile Arab world. Whether these attitudes will survive remains to be seen. South Africa and Northern Ireland were each a paired minority conflict—the Queen's willingness to shake hands in June 2012 with one of the leaders of the Irish Republican Army was immensely symbolic, but bitter feelings remain on both sides. There were elements of such a conflict in Brazil's relationship with Argentina, and in the Greece-Turkey pair, the latter having echoes in Cyprus. At the internal level, Sri Lanka has a paired minority conflict between the numerical minority Tamil population and the Sinhalese.[55] The former believe they are under a comprehensive threat from the more numerous Sinhalese, and the latter believe *themselves* to be the threatened minority, with 60 million Tamils positioned across the Palk Straits. Some, including the Tamil Tiger movement, argue that Tamils can never be secure unless there is a Tamil homeland on the island.

Paired minority conflicts can also be fomented by a strong-weak identity. Israel broadcasts the idea that it is irresistibly powerful but uniquely vulnerable—what Levi Eshkol, prime minister at the time of the 1967 war, described as the "poor little Samson" narrative replacing the perception of David against

Goliath.[56] For their part, the Palestinians play up their victim status while also portraying themselves at the forefront of the Arab (or Muslim) defense against an assertive Israel, which in turn is the Western/Christian dagger aimed at the Arab heart. For the Palestinians, the chosen grievance—the tragic moment—was the Nakba—the dispersion of the Palestinians celebrated on the date of Israel's independence day.[57] India and Pakistan do this as well; while their chosen grievances differ, they share in mourning the partition and the unjust behavior of the other side in subsequent decades, the disinterest of outside powers in their plight, or the tilt of outsiders.

One must add, however, that a number of seemingly intractable disputes have been resolved or at least successfully managed. Some of these are civil or domestic wars, such as those in Colombia, Cyprus, and Northern Ireland. In other cases, notably Indonesia in Southeast Asia, a strategic realignment has provided a framework for normalcy, evident in the operations of the Association of Southeast Asian Nations (ASEAN), or in South America with the gradual emergence of normal relations among the major powers under both the umbrella of the United States and the diminution of strategic ambitions of Brazil and Argentina. A similar process is under way in Africa, with stable relations between the region's major military power, South Africa, which has provided the muscle and brains for African military intervention in several troubled states, and other African states. Europe, too, provides examples of strategic adjustment leading to normal political, economic, and cultural ties. The Franco-German dispute—in which each side considered the other implacable and domineering while it was weak and vulnerable—faded with the destruction of Germany and the rise of the Soviet Union as a general threat, which brought the two states to the same side. In the past twenty years Russia has become a more ordinary state, albeit a difficult one to deal with, and its relations with all of its neighbors, notably Ukraine and Poland, have changed; it is no longer feared, nor is it a fearful state.

Paired minority conflicts display a moral dynamic, wherein both sides claim ownership of the high ground as victims of unprovoked aggression. With time, these conflicts grow more complex as they become integral to each side's identity.

Some paired minority conflicts take the form of a civil war, at times propelled by deep and enduring rivalry between religious, ethnic, or linguistic groups. Rivalry of this nature does not readily lend itself to the kind of sustained dialogue that leads to regional peace. But neither does it imply that war is likely. Other paired minority conflicts have been moderated or appear on the road to resolution, or at least manageability. In the case of India and Pakistan, six attributes perpetuate the conflict.

First, insecurity and distrust permeate the relationship. Conflicts such as this seem to draw their energy from an inexhaustible supply of distrust. As a result, it is difficult for one side to offer reassuring concessions or compromise on even trivial issues, since doing so only confirms one's own weakness and invites further demands. Compromise is resisted even when one has the advantage, believing that as the stronger side one can bend the other side to one's will. As if on a teeter-totter, the two sides take turns playing the role of advantaged or disadvantaged party. They may briefly pass through an equilibrium point, but their state of dynamic imbalance reduces the prospect of serious negotiations.

Second, both sides are certain that they are threatened by attributed identities of the other and oneself. For instance, when attempting to garner support for international war, the attacked side routinely portrays itself as a band of righteous innocents and the enemy as an assailant of not just national security but also morality.[58] Distrust also extends to those who advocate compromise, whether outsiders or members of one's own side. The former may be fickle; they may shift their support to the other side for one reason or another.

Third, *time* is a critical component of these conflicts. Each side is spurred by the hope that in time it will achieve some special advantage or the other side will collapse. Do long-term demographic trends, real or imagined, appear to be threatening? Is the country or group acquiring some special advantage in terms of technology, alliances, or economics that will change its relative position of power in the future? In brief, does the calendar work for or against it? If either side believes that time is not on its side, then the resolution of the conflict remains very unlikely.

Fourth, one or both sides tend to exhibit a "persecuted minority" syndrome. They not only see the other as an existential threat but also themselves as a victim. This status is used to justify resisting compromise as well as resorting to violence. The syndrome is rooted in the belief that the side has been wrongfully harmed, could not prevent the initial attack, and is the morally correct side, hence deserves sympathy. If both sides claim to be victims, the conflict tends to be perpetuated.

Fifth, paired minority conflicts are morally energized as the search for justice overlaps with the pursuit of power. In South Asia conflict is goaded by a sense of injustice and the notion that it is the only way to protect the threatened group. As already mentioned, the group considers itself threatened because it is morally or materially *superior* and thus the subject of envy. Even past defeats and current weaknesses are "explained" in terms of one's own virtues, which invite the envy of others.

Sixth, outsiders may be unable or unwilling to intervene in such conflicts. Over the past several decades, India and Pakistan have constructed their relationship in part through a search for outside allies against each other. At times outsiders have willingly become their allies, but usually they have been reluctant. Some of their most important allies—the Soviet Union, the United States, and China—have taken a noncommittal stance or have directed their support toward particular initiatives.

The Soviet Union, for instance, was for a time India's major ally in its competition with Pakistan, supplying it with vast quantities of arms and diplomatic support, among other things. However, this support was directed not so much against Pakistan as it was at ensuring that India would not tilt toward America and would also harden its policies on China. When the Soviet Union under Mikhail Gorbachev began to normalize relations with China, its support for India gradually declined. Similarly, the United States was more concerned with opposing the communists than with fostering regional unity in South Asia. The United States stopped supporting India in the mid-1960s when it failed to accommodate U.S. and U.K. concerns about Kashmir and revived the relationship only upon the Soviet invasion of Afghanistan in 1979, keeping South Asia itself a minor concern. Normalization was never important because the lobbies were too small and Kashmir was considered an obstacle to a strategic alliance against China. Similarly, when Pakistan has attempted to enlist several powerful allies in order to balance Indian power, the United States has resisted extending the security umbrella to cover an attack by India. China has been less restrained, providing more military assistance to Pakistan than to any other state. China's support for Pakistan served a double duty, since a stronger Pakistan could counter the Soviet Union and resist Indian pressure. However, China has now moderated its support for Pakistan's claims to Kashmir and gradually normalized its relationship with India. So far, neither the United States nor China seems to be actively seeking India-Pakistan normalization. U.S. policy (discussed further in chapter 7) is confined to wishfully urging the two states to better manage their relationship. China, concerned about Pakistan's growing Islamic extremism, has yet to broach the subject with Indian officials, although it has unofficially discussed this with the United States and in private dialogue with foreign scholars. The unwillingness of outsiders to intervene in the India-Pakistan conflict is likely to continue indefinitely.

Strategies

Rejection and ambition have influenced the behavior of every nationalist and identity group. When Gandhi was rejected by the British even though he had a British law degree and the Nehru family rejected even though it belonged to India's highest castes and was highly accomplished by British standards, some Indians responded by mobilizing mass political parties, and even armies. Subhas Chandra Bose, Nehru's rival, joined the Axis powers during World War II, for example, and created his own army out of captured Indian soldiers. A personal slight from the Congress Party was one of Jinnah's motives for going his own way, leading many Indian Muslims into Pakistan.

Being rejected can be a critical factor in developing an identity, in that it may generate a feeling of being special, or chosen. Bangladeshis have been thrice rejected: first by the British (as Bengalis), then by Indians (as minority Muslims), and then by West Pakistanis and Punjabis (again as Bengalis). In other words, they have been rejected as an ethnic group, as a religious minority, and then again as an ethnic group, and always as a poor people.

Inevitably, the rejection syndrome is transitive: people appear to need a fixed quantity of threat and hostility to make them whole. If the British could not provide it for South Asians, the Americans could. What often passes for strategy and high policy is often a pretext for elites to shift their chosen grievance from one party to another; the process of doing so is the concrete and landfill of politics, on which policy superstructures are erected by publicists, journalists, and self-appointed strategic thinkers.

States or groups can cope with a paired minority conflict in several ways. They can *flee* the relationship psychologically or physically; they can *demonize* the other side; they can *assimilate* with it or *accommodate* it; they can also *compromise* with the other side, or try to change its *perception* (through people-to-people diplomacy, persuasion, or bribery); they can use *outsiders* to redress the balance of power; or they can change the *balance of power* by war or other means (such as growing one's own economy or population faster than the other side). Over the past fifty years India, Pakistan, or third parties have contemplated all of these strategies.

India and Pakistan have in fact tried to flee their relationship several times. The first instance was a physical escape, the others symbolic, psychological, and strategic flight. Pakistan's founders fled India to establish a new "homeland" for the subcontinent's Muslims. The key West Pakistani leaders were from Uttar Pradesh, Delhi, and Bombay; the key East Pakistani leaders were Bengali Muslims. Most of these founders were secular politicians worried about being outnumbered in a democratic India, where Hindus would have a controlling majority. They had no interest in creating a theocratic state but rather a tolerant Muslim-majority state where Hindus, Sikhs, and Christians would live as contented minorities.[59] Indeed, some Islamist groups such as the Jamaat-i-Islami originally opposed the idea of Pakistani independence on the grounds that Islam could not be contained within a single state.

Intermittently, India has attempted to escape the relationship with Pakistan psychologically through the "look East" policy, or by ignoring Pakistan—simply refusing to engage in serious negotiations with it. The late Sisir Gupta used to argue privately that India might well encourage Pakistan's ambitions to be a Middle Eastern country, if that would temper Islamabad's obsession with India.[60]

Demonization is another coping strategy. If the leaders of the other country are evil, misguided, or corrupt, then there is no need to talk to them. Indeed, dialogue with such a country or its leaders is immoral and dangerous. For many Indians, Mohammed Ali Jinnah, the founder of Pakistan, has long personified the evil leader who was seriously misguided: he challenged India's civilizational unity with his two-nation theory, began the militarization of Pakistan by seeking arms from the West, and was aloof, cold, and undemocratic, jealous of Indian rivals, whipping up hatred and fear of India.[61] His successors, by and large military officers, are demonized as well, but for other reasons: for not having even Jinnah's leadership qualities and for lacking the moral authority to place their country on a solid footing. Complaints are also leveled at Pakistanis in general, who are said to be insecure because most were converts from Hinduism to Islam, a religion that is notably illiberal.[62] Some blame Pakistan's leaders for the "psychological" origins of the India-Pakistan dispute, and for allowing their hatred of India to entice them into becoming "the plaything of external forces," while being dominated by the military. As General P. N. Kathpalia has summed up: "There is no doubt that the troubles of India and Pakistan are basically of the making of the leadership. In the last forty-one years the leadership of one country has consistently fanned popular hatred and suspicion and pursued it as an instrument of policy."[63] Today, Indian diplomats despair of negotiating with Pakistan, a chronically weak state under the control of the most anti-Indian elements, such as the military, the intelligence services, and the Maulvis.

Pakistan's image of the Indian leadership is no less hostile. An important component of Pakistan's founding ideology was that Muslims could not trust the "crafty" Hindus, who still suffered from an inferiority complex.[64] While Gandhi and Jinnah were once respected rivals, their successors in both states lacked even professional respect for each other. It has come as a surprise to those few on both sides who have had a chance to interact to discover that the "other" was not so evil as had been portrayed in official and semiofficial circles. A retired senior Pakistani officer, Mahmud Durrani, recounts that after meeting an Indian counterpart at an American military school, "the adjectives that are normally associated with the Indians, as we learned in Pakistan—treacherous, dishonest, devious, crafty, sly and stingy—were not evident in Kapoor."[65]

When it comes to accommodation or even assimilation, some Indians still think that Pakistan might rejoin India. Yet Pakistan's leaders have never contemplated assimilation, although some important linguistic and ethnic minorities would have accepted a place in the Indian Union. In the last elections before independence, the dominant political party in the Punjab was the Unionist Party, an alliance of Hindus, Muslims, and Sikhs, and both the North-West Frontier Province and Sindh had Congress governments. As for India, most of its leaders assumed that the Pakistan experiment would fail and Pakistan would come back to the fold.

Although Indians no longer openly refer to the reintegration of Pakistan into India, there are many (generally private) discussions of how India might establish friendly relations with successor states to present-day Pakistan. Many Indians regard Bangladesh as an acceptable neighbor and believe that they could develop a similar relationship with a Sindhu Desh, an independent Baluchistan, or a separate North-West Frontier state, and even a militarily diminished West Punjab. Bangladeshis may not like or love India, but they fear and respect Indian power and would not dream of challenging New Delhi the way that Pakistan has.

Pakistani strategists, on the other hand, view the accommodating strategies of Nepal, Sri Lanka, Bhutan, and even Bangladesh as precisely the wrong model for Islamabad. These states have lost their freedom of action, they have been penetrated by Indian culture, and New Delhi has undue influence on their domestic politics, even intervening by force where necessary. Accommodation can also invite absorption (as in the case of Sikkim), direct intervention (as in Sri Lanka), and a military presence (as in Bhutan). But, the strategists say, Pakistan is larger and more powerful than any of these states, so it does not need to accommodate India. This resistance to accommodation or compromise with India is especially powerful in Pakistan's armed forces. Pakistan, its officers argue, may be smaller than India, but it is not weaker. It is united by religion and a more martial spirit than India and need not lower its demands of India, especially on Kashmir.

A fourth strategy for coping with conflict is to focus on changing the enemy state's perception of oneself, for example through diplomacy, people-to-people exchanges, persuasion, and, if necessary, bribery. This approach is closely related to and possibly even a substrategy of assimilation and accommodation, and in stark contrast to the strategy of demonization. Based on the idea of soft power, as defined by Joseph Nye, this amounts to "the ability to get what you want through attraction rather than through coercion," developed "through relations with allies, economic assistance, and cultural exchanges" and eventually resulting in "a more favorable public opinion and credibility," either generally abroad or in a particular country.[66] Many Indians involved in the Track II dialogues have been arguing for just such a bottom-up approach, on the assumption that more people-to-people and other cultural exchanges and confidence-building measures will eventually improve Pakistani popular perceptions of India and force the Pakistani establishment to take a softer line with India. While less prevalent in Pakistan, this strategy has some adherents among Pakistani moderates and liberals who see Hindu nationalists and their negative perceptions of Pakistan as a major obstacle to peace.

Balancing is yet another strategy, consisting of external and internal dimensions. External balancing refers to a state's capacity to sway the international balance of power and alliance politics in the direction of its immediate regional interests. In other words, this is the capacity to perform diplomacy and use outside powers and interests to achieve security against the enemy state and, if possible, a strategic advantage. Both Pakistan and India have, since 1947, been playing this game, but without definite success, though each complains that this strategy has been used more effectively by the other side and that it is merely responding to and counterbalancing the other. For Pakistan, the United States and China were initially important external allies to balance an India that was a leader of the nonaligned block, while for India, the 1971 quasi alliance with the Soviet Union was motivated by Pakistan's involvement with the United States and China.

Internal balancing focuses on increasing domestic resources and capabilities—military, economic, demographic—that will drastically alter the status quo so as to give the state such an overwhelming advantage that it will effectively translate into latent but acknowledged dominance over the rival. India has been developing this preponderance over the past two decades, increasing the asymmetry over Pakistan in almost all criteria of domestic power. Even discounting parity in nuclear terms, this domestic advantage is far from being acknowledged by Pakistanis, who still see their country as being of equal global rank and status with India, and has thus proved unsuccessful in terminating the rivalry.

An Eternal Rivalry?

The India-Pakistan rivalry is strongly generational, passed down from year to year, but it mutates over time. It consists of many layers of significance to many audiences. Kashmir is often identified as the root of the conflict, but it is as much a symptom as a cause, representing primarily a dispute about justice and people, but with complicated territorial dimensions. As in many intractable relations, it is also hard to tell where domestic politics ends and foreign policy begins; the rivalry has indeed become firmly wedged in the internal politics of both countries.

What makes this conflict so intractable and thus rare is its structural complexity: Indians and Pakistanis are divided as to the very nature of their differences. Is the dispute basically about territory (for example, Kashmir), authority over people (over Kashmiris, but also India's Muslims), ideology, or a simple struggle for power between two powerful states? In a sense it resembles a latent and protracted civil war, in which some elements on both sides argue that they will never have a normal relationship until one side or the other gives in completely—whether on the territorial issue, the "people" issue, or the ideological issue—or all three.

Even if the proximate causes of conflict are manageable, these deeper ones cannot be changed even by war. The conflict has gone on for so long that it may be, in its deepest manifestations, immutable. Events of the past, carried forward in the collective memories of Indians and Pakistanis, are a major component of the relationship. Over time the "facts" of history—real or imagined—become as hard to change as geography.

The logic of the situation demands that Pakistan (as the state most dissatisfied with the status quo) be the short-term instigator of conflict, India the long-term one as it has a potential to eliminate Pakistan and transform the status quo. It contemplated this twice: in 1971, in the war that broke up Pakistan, and in 1987, during the Brasstacks crisis, the last opportunity India had for a military victory before Pakistan went nuclear. For better or worse, India does not have a leader as ruthless as Indira Gandhi, nor is it likely to again produce a combination equivalent to Rajiv Gandhi, General K. Sundarji, and Arun Singh. The introduction of nuclear weapons into the subcontinent does not change this logic but makes it difficult to contemplate a large-scale war, and increasingly, to imagine and implement a limited one. Nehru once spoke of the impossibility of one state defeating the other by war—he hoped for a peaceful reconciliation and even reunification.[67] Yet if war cannot bring about a solution that might be acceptable to even one side, other approaches seem to be no more promising, as explained in the following pages.

CHAPTER SIX

Prospects

In 1947 no one seemed to envisage a protracted conflict between the two new states of India and Pakistan. Today their inability to resolve disputes is widely acknowledged to be a tragic failure, and the prospects for full normalization are not bright. There could be further warfare, the absence of normal trade hurts both countries, they are culturally cut off from each other, and their substantial nuclear weaponry changes the nature of the dispute—it is no longer merely a regional matter. Despite the poor prospects, unofficial, nongovernmental, and outside attempts to resolve specific India-Pakistan disputes have not been abandoned, and the governments themselves are engaging in back-channel diplomacy.

Track II and Unofficial Attempts

Unofficial dialogue between India and Pakistan has a long and erratic history.[1] In the hope of promoting better understanding, many foundations, governments, and individuals have supported private diplomacy and efforts to change the *perceptions* of Indians and Pakistanis. Over the past ten years, there have been at least a hundred efforts to bring together students, journalists, politicians, strategists, artists, intellectuals, and retired generals from both countries. Much of the goodwill thus created was washed away by the Kargil war and the Indian Airlines hijacking to Kandahar in 1999, followed by the even more traumatic (for Indians at least) assault on Mumbai in 2008 by Pakistan-based murderers.[2]

Compared with other conflict-laden regions, India and Pakistan have engaged in few dialogues over the past decade. They have behaved more like the United States and the Soviet Union during the cold war, motivated in large part by the same concern—the danger of a nuclear war. Fear, rather than opportunity, is the reason, and most funding for any such activities comes from foundations and governments outside the region. A 1997 Ford Foundation study optimistically observed that "non-official dialogues are beginning to generate momentum and achieve some tangible results," but this was premature.[3] The following years were conflict-ridden, and unofficial diplomacy suffered major setbacks, notably because of the Kargil war and the attacks on Mumbai. These alienated many Indians from unofficial attempts to bring about normalization or peace.

Current India-Pakistan dialogues are still bedeviled by wild swings between two views: that the countries are so different that no accommodation is possible (often the Pakistani view), or that they are at bottom quite similar (often an Indian view) and therefore accommodation would be easy if only Pakistan's misguided elite or its recalcitrant military were less obsessed. Nevertheless, nuclearization has reinvigorated Track II dialogues and sparked new, high-level back-track diplomacy. When the 1998 tests traumatized the Western powers and Japan, and foreign-sponsored efforts to prevent the tests were deemed a failure, some Indian and Pakistani business leaders organized talks on their own. In March 1991 they sponsored two sessions of an India-Pakistan dialogue, held in Islamabad and New Delhi. This effort was organized by O. P. Shah, a Kolkata-based businessman, and brought together nearly fifty professionals to discuss cultural and economic issues. These dialogues even brought representatives from extremist organizations in the two countries face to face.

Meanwhile, the two governments themselves sought to ease global fears of an imminent nuclear holocaust by initiating secret talks. These had to be kept private to avoid arousing the Pakistan army, which was suspicious not only of India but also of its own prime minister, Nawaz Sharif. Meetings were held between R. K. Mishra, chairman of a private Indian foundation, and several Pakistani interlocutors, including former foreign secretary Niaz A. Naik. No government officials participated, but India's prime minister Atal Bihari Vajpayee and Pakistan's prime minister Sharif were informed of the meetings. Naik and Mishra would visit each other's country under the pretext of attending a wedding or some other innocuous function. The meetings laid the groundwork for Vajpayee's historic visit to Lahore in early 1999, which led to a hopeful declaration and the opening of a broad range of ties. However, the goodwill generated by the visit evaporated when the Pakistan army discovered the Mishra-Naik tie (Sharif had tried to keep it from them) and the Indian army discovered Pakistani infiltrators in the Kargil region of Kashmir, triggering nationalist fervor throughout the country. India's feeling of betrayal deepened when the seized diaries of Pakistani military officers revealed that the Kargil infiltration was being planned even as Vajpayee was visiting Lahore. Secret diplomacy ended, back channels were closed, and the ever-hopeful Track II dialogues ground to a halt. People-to-people contacts were virtually suspended after Agra-Kargil, although a few peace groups maintained contacts, which on several occasions involved standing on both sides of the frontier in a candlelight vigil.

It took three years for the back channels to reopen. In 2003 Brajesh Mishra, then India's national security adviser, and Tariq Aziz, a senior civilian adviser to President Pervez Musharraf, engaged in a fresh round of secret diplomacy, this time with the knowledge of the Pakistan army. Their talks led to the successful meeting between Musharraf and Vajpayee during a gathering of the South Asian Association for Regional Cooperation (SAARC) in Islamabad in January 2004.[4] This held out the promise of expanded road, rail, and air contacts, as well as people-to-people exchanges, a new look at regional economic cooperation, and even a discussion on Kashmir. Subsequently, a number of unofficial dialogues sprang up, including a revived dialogue between retired U.S., Indian, and Pakistani strategists and officials called the Neemrana group, visits of high-level Indian businesspersons to Pakistan, and the prospect of cooperation between Bollywood and Lollywood—India's and Pakistan's film studios in Mumbai and Lahore.[5] One unusual effort was mounted in 2005 by American physicians of Pakistani origins, who made a successful trip to New Delhi.[6]

After the 2008 attack on Mumbai these official and unofficial normalization dialogues ground to a halt, but the process was again revived in 2012 with the announcement of Pakistan's positive response to the proposal that it give India most-favored-nation status. Again there was a surge in people-to-people diplomacy, this time substantially strengthened by the availability of social media, with websites, Facebook pages, and tweets providing the activists with better communication with each other than the two governments had.

All unofficial dialogues, whether Track II or people-to-people talks, are of marginal value if the governments are uninterested in addressing fundamentals. Neither India nor Pakistan has been enthusiastic about authentic Track II diplomacy or nongovernmental initiatives. Pakistan does not trust its own civilians, while India does not trust the other side. As one senior Indian foreign ministry official told me in 2013, the problem is one of getting the right people to talk to each other, meaning Indian civilians across the table from Pakistani generals, an arrangement that cannot be made public. It would do no good to get Pakistani and Indian officers talking to each other, although that might be an important confidence-building step, reassuring the Pakistan army that it is India's civilians who are powerful in New Delhi, not its generals.

Further, many of the most important issues dividing the two countries (Siachen, water, and Kashmir's status) might involve China, which occupies territory in Kashmir and along the India-China border—some granted to it by Pakistan, but most of it taken by force. While China may have concerns about developments in South Asia, its involvement at the unofficial level is ritualistic and tightly regulated by both the Communist Party and government.

India and Pakistan (and China) each believe that truly independent dialogues cannot be trusted to present their government's perspective. If held, they must be deniable—since the political risks are tangible—and private to avoid embarrassment. The best way to back away from informal commitments made in such sessions is to keep them secret. This kind of diplomacy must also be timely, that is, geared to developments on the ground; private talks must match up with a state's own timetable of decisionmaking, and that of the other party. Track II dialogues that take place too late or too early may not be effective and might even discredit such contacts.

Very few dialogues meet these criteria. Put another way, Track II dialogues must take place when an issue is "ripe" for new or innovative policies so that they contribute to the process, not be irrelevant to it. It is dangerous for either government to engage in serious private conversation in an era of open public diplomacy, Wiki Leaks, and e-mail. Both countries tend to prefer no serious dialogue rather than one that might go awry. Track II dialogues are also apt to be exposed prematurely by parts of the government that do not want to move toward a real or serious discussion, as in the case of the Mishra-Naik talks, which were sabotaged when the Pakistan army found out about them.

Another complication: at times unofficial dialogues may function as a form of strategic deception, to give the impression of a willingness to talk; they can also be part of a strategy of inaction, especially if third parties are eager to see a dialogue at this level. Typically, the United States, Japan, and some European nations want the two countries to talk unofficially when their officials have been unable to do so. Although these countries and their private foundations have poured out millions of dollars in travel, lodging, and honoraria to encourage Track II diplomacy, and both sides have obliged by talking a great deal, most dialogue participants remain fixed in their ideas about critical issues and would not even try to persuade governments to review their policies. Such meetings may be enjoyable and provide an opportunity to renew old friendships or revisit the battles of the past, but there is zero impact on policy.

To illustrate the state's interest in ensuring that even its private citizens are kept under control, Indian and Pakistani scholars and journalists alike often come under pressure *not* to participate in dialogues at certain moments. Sometimes the evidence is mixed: the distinguished Indian journalist (and parliamentarian) Kuldip Nayar has been scathing in his remarks about the Ministry of External Affair's secrecy and has filed freedom of information requests regarding documents in its possession. But the Indian government has warned its citizens about participating in events such as the Kashmir Action Council's Washington conferences; these were disclosed in 2011 to be supported by Pakistan's intelligence agency, the ISI.

Because Track II is often a way of avoiding real dialogue, the interlocutors tend to be former government officials or citizens with links to their governments. As a result, they do little to promote understanding and wind up rehashing old arguments, often for the sake of participants from outside the region. History is used—and abused—to emphasize the legitimacy of one's own side and the misguided arguments of the other. Such dialogues take the form of a duel between long-time adversaries, each knowing the moves of the other and the proper riposte to every assertion or claim. Meetings rarely last long enough to systematically discuss the differences between the two sides and how those differences might be ameliorated or accommodated.

Indians and Pakistanis engaged in Track II can usually be trusted to stay within their brief, but they can also be sent on exploratory or deceptive missions without compromising the reputation of serving officials. Thus a number of unofficial dialogues and meetings have attempted to circumvent governments considered hidebound by tradition, excessively cautious, and not really interested in genuine peace or reconciliation. This is not the case with true back-channel talks, such as those initiated in 2007 by Musharraf and Singh, with envoys Tariq Aziz and Satinder Lambah meeting over several months in Bangkok, Dubai, and London in a continuation of the Aziz-Mishra talks.[7]

Some unofficial dialogues have tried to create extra-governmental links between the like-minded—for example, workers, laborers, or ethnic or religious cohorts—in the hope of creating an *alternative* to official or officially blessed diplomacy, the assumption being that groups in different countries have shared interests. Although World War I disproved the notion of workers' solidarity, people-to-people diplomacy persists in the hope that common social, economic, and ideological interests will override the siren call of nationalism.

Another type of unofficial interaction consists of contacts between professional or academic individuals and groups. These contacts may or may not acquire strategic importance. Businessmen, students, intellectuals, religious leaders, tennis players, or journalists of both states may meet for purely professional reasons, but their meetings turn out to have political implications. Two examples would be the "Ping-Pong" diplomacy between the United States and China, and to some extent the "cricket diplomacy" between India and Pakistan—when President Zia came to India ostensibly to watch a cricket match, but really to engage in further conversations with Indian leaders.

Interaction can also take place between advocacy groups—human rights, environmental, antiwar, antinuclear, and women's activists—many of which operate globally, often through national chapters. Being weak claimants to power within a state, they often try to mobilize external support and at times can help manage relations between antagonists or provide a forum for dialogue. For example, the Pugwash movement, which brought together scientists and strategists from many countries, facilitated the development of nuclear risk–reduction measures between the United States and the Soviet Union, although it was less effective in dealing with proliferation matters. Originally viewed with hostility by both the East and West, Pugwash later became a vehicle for superpower diplomacy as well as an independent source of ideas. Washington and Moscow also used other dialogues between scientists and intellectuals to explore ideas and strategies, especially in the management of nuclear weapons.

Because India and Pakistan fear the independent voice in their dialogues, they avoid it, but a greater failing is their reluctance to rely on the institutions that they *do* control—the officially sponsored think tanks, key newspapers, and commentators that hew to the official line, or are made to do so. Of course, these institutions may introduce some risk: at times officials may allow dialogues to get out of hand and have to be disciplined, and intelligence agencies are always suspect until proven otherwise. Nevertheless, if India and Pakistan gave their own think tanks and strategists more latitude, it might improve the quality of regional dialogue.

If the two states decide to continue along the unofficial path with dialogues funded by outside sources, such talks can only make headway if they are more purposeful, their time-frame matches regional needs, and they are not the whim of a program officer or held simply to use up unexpended funds. Most of these wind up being one-shot talkfests; while enjoyable and diverting, they tend to be a waste of time and money. One example of a sustained dialogue is Balusa, which failed to show results not because of conceptual shortcomings but because of regional tensions. Another example is the Kashmir Study Group (KSG), which has made an impact through published studies, meetings in India, Pakistan, and outside the region, and contacts with government officials in a number of countries. The KSG is the gold standard for reasoned discussion and the development of new and creative ideas; it also has the advantage of being able to contribute to a wider understanding of the issues even if its Track II or diplomatic functions are on hold.[8]

South Asia needs more discussions of technical issues that improve regional expertise, especially in the nuclear arena. To some degree, the ill-fated Neemrana dialogue was moving in this direction—it had military, economic, and political expertise, and added journalists to its membership. A group that appears to be replacing Neemrana is organized by the Atlantic Council of the United States, and while foreign-funded, it is being operated by Indians and Pakistanis themselves.[9] Such a group should not attempt to cover all problems but, like the Kashmir Study Group, should focus on one issue from a multidisciplinary perspective. Balusa's study of pipelines is a model of its type.[10]

If outside foundations are to do something useful, an important step would be to enhance the expertise and capabilities of younger Indians and Pakistanis. If the region can avoid catastrophe, and if the political circumstances permit, the *next* generations will be called upon to grapple with extremely complex technical and political issues. This is one area in which South Asia has surpassed many other regions, and the Regional Centre for Strategic Studies (RCSS) workshops on conflict resolution and arms control are superb examples of a low-cost, intense program aimed at this generation. If they are sustained (the RCSS dialogues lasted for nine years before running out of money), they can develop regional and national informal alumni associations.

Just as Track II diplomacy may be the last refuge of a desperate political leadership, people-to-people diplomacy is often the last resort of angry and frightened citizens. As South Asia's crises grew in size and frequency, people-to-people dialogues multiplied. Many have been naïve, all have been dismissed by the hard men on both sides of the border, but they represent an important feature of the region—one does not see the Chinese, Saudis, or citizens of a dozen other wealthy but restrictive states engaging in spontaneous people-to-people diplomacy. Instead of denigrating nongovernmental efforts, governments should be more attentive to them, even in the case of a feeble but well-intentioned effort to create a joint school history for both countries that would be available on the World Wide Web.[11] Alas, the mind-set in officialdom is like that of the British Raj—that is to say, the people are more democratic than their elected governments, and history textbooks would be a worthy subject for the newly revived Joint Commission. The region's dangers suggest more, rather than less nongovernmental diplomacy is needed, and India and Pakistan should be held to their own public commitments to the free movement of ideas and people.

Instead, the two governments share the honor of being the greatest obstacles to effective unofficial dialogue. In the past New Delhi's haughty disdain and the Pakistan army's faith in force as a means of diplomacy meant that Track II or unofficial dialogues have never come to much. In the understated language of *Beyond Boundaries*, the most comprehensive review of unofficial dialogue, "The Indian government has not played a strong leadership role in promoting bilateral or multilateral dialogues in the region."[12] The same could be said of Pakistan. This lack of interest is especially striking when compared with Indonesia's approach to the Association of Southeast Asian Nations (ASEAN) after the 1962-66 *Konfrontasi* period, and subsequently Indonesia's and China's willingness to participate actively in the quasi-official Council for Security Cooperation in the Asia Pacific (CSCAP).[13] The authors of *Beyond Boundaries* wrote that official and unofficial diplomacy and dialogue are mutually supportive, but that without pressure from below "track one is not likely to move at all."[14] This is a polite way of saying that the governments involved do not want to move—that they are content with an arrangement in which they control contacts between their citizens.

Outside Interventions

The countries outside the region most involved in encouraging normalization between India and Pakistan have been the United States, Great Britain, the European Union, and the Soviet Union, in that order. With China's emergence as a real power, and with its growing ties to both India and Pakistan, the Chinese could be important in the future.

America has dominated these outside interventions, its South Asian policy from 1947 onward being a function of primarily cold war calculations.[15] The vehicle for American policy early on was often the United Nations, or had UN cover, in the belief that this would have a greater impact on India, which was an early supporter of the organization and had itself brought Kashmir to the UN forum.

U.S. policy oscillated during the cold war years. India was important as a balancer of communist China (at least until the Nixon administration) and as a proto-ally of the Soviet Union. It was in this context that the first Bush administration attempted to normalize with India after the Soviet invasion of Afghanistan. It was concerned about protecting Pakistan's rear flank, while the Indians were dismayed by the actions of their Soviet patrons. At no time was India or Pakistan valued per se, except by the occasional policymaker who thought that India was important for its democratic orientation and its developmental potential; Pakistan was always viewed solely in terms of alliance politics, an assumption that led to catastrophic misunderstandings between Washington and Islamabad after 9/11.

After 1989 nuclear proliferation displaced the cold war as the guiding star for U.S. policy (and Britain's, too). Wielding sanctions and threats, Washington tried to stop India and Pakistan from "going nuclear" without addressing the underlying insecurities that drove the process forward. As Shirin Tahir-Kheli noted in 1995, there were differences between American arms control specialists—then pressing for a three-stage process of capping, rolling back, and eliminating nuclear weapons programs—and the regional experts who believed that proliferation was a fact of life that had to be accepted until both states achieved normalization.[16]

The United States rarely if ever saw regional normalization as a prime goal, only as a means of securing India or Pakistan in the cold war struggle, or in the past fifteen years it saw the two as guilty parties in the nuclear proliferation process. There was no lobby for a normal India-Pakistan relationship in the United States, while both governments spent large amounts of money organizing their own supporters, who then spent most of their time and money battling each other. The United States considered Kashmir an obstacle to a strategic alliance with India against China or the Soviet Union, or latterly, as a trigger that could set off a nuclear war between the two irresponsible and very frustrating countries.

Neither the advent of regional nuclearization nor the transformation of American policy after 9/11 elevated India-Pakistan relations to anything but a third-tier issue, except when the two states were in a crisis, and Kashmir was usually regarded as the cause of regional conflict (this point is taken up further in chapter 7). The Obama administration's one attempt to address the region as a whole collapsed in 2011 when India refused to work with the American special representative for Afghanistan and Pakistan. The job description originally included India until Indian officials made it clear that they opposed this expansion of the remit. The American, Richard Holbrooke, at one point was subtly denied entry into India.[17]

Yet inch by inch, Indians, Pakistanis, and Kashmiris have begun to understand that the international community has changed its views on Kashmir. The specter of an escalation to a catastrophic nuclear war has now made regional normalization and stability the primary goal pursued by the United States and others—although no solution will last very long if it is not considered as just by a good number of those involved. For outsiders, stability is more important than content. This favors India as the status quo power, so New Delhi should be less concerned about the consequences of outsiders playing a role in addressing the Kashmir issue. But New Delhi still opposes such a role, although its own policies toward the people of Kashmir are moving slowly—very slowly—in the direction of accommodation.

The European Union has normally avoided involvement in the India-Pakistan rivalry, but it occasionally offers to "mediate," and it also funds various Track II dialogues, mostly on "conflict resolution" and the Kashmir issue. The EU member states have funded innumerable academic conferences and research projects on the possible "lessons" of the European integration process for South Asia and on comparing the European Union to the regional organization, the South Asian Association for Regional Cooperation (SAARC).[18]

Europeans compare the India-Pakistan conflict to the old Franco-German dispute that sparked several wars and assume that their post–World War II experience makes their countries a role model for other conflict-ridden regions. This analogy overlooks the important role the United States played in inducing normalization and sponsoring economic integration, as well as the additional incentive provided by a commonly perceived outside threat—the Soviet Union. These kinds of forces are absent in contemporary South Asia, and thus in the words of one observer, "unless the 'original sin' of Partition is, in one way or another, made irrelevant, the SAARC or a new limited avatar (of the EU in South Asia) will not go very far."[19]

India has reluctantly permitted the European Union to look into Kashmir through annual ambassadorial "fact-finding missions," also known as "troikas," although it sees them as a form of meddling in domestic affairs. At the same time, the Indian government believes such missions indirectly legitimize its sovereignty over the state.

The European parliament also commissioned a study known as the Nicholson report on the rising Islamic militancy creeping into Europe from Pakistan, and on the impact of the earthquake of October 8, 2005, which devastated parts of Kashmir (especially on the Pakistan-controlled side). The report met with scathing remarks from pro-Pakistan nongovernmental organizations (NGOs) and commentators, for it was very critical of Pakistan's administration of the parts of Kashmir under its control and did not support a plebiscite. It also took an unfavorable view of the way the Pakistani constitution addressed fundamental freedoms and the rights of women, children, and minorities.[20] A quasi-official Indian think tank took a selective view of the report, liberally citing its criticisms of Pakistani practices and ignoring its comments on Indian policies.[21]

Many Eastern European, but also Austrian, Scandinavian, German, and British parliaments have pro-Kashmiri lobbyists, and the European Union even observes a "Kashmir Week."[22] The Kashmir Action Council's office in Brussels plays an influential role in pressing these Euro-parliamentarians to expose human rights violations in Jammu and Kashmir, and some even support the idea of its secession from India or accession to Pakistan. The European parliament also hosts a general group for "South Asia," which tends to be more focused on political and economic cooperation and fostering regional integration through SAARC.

While the self-defined European human rights activists continue to raise the Kashmir issue, the European Union's official approach to the region and India-Pakistan rivalry has shifted in recent years. The Nicholson report on political freedom and development progress in both Indian and Pakistani Kashmir marked a turning point, in that it took a less investigative approach to India while exposing significant democratic, human rights, and economic shortcomings on the Pakistani side. It is the first official European document to acknowledge fundamental violations and shortcomings in Pakistani Kashmir. Despite significant opposition from Islamabad, it was adopted after many amendments.[23] It met with a positive response from Indian Kashmiris.[24]

The shift in European thinking about "the region" is reflected in the words of the European Union's ambassador to India during a visit to Srinagar, Kashmir's capital, in 2011: "We are not coming here with a particular mandate [to solve the Kashmir issue]. What is happening in this part of the country has to be solved by the people who are living in the region."[25] The ambiguity about *what* region was being referred to—Kashmir or South Asia—was deliberate, signaling Europe's attempt to reduce the traditionally central role Kashmir has played in its relations with India and its willingness to focus on more substantive political and economic dimensions of the EU-India "strategic partnership" signed in 2000, including a much awaited free trade agreement.

Historically, the Soviet Union (now Russia) and China were disinterested in normalization between the two major South Asian powers. In the late 1960s they developed security agreements with India and Pakistan, respectively, which expanded in the wake of the failed U.S.-U.K. attempts to resolve Kashmir after the 1962 India-China war. For them, as for the Americans, cold war and balance of power considerations were uppermost concerns; India and Pakistan were seen as proto allies, and at times loose alliances were formed between India and the Soviet Union, on one hand, and the United States, Pakistan, and China, on the other.

There were a few important deviations: the Soviet Union brokered a peace agreement between India and Pakistan at Tashkent in 1966, and it tried and failed to get the two countries to issue declarations of peaceful intent. In November 1986, in an address to the Indian parliament, Soviet premier Mikhail Gorbachev called for the establishment of a UN center on reducing the risks of war, a conference on the Indian Ocean as a zone of peace, and a conference on the relationships between arms and development. Gorbachev also proposed a third world space research center to be based in India. He discovered to his dismay that Indian officials did not really care for his Asian peace proposals because they involved substantive talks with Pakistan.[26]

Neither Russia nor China wanted to see a major conflagration to its south, and neither India nor Pakistan matters very much to either in terms of its own balance of power. Russia now sells the same weapons to both New Delhi and Beijing, and military hardware to Pakistan; trade and weapons are its major interest, while the Chinese share India's trepidation regarding Pakistan's organized support for Islamic extremists—and now for dissident Muslim Chinese in China's Xinjiang Province. Theoretically, China could take advantage of its growing economic position in both India and Pakistan and facilitate trade, perhaps by using different branches of the same company. In the past American firms were unwilling to do business in Pakistan for fear it might hurt their operations in India, and the idea of doing business in both was not part of their corporate strategy. For this to happen, Chinese (and American) companies would want reassurance that this cross-border knitting together would pass a political test in both New Delhi and Islamabad.

Prospects

The history of India-Pakistan relations can be summed up as demonstrating an inability to move very far on the issues discussed in chapter 2. The two countries have also been unable to comprehensively address concerns such as regional arms control and security arrangements—but then neither were the Soviet Union and the United States able to come to any but the most anodyne agreements in these areas. Cynically, the alternation between proposals for "joint defense" and "no war" is actually one subject on which India and Pakistan have *agreed:* they will keep the process going and periodically raise a new idea—or a variation on old ones—to demonstrate their own sincerity and the obtuseness of the other side. The major purpose of these exercises has been to reassure outside powers and to persuade their own leadership of their righteous and forthright position; there is little belief on either side that these proposals are to be taken seriously (see box 6-1). While the agreements on trade and visas were warmly greeted by the two populations, deep suspicions remain, and the pattern of the past could reassert

Box 6-1. *The Perfection of Insincerity*

Both India and Pakistan have become skilled in offering each other proposals they know will not be accepted. In 1949 Nehru offered Pakistan a "no-war" pact, but Pakistan did not respond. Then in 1958 Ayub Khan offered India a "joint-defense" agreement provided the Kashmir dispute was solved, after which Nehru again reiterated India's offer of a no-war pact. According to one recent study, General K. S. Thimayya, head of the Indian military and worried about the rising China threat, favored such an agreement. Opposition by Nehru's close adviser and minister of defense, Krishna Menon, killed the idea and actually generated suspicion among some civilians about the reliability of the Indian military.[a] Several years later, with the U.S.-Pakistan alliance revived after the Soviet occupation of Afghanistan, President Mohammed Zia ul-Haq offered Delhi a no-war proposal, advised by an American that this might get some dialogue going. This flabbergasted the Indians. Of course, neither proposal was serious, their purpose being to impress outside powers of Indian (or Pakistani) sincerity.

The two states also changed positions on the question of the original Line of Control. In 1954 Pakistan's governor-general Ghulam Mohammed explored with Nehru the possibility of formalizing the cease-fire line in Jammu and Kashmir as an international boundary. Nehru rejected the proposal. Then in 1963 India, at the Bhutto–Swaran Singh talks, proposed formalizing the cease-fire line in Jammu and Kashmir as an international boundary. This time, Pakistan rejected the proposal. Finally, in 1972 an Indian delegation led by P. N. Haksar and a Pakistani delegation led by Aziz Ahmed agreed to establish a line of actual control in Kashmir to separate the respective areas occupied by India and Pakistan. The Line of Control has been violated numerous times by both sides, notably when Pakistan initiated the Kargil war. Furthermore, many areas, including Siachen, are disputed.

Much the same can be said of recent proposals for the institution of confidence-building measures (hotlines, summits, dialogues, and various technical verification proposals) between the two countries. While outsiders regard such measures as no-risk high-gain arrangements, in the India-Pakistan case any cooperation is seen as low gain and high risk. If cooperation fails, losses will be public and politically damaging; there might also be a multiplier effect in that the risk of conflict might increase if an active attempt at cooperation fails and if the costs of conflict are very high.

a. Srinath Raghavan, "Soldiers, Statesmen and Strategy" (www.india-seminar.com/2010/611/611_srinath_raghavan.htm).

itself because these understandings do not address the unaddressable—deep conflicts over identity and strategic assumptions. One knowledgeable Indian strategic thinker, skeptical about even this limited agreement, has suggested that both governments should be asked to announce exactly how many visas they have issued, year by year, after the agreement is concluded.

Yet a disheartening history also includes events and developments, some recent, that could change the context in which the two countries approach each other and their common problems. They have stabilized their nuclear deterrents, although they are still both groping for a common understanding of stability. They have begun some limited trade. And the official invective has been moderated.

In a series of interviews with recently retired and senior Indian and Pakistani officials—both civilian and military—I detected a new optimism in their ranks, although more so in Pakistan than in India. These discussions raise some important points about the prospects for normalization.

First, as just mentioned, a qualified optimism is emerging on both sides (and enthusiasm among Pakistanis), especially after the decision in 2012 to accept Indian trade terms. Civilians in Pakistan were relieved that the army allowed the process to move ahead, although generals had been complaining about Pakistan's bad economic prospects for at least twenty years.

None of the professionals on either side believe that a major breakthrough is likely, and all point to the obstacles in various areas and to the larger problem of Pakistani coherence and India's ability to compromise; yet their estimate is realistic on the whole. As one Pakistani official with experience in negotiating with the Indians told me, "Get rid of some of the minor issues such as Siachen so that trade can flow between India and Pakistan. Also, India needs to do more than Pakistan on the so-called trust deficit" (see box 6-2).

Their pessimism reflects professional candor and the reality of a relationship that could be blown apart by a serious miscalculation on either side, by a clumsy foreign intervention, or by one or more terror groups bent on disruption. Deeply pessimistic voices remain, but they are found mainly in the ranks of the retired.

This generational difference remains a problem. Indians and Pakistanis with long memories are numerous; those with memories of good relations with the other side are few and far between. Some in a younger generation, especially in Pakistan, see the importance of normalization. In 2012 one senior Pakistani official with experience in many posts, including India, told me that trade can lead the way and that with the army's decision to accept the process of trade normalization, South Asia can catch up with other regions. He praised the normalization taking place between India and Bangladesh

Box 6-2. *Trust Deficit*

A frequently heard explanation of India-Pakistan rivalry is that it centers on a massive deficit of trust. This is not quite correct. The deficit in India-Pakistan relations pertains not to trust but to verification. Neither side can independently or reliably verify the actions of the other. The intelligence agencies on both sides are not equipped to do so either technically (as in the case of military withdrawals or trade flows) or temperamentally (they each have strong biases), although the recent joint statement between two former intelligence chiefs is a large but belated step in the right direction.[a] While the rivalry continues to be sharply contested and is far from normal, the verification/trust deficit could be addressed in several areas. These could include independent verification of water flows, meetings of serving officers of middle rank on a regular basis, and an expansion of the new visa agreement to include scholars. Third parties are limited in playing the role of facilitator as outside powers are considered not only biased but also motivated by their own interests in outcomes, although sometimes their technological capabilities can be put to good use. Pakistan has been more willing to accept outsiders—even encouraging their engagement—but in India a "principled" opposition to outside intervention permeates the bureaucracy because of hangovers from nationalist attitudes.

a. Amarjit Singh Dulat and Asad Durrani, "India-Pakistan: Need for Intelligence Cooperation," *The Hindu*, July 14, 2011.

as a model, noting that the army had begun to support a democratic process in Dhaka and hoped for the same pattern in Islamabad, cautioning that "the problem is still India's insecurity, but now that India is becoming more powerful as a state, that should disappear." It remains to be seen whether the trade initiative is a deeply thought-out calculation on the part of the army or the product of panic caused by Pakistan's poor economic prospects. One Pakistani official who has been part of these talks assured me that the military had changed its position on trade talks after 2002, but explained this had little impact because of Indian recalcitrance and Musharraf's weakened position.[27]

The "formers," the retired diplomats and soldiers, tend to subscribe to the long-held views, although there are exceptions. The catastrophe of the 1971 defeat, for example, still resonates with some in Pakistan, just as Pakistani-sponsored terror attacks against India have traumatized a younger generation of Indians. This is one reason why Track II meetings involving the formers are rarely productive: many retired officials talk as if they are still in government upholding the hardest line possible toward the other side. Yet they will readily agree to peace and cooperation in the abstract, on the condition that the other side will also yield equally on long-held policies. They are living in a comfortable if confrontational past, and few can imagine a future in which cooperation is the norm. As one senior Indian journalist quipped at a meeting in Salzburg where the formers were suddenly and most insincerely advocating peace, "We ought to extend the age of retirement, because it seems as if once an official retires he becomes committed to peace with the other side." Few if any of the formers understood the sarcasm.

However, generation is not an absolute predictor, as indicated by the following remarks of a former senior Pakistan army official with strong ties to the intelligence community:

> I have met both Jaswant Singh and Yashwant Sinha, and I agree they are pragmatic and one can do business with them. "Verify but trust," the words left me dumbfounded. What wisdom! I am not sure if those who make and implement policies can fathom the depth. None on our side at least. I suggest you give it a try when you meet them next.[28]

Further, two of the leading Pakistanis in favor of an accelerated peace process are generals: Mahmud Durrani and Talat Masood. Both are prolific and serious participants in various Track II and unofficial dialogues. On the Indian side, several former generals and admirals seem to be equally committed to dialogue and normalization and have been participating in military-military dialogues.

A second observation arising from discussions with formers is that past irritations recur often enough to keep levels of suspicion high. Both Indian and Pakistani diplomats recount episodes in which the other side failed to adhere to positions set out in preliminary negotiations or public statements, or in which they behaved badly toward the other side. Yet in the first instance, there is no shared understanding of the reasons why the 1972 Simla summit did not lead to an agreement on Kashmir, or why the 1989 Siachen agreement was not consummated: it was presumably wrapped up and completed pending Rajiv Gandhi's reelection. More recently, Indian and Pakistani professionals cannot seem to understand why the 2001 meeting at Agra ended in catastrophe. Indian officials still complain about Pakistan's slowness in reciprocating the offer of most-favored-nation status made to Pakistan as part of the World Trade Organization process back in 1994. As for high-level visits, while Pakistan seeks them, officials in New Delhi are skeptical, reportedly in response to the lack of Indian domestic support for the prospective visit of Prime Minister Manmohan Singh, even in Punjab, which is usually eager for a peace initiative. "Officials in the know" have stated that India would wait until the Pakistan army gave the People's Pakistan Party civilian government a relatively free hand, improved visa regimes, and promoted trade and people-to-people contacts.[29]

Since there was no substantive movement on areas where the Pakistan army is involved (Siachen, Sir Creek, cross-border terrorism, and Afghanistan), the assumption was that it still called the shots in Pakistan, and India could not find a way to deal with that. One Ministry of External Affairs official noted that Pakistan president Asif Ali Zardari had even reversed Musharraf's liberal position on Kashmir, reverting to Pakistan's original plank of self-determination for Kashmiris, a UN proposal that India believes is superseded by the bilateralism of the 1972 Simla Agreement.

However, there is one important point on which virtually all serving officials (and most who are retired) can agree, but none will say this publicly: it is that the present Line of Control in Kashmir will and should become an international border between the two countries. This was, briefly, Pakistani policy, and it has been Indian policy—but privately—over many years, complicated by a parliamentary resolution declaring that no Indian territory can be transferred to any foreign country. Both states are a long way from reaching this point.

Present and future negotiations will be carried out by officials who have had a bad experience with the other side, or whose diplomatic tradition cautions them to be ultra careful. One Pakistani diplomat recounted the way in which India "bargained like dogs" on the initial round of trade talks—before Pakistan's change in position. Earlier India had pressed for talks on trade; later it shifted grounds and refused to talk until the subject of terrorism was addressed, while Pakistan insisted on dealing with Kashmir. This was reminiscent of the policy flip-flops two decades earlier on the question of joint defense versus a no-war pact. To add to grievances on both sides, embassy staff have been subjected to rough treatment by their host's intelligence agencies, which are not much beholden to political direction and often act on their own. Those who want to help normalization proceed should be supporting collaborative India-Pakistan studies that set out, as best the record allows, an objective history of the past, so that both sides will be encouraged to rely less on myth and gossip in their assumptions about each other.

Third, the professionals interviewed expressed real doubts about the ability of one or both sides to sustain a normalization process. The astute ones are well aware of the difficulties of negotiating within their *own* country, let alone with the other side. The "process problem" will not disappear.

All of the officials interviewed for this study note that Pakistan's positions on all India-related issues are highly dependent on the military, and that Pakistan is not as politically stable as it used to be. Meanwhile, India has allowed the armed forces to enter into security matters, notably border issues, and the intelligence services still have a heavy but veiled role. The armed services and the intelligence agencies may have a veto, depending on the strength of the serving Indian prime minister, while the veto is taken for granted in Pakistan. The fact that no official can openly say that the solution to Kashmir is the present Line of Control is a perfect illustration of the problem in advancing normalization.

As India enters its second decade of coalition governments, policies of national importance may hinge upon the views of political parties that have little or no interest in foreign affairs. The one exception is economic normalization with Pakistan, for just about every state has something to gain from increased trade, including the border states, Rajasthan and Gujarat. In the latter the chief minister, Narendra Modi, is notoriously anti-Pakistan but has been cautious in statements on expanding trade and cross-border contacts. In Pakistan, as one official proudly noted, all of the major political parties—except for the fringe Islamic ones—have come out in favor of economic normalization. Whether they will remain so may depend on the terms of such agreements unless they are consulted by the government beforehand. The one certainty is that the political balance in both countries will have to be carefully calculated before major steps can be taken. Center-state or provincial negotiations will have to be a feature of the overall normalization process; this could be helped by greater economic ties as well as cross-border conflicts, both of which could build lobbies in favor of agreement.

Pakistan faces multiple potentially fatal threats to its standing as a country: an economic crisis, a decline in educational competence, a shrinking state, and, above all, still no consensus on what exactly Pakistan stands for as a nation and a state.[30] Most countries have more or less functional "ideas" of who they are. Pakistan's is still a work in progress. The debate over the idea of Pakistan has been accelerated by a free but still not responsible press, the influence of extremist Islamic ideas coming from the Middle East, and the temptation of India's plural secularism as a model—one that dare not be openly followed but that is greatly admired by many Pakistanis who are envious of India's economic role and new international standing. Pakistan is groping toward a workable identity, even as it attempts to repair the damage done to its economy, society, and culture by several generations of rapacious civilian leaders or incompetent military ones. Can it sustain the process of redefining and rediscovering an identity that does not inherently challenge its neighbors and other parts of the world while simultaneously conducting a diplomacy that normalizes relations with is historic foe, India?

This question is a mark of the great uncertainty Pakistan lends to the prospects for normalization, especially when its overall political stability remains shaky. As time passes, Pakistan's deeper dysfunctionality could come into play, as will Indian doubts about concluding agreements with a failing or erratic state.

The professionals have also expressed some consensus on the role of outside powers. On the one hand, they look to outsiders for validation of their identities and their policies. India in particular craves recognition as a major power, even as a world power, yet Indian officials are aware that it barely leads one of the most dysfunctional regions in the world, and that many of its neighbors—notably Pakistan—regard it with suspicion. Meanwhile, Pakistan just wants to be treated as an important country and have its sovereignty respected. The suggestion that there might be a role for outside powers in helping India and Pakistan settle their disputes is now widely rejected—with a caveat. Even Pakistanis understand the Indian view that bilateral negotiations are the only route to a settlement of Kashmir, and that there is no important role for outsiders in other matters, including Siachen and Sir Creek—although both states are committed to abiding by the International Court's judgment on the Indus Basin. A few Pakistani diplomats, especially of an older generation, may hope that the United States will side with them against India on Kashmir, but their experience with Washington over Afghanistan has created a new, tougher approach to the United States. Islamabad will still try to use America to pressure India, but without expecting significant results. What is new is that Indian diplomats and officials have become accustomed to working with the United States to coerce Pakistan, a result of the Clinton administration's 1999 Kargil intervention. Privately, they acknowledge that this has been helpful in their own diplomacy, but none want an overt, declared American role on any dispute involving Pakistan.

Looking Ahead

I have argued in this book that three sets of factors perpetuate the India-Pakistan conflict:

—The visible disputes between India and Pakistan over matters such as Kashmir, river waters, and different territorial claims.

—Identity issues, not between the two peoples having huge commonalities, but between the identities of the states that evolved after 1947.

—Strategic pressure points that are shared by the two states, Afghanistan being the most notable one.

The variety and complexity of these factors make somewhat irrelevant the chicken-egg debate as to how hostile or unfriendly states normalize their relations. Put crudely, the "bottom-up" school argues for increased trade, people-to-people relations, Track II diplomacy, and greater cultural understanding. Out of this, many say, there will flow greater understanding and the eventual realization that the two countries can normalize or negotiate away their territorial or strategic differences. The "top-down" school, represented by scholar Charles Kupchan, stresses the supreme importance of strategic accommodation at the top, after which trade, people-to-people exchanges, and other ties will develop.

In the case of Pakistan and India, it is extremely difficult to assess whether core strategic and military policies of each country will be shaped by growing links, or instead by developments within each country that are not affected by greater trade and investment, such as common culture and values, plus domestic and bureaucratic politics. The answer is complicated, of course, because simultaneous processes are involved, and not all of them are moving in the same direction. It is possible for two states—often hostile although culturally not very distant—to achieve normalization along some dimensions, but not others. The outstanding case is that of America and China, although Israel and Egypt fall into the same category. In both cases relations were normalized along one dimension only—strategy. Could India and Pakistan normalize their relations along economic lines, leaving Kashmir, Siachen, and other disagreements untouched? One way of answering this question is to turn to a generational model that combines elements of both the top-down and the bottom-up approaches.

If, as think tanks are wont to do, one assesses the impact of economics, security, and strategy on country relations separately, each can be said to be a "driver," but that approach fails to include the impact of the relationship *between* these sectors. They do influence each other and thus the overall perspective of a country, although a generational time lag will also play a role in this. A "generation" does not pivot quickly in its attitudes:

—First, the new generation will be exposed to new and different interpretations of another country.

—In a second stage there might be a debate within a strategic or political elite about these assumptions.

—In the third stage new policies or interpretations are hesitantly trotted out.

—Finally, if there is congruence between the two states, and the reinterpretation process has proceeded apace in both, a new relationship may evolve.

In considering the prospects for normalization between politically complex countries such as India and Pakistan, it is essential to account for all dimensions of each: their national identities, domestic interest groups, and regional and coalition politics, and their interrelationships. These may all march to different drummers. In Pakistan there is a clear difference between the army, with its associated civilian hard-liners, and the rest of society; in India the intelligence services and the military differ from the civilian businessmen and the "peace" lobby. A change in strategic policy may be acceptable to some but effectively vetoed by others. The four-stage model is complicated by a federal or multipolar political order, and it is vulnerable at many points and at any time. Indeed, it is a miracle that states ever do normalize their relations without violence and war; of the world's hard-core disputes, most eventually do get resolved by a combined process of top-down, bottom-up, or changed strategic circumstances.

India and Pakistan are only in the first and second stages of this process. The trade agreement plus the potential agreements on a greater exchange of people could lead to a wider debate in each country about alternative futures and policies. The process is both accelerated and slowed by the revolution in communications between and within each country: Facebook, dozens of TV channels, and hundreds of websites are neutral media by which opposition to normalization is strengthened as well as encouraged.

It remains to be seen how these new contacts and the prospect of economic growth at least in India will affect other differences between the two countries, especially the respective and somewhat incompatible identities that they have embraced. Many have recognized this as a factor that makes this case different—but few have offered useful ways to resolve these differences. Perhaps the most insightful commentary comes from a little-known Mumbai think tank, the Strategic Foresight Group (SFG), which asks that the Pakistani people stop thinking of their country as the "un-India" but simply as a progressive and normal state—the argument that Pakistani liberals have been putting forward, and losing, for decades. But the SFG also challenges India to accept a mind-change that reinterprets India's dominant role as a partnering one, such that it will treat Pakistan and other neighbors as partners in progress.[31] This, again, is what many Indian and Pakistani liberals have called for. However, it remains to be seen whether normalization with Pakistan will become a major component of the Congress Party's platform, let alone a policy supported across the political spectrum—and what little of this will be acceptable to Pakistan's guardians: the army and its hard-core elements.

Looking ahead two, five, or ten years, let alone to 2047—my best prediction is that a hurting stalemate will likely continue, albeit one with less tension, as the trade and visa agreements of 2012 indicate. There will be cautious movements toward dialogue, punctuated by attempts on both sides to press unilaterally their advantage in Kashmir and in international forums. This is a conflict that Pakistan cannot win and India cannot lose. Reinforcing this conclusion is the strong possibility that stalemate may be more attractive to each side than some of the solutions that have been put forward. From the perspective of Pakistan's army, tying down Indian forces in Kashmir remains an important side benefit of the dispute; cynically, it could be said that Pakistan is willing to fight India to the last Kashmiri. As long as Pakistan sees itself as militarily disadvantaged, it will try to equalize the military balance by any means possible. This includes the nuclear program, but also a strategy aimed at forcing India to divert important resources to a military front (Kashmir) where the terrain and political situation are in Pakistan's favor. For India, Kashmir has so many links to India's secular political order—especially the place of Muslims—that any settlement appearing to compromise this order is unacceptable. Kashmir is thus linked to broader issues of the military balance and the identity of the two states. While more could be done to ease the suffering of the Kashmiri people—a cease-fire, some drawdown of regular and paramilitary forces on the Indian side, and some reduction in support for extremists coming from the Pakistan side—no lasting settlement is possible without attending to these larger strategic and ideological concerns. A hurting stalemate can settle in even if there is an increase in trade. The latter may grow, as might an increase in the flow of people between the two countries, without significant movement on any of the core disputes I have discussed.

However, there are futures worse than a continuing stalemate. Until a few years ago, the prospect of a failed Pakistan did not disturb India to any degree. The rise of Islamic extremism, Pakistan's acquisition of nuclear weapons, and its faltering economy mean that a failed Pakistan is an increasingly likely prospect. This kind of Pakistan could spew out millions of refugees, might accelerate the spread of nuclear weapons to hostile states and terrorist groups, and could serve as a base for radical Islamic movements that recruit Indian Muslims and target India. Strategically, a failed Pakistan might draw outside powers into the subcontinent. Conversely, a more normal India-Pakistan relationship could help India assume a place among the major Asian and even global powers. It would not be a question, as it is now, of Indian power *minus* Pakistani power, but of an India free to exercise its influence over a much wider range, without the distraction—and the cost—of a conflict with a still-powerful Pakistan.

Indians need to more fully debate their relationship with Pakistan. The problem is that events may outrun India's capability to understand them. In recent years, for example, Pakistan has experienced a summit, a war, and a coup in rapid succession. Nonetheless, New Delhi may still seek agreement with Pakistan on Kashmir and other disputes. The most important question to ask in these negotiations will not be whether Indians or Pakistanis can be trusted to fulfill obligations incurred in agreements where they had little incentive to comply, but whether, under the influence of a pessimistic vision of the region's destiny, they can be trusted in cases where it *is* in their self-interest to comply.

The rest of the world should be worried. The root causes of regional antagonisms remain intact. Both sides believe themselves to be the victims of an unjust international community and a clever and sometimes malevolent rival. Both also feel strategically threatened by a coalition of hostile powers: for India, this is the China-Pakistan axis; for Pakistan, the apparent India-U.S. axis, in which Pakistani Islamists would include Israel as a third member. As a result, strategic competition must be added to the list of factors—economics, timing, domestic politics, and nuclear weapons—that together will control the pace and direction of normalization.

Indian economic growth, recognized and admired by Pakistan, has not changed the fundamental paired minority conflict, although Pakistan's weak economy has brought its people to a point where they want to benefit from this growth. As one former Pakistani ambassador to the United States put it, "Pakistan is negotiating with India after a clear discussion in Islamabad of priorities: with a new threat from and on the West, we need to normalize relations within South Asia." Some would argue that increased trade and people-to-people exchanges will change attitudes over the next few years—but this bottom-up approach to peace and national accommodation is still a theory that has to navigate two separate reality tests. One is the actual conclusion of an agreement to expand and liberalize trade; the second is proof over the next few years that the agreement is politically workable. Only then will the hoped-for results of expanding ties become visible.

An optimistic case for the future was made by a leading Pakistani émigré, economist Shahid Javed Burki, who foresees relations evolving in a "Three-Step Tango." Pakistan, he points out, agreed with India that it would be more practical for the two to focus on economic and trade issues and place the more contentious issues such as Kashmir on a back burner, and the two arrived at additional agreements in mid-2012. These include the resumption of cricket matches, a hoped-for visit to Pakistan by Indian prime minister Manmohan Singh, and an Indian decision to allow individual Pakistanis and Pakistan firms to invest in India.[32] This optimism is routinely balanced by Indian statements, usually from the Ministry of External Affairs, that a visit by Manmohan Singh is unlikely to take place because Pakistan has not responded to Indian concerns about terrorism, or more dramatically, that the "scar" of the Mumbai attack has not yet healed.[33]

A future worse than stalemate could be rivalry in other areas, especially in Afghanistan (see chapter 7). Although there is a natural market in the exchange of goods between India and Pakistan, and it is possible that they will reach an agreement on trade, there is no natural market in strategic pressure points. Both inherited the same choke points and proceeded to fight each other over them.[34] The wish of senior British Indian army strategists that somehow a moderate Pakistan would defend the entire subcontinent from radical Islamist movements, as well as from Soviet probes, is unfulfilled. Instead, India has become certain that Pakistan is part of an American-Chinese-Pakistani encirclement project, while Pakistani strategists now see India boosted by new and powerful allies of its own. Both sides view the various approaches to South Asia, notably Afghanistan, in terms of strategic "choke points." There was a single strategic pressure point before partition; today there are many such points of rivalry, intensified by the use of intelligence services, bribes, information programs, and other means.[35]

Pressure points cannot be traded off, as was the practice in classical nineteenth-century diplomacy. Public opinion makes that difficult in more or less open societies, especially when that opinion has been manipulated into a hawkish stance by each government. The importance of strategic pressure points is hard to measure with the same precision as trade agreements; for example, India can measure its benefits and losses with Pakistan (and vice versa) on an exchange of territory, or on their respective positions in Afghanistan or other countries, because hawks will define all strategic pressure points as "strategically vital," without any serious discussion of what vital means. It is possible to measure the gains and losses in trade between them, as it is measured with other countries, including China, but security issues are defined by each state in accordance with received myths and sometimes simplistic understanding of what is threatening and what is not.

The most urgent new development in this regard is an expanded rivalry in Afghanistan, which could make impossible an economic and trade agreement. The conflict between the two states in Afghanistan replicates their struggle over Kashmir. Their presence in Afghanistan is like the cold war proxy wars in which intelligence services battled it out without fear of direct escalation.

This classic Raj pressure point remains important to each, but not for the same reasons that motivated the British. The danger is no longer a German or Soviet invasion of South Asia, but the rise of extremist, militant Islam, which threatens both countries (whereas the expansion of Chinese power is feared by India but welcomed by Pakistan). Both see Afghanistan as a zero-sum zone of strategic competition, with Pakistan supporting the Taliban and a few Afghan leaders as its surrogates, while India, tongue-in-cheek, claims to have merely provided economic assistance to the Afghan regime. This conveniently ignores its long and important support for the Northern Alliance against the Pakistan-supported Taliban from 1992 to 2001. Once American forces in Afghanistan are greatly reduced, it seems doubtful that enough troops will remain to allow the Karzai regime (or its successor) to maintain control over most of the country. The default option for both India and Pakistan seems to be to renew their competition in Afghanistan, possibly fueling a new civil war in that state. One could argue that this is better than another confrontation along the Line of Control, but there should be better options, as discussed in chapter 7.

A third future worse than stalemate could transpire if one or both states took the irresponsible step of expanding their nuclear weapons programs, or if they viewed the weapons of the other side as inherently dangerous. Few Pakistanis or Indians can imagine the devastation one or two nuclear weapons, let alone a larger strike, could unleash on key cities—the reality is that each country is capable of turning the other into a vast graveyard, unlivable for decades.

Both states have had a difficult time dealing with the dilemma all nuclear weapons states face: that of balancing the competing requirements of secrecy and transparency. They have to be transparent enough to reassure the other side—and the world—that their nuclear operational procedures and doctrines are not provocative and irresponsible, lest they encourage the other side to strike first. Yet they cannot be too open, lest they provide information that would be useful to the other side (or conceivably a third party) in formulating a strike against their own forces. Recent studies show how far they have to go in developing this balance.[36]

Without greater transparency, and perhaps additional agreements that would reassure each country, myth and bad intelligence are likely to play a role. For example, some Indians assume that Pakistanis will be deterred from striking India with nuclear weapons because its two largest cities, New Delhi and Mumbai, contain huge numbers of Muslims, and the Pakistani leadership has ties to both. Would this still be a consideration if Pakistan was coming apart as a country—or would some Pakistani extremists, Hitler-like, believe a final cataclysm is justifiable? The irony of India's position is that while many of its military officials and strategists belabor Pakistan for its support of extremists and its irrational behavior, they think that Pakistan will act rationally in moments of crisis. Perhaps they are projecting their own supposed rational crisis behavior on Pakistan, or perhaps they are misinformed. In any case, the history of regional crises does not inspire confidence, as both sides have made serious mistakes. No one knows how leaders in India and Pakistan judge which of their cities will be spared and which will be targeted, which will be defended by an antiballistic missile shield, now in the development stage, and which might be sacrificed. If relations between the two states are normal, as they are between America and Russia, these concerns will be irrelevant, but the India-Pakistan pair could slip into one or more crises in the future. The further testing of nuclear weapons by one or both, or their use in a very limited war, would be historically significant events, but anything larger than a demonstration-effect strike is unimaginable.

One of the paradoxes of this relationship is that the fear of such a war ensures the continuation of the rivalry; it rules out a conventional war that could establish Indian strategic dominance. In this, the Pakistani nuclear hawks are correct—that is, if rationality prevails on both sides. Any new Indian policy toward Pakistan has to run the gauntlet of the political parties, both national and regional, as well as the foreign and security policy bureaucracies, which are expert at stifling change and are notable for their lack of original thinking. As Indian strategist Bharat Karnad points out, India's very size and complexity reduce its ability to run this gauntlet nimbly. Furthermore, Karnad wryly comments, the Indian attitude to the state's physical security, which arises out of a habit of mind defined by geography and subcontinental size, is "lax to the point of exasperation."[37] As is well documented, the Indian bureaucracy is slow and cumbersome even in the face of threats such as another Mumbai attack or in other security matters, plus has a weak planning process (except in economics).[38] This applies manifold to all policy matters regarding Pakistan. As discussed in chapter 3, Indians are, for the most part, skeptical if not opposed to normalization with Pakistan, and dead set against any role for outsiders. India's Ministry of External Affairs is not unlike Pakistan's Inter-Services Intelligence Directorate in this regard: both are capable, influential, and hard-line when it comes to regional normalization. India's civilian bureaucrats certainly exert greater influence than their American counterparts—being more like British or French civil servants. Moreover, its intelligence agencies have considerable clout because they are not fully accountable to the public or parliament. They mix domestic and foreign intelligence, which is perhaps inevitable in dealing with Pakistan, but this can work at cross-purposes with diplomacy. In addition, there is a notable absence of strategic planning in India, with rivalries between the prime minister's secretariat and the Ministry of External Affairs, whose policy planning division has long since atrophied.

By contrast, India's armed forces are confined to their narrow operational and organizational spheres. Their policy suggestions are based largely on their own organizational requirements, not an overall national strategy. The glaring exception is the army's public announcement that it would oppose any settlement of the Siachen Glacier dispute that might reverse what it regards as a hard-won victory over Pakistan. The military finds it difficult to make long-range plans because of the turnover of political leadership, the latter's lack of expertise, and disarray over defense budgets and weapons acquisition strategies.

The prospects for normalization will also be affected by several forthcoming events, one being the International Court of Arbitration's ruling sometime in 2013 on the alleged Indian infringements of the Indus Waters Treaty. This will be an opportunity for both India and Pakistan to demonstrate that they are willing to accept international arbitration, although the history of arbitration over the Rann of Kutch is not encouraging (it hurt Ayub Khan politically, and it made the Indians wary of outside arbiters). The Soviet attempt to broker a larger agreement between Ayub Khan and Prime Minister Lal Bahadur Shastri following the 1965 war fared no better. An outside decision on the Indian headworks, suitably verifiable by Pakistan, could pave the way for larger talks about sharing the river waters. Here, India's recent experience with Bangladesh has been encouraging, and some Pakistani diplomats have told me that this might be a precedent for India-Pakistan talks on water issues.

The recent normalization breakthrough in the form of trade liberalization negotiations will follow its own diplomatic and economic logic, undoubtedly with much tough bargaining. Still, there is no reason why some milestones should not be reached in 2013 and 2014. The example of other regions should be powerful and relevant here, and outside powers might offer inducements to ensure that the process of trade liberalization is rewarded.

Another significant event in 2014 will be the reduction in America's military presence in South Asia. India will also hold national elections that year, while Pakistan will be doing so in 2013, if the political system remains stable. Election results in India are likely to show political power shifting further to the states, only a few of which are really interested in normalization with Pakistan. Even New Delhi has only a tiny elite following foreign policy closely. Pakistan is likely to see the People's Pakistan Party win another victory, but there are regional movements against the Punjab's domination, and a "Punjabi Spring" is under way that puts the politics of that key province in play.

Over the next five or six years a new factor might shape India-Pakistan relations that was unthinkable five or fifteen years ago. This is Pakistan's very integrity as a state. In a recent study of the country's future, I was unable to peer beyond the next seven years.[39] This raises time-bound questions about the present normalization process. Can it succeed in taming the hostilities on both sides of the border, and even if it does, will Pakistan hold together long enough to keep any side of an agreement that it might reach with New Delhi? Will the priorities of other countries also be affected? While the India-China rivalry is looming, it is going to be antedated by further crises in India-Pakistan relations if the latter should deteriorate further, or if it fails to move toward normalcy. The next five years will be critical: India will not want to make concessions to a Pakistan that is clearly failing and cannot be transformed into a normal partner—some in New Delhi might even want to give it an extra push and hasten the process.

Judgments are being made in both countries as to whether time is on their side. If Pakistan concludes that pressure on India has not worked, it could decide to escalate and accept higher risks or consider alternative solutions for Kashmir. If India decides that its practice of absorbing punishment has become intolerable, then it also might decide that a riskier strategy should be employed sooner rather than later. Even more dangerous, both sides may simultaneously conclude that time is working against them and that they might gain from a confrontation if it took place sooner rather than later. Even if both sides try to avoid a major conflict, one could come surprisingly soon, as in early 2013 when the alleged beheading of an Indian officer by Pakistani forces along the Line of Control temporarily strained relations. However, the event showed that India-Pakistan relations are likely to stay within a band—not escalating to all-out or nuclear war, but not moving toward normalization or peace either. The armed forces of both states are unhappy with some aspects of normalization, which is one reason why the incident received so much publicity, and their close proximity along the Line of Control in Kashmir and along the international border provides opportunities for mischief, miscalculation, and subordination of the slow and not inevitable move toward normal relations.

What Can Be Done?

When I broach the idea of normalcy to Indians and Pakistanis, as well as Americans, I receive three kinds of responses. Many Americans and some Pakistanis and Indians believe that nothing can be done, that this is an eternal strategic rivalry, what I have called an intractable paired minority conflict. The policy prescription that flows from this judgment is to avoid involvement and hope that time will alleviate some problems.

For Indians, this means waiting Pakistan out, avoiding a major conflict, and hoping that the political process in Islamabad will eventually produce a leadership that is willing to address Pakistan's identity crisis and consider a compromise over Kashmir and other issues. Pakistan's identity as an Islamic state still threatens Indian pluralism, and when it is given muscle by Pakistan's intelligence agencies, it becomes a domestic political problem for India, leaving aside the ambivalence of some Indian Muslims.

For Pakistanis, the notion of a perpetual conflict means finding a way to live with a more powerful and still-threatening neighbor, strengthening the one technology that assures Pakistan that India will not seek a military victory—nuclear weapons—while searching for a way to overhaul the economy. From an orthodox Pakistani position, normalization will come if and when India backs off on the key symbolic and strategic issues that have been there for sixty-five years, notably Kashmir. Meanwhile, the Pakistani state will continue to endorse and support elements of the Pakistan identity that make it distinctive, including hatred and fear of India, with a few hawks still arguing that India, not Pakistan, is an artificial state and that Pakistan need only wait until India comes apart.

If the future is to be "more of the same," then meetings between Indians and Pakistanis will come to the conclusion that nothing can be done, because individually neither side is willing to do anything, and that both sides prefer, as they have for sixty-five years, to wait and watch. Foundations should insist that any Track II dialogues that they fund actually go beyond current government policies and publicly offer new ideas—otherwise they are a waste of time and money.

The second response that I have received—largely from some Americans and Indians—is that Pakistan is a fatally wounded state trying to meet the challenges of the modern era. Normalization will have to be postponed indefinitely. The present era is massively different from the years in which Pakistan was first imagined and then enjoyed substantial international support. It is undergoing complex and unpredictable transformations brought about by global revolutions in the movement of people, goods, and ideas. When faced with these developments, Pakistan, with its 1930s-style identity and emphasis on religion as the tie that holds Pakistanis together, becomes a dysfunctional state. Some Pakistanis understood the significance of the loss of East Pakistan, but the army and the Islamists dismissed it as the result of India's machinations and Pakistan's failure in attempting to impose true Islam on its population. This has opened the door to more totalitarian strands of Islamic thinking. Pakistan's political domination by the India-obsessed military, with its clumsiness at governing a complex state, seals its fate. It may last five years or more, but the end point is evident. Some Pakistanis have already reached this conclusion, as have more and more Indians; the former are looking for careers and homes outside of the country in increasing numbers, while the latter watch with trepidation. A few Indians believe that they only need to wait until Pakistan collapses and then can pick up the pieces.

In the event, India would become the dominant power of Southern Asia. However, many Indians understand that a collapsing Pakistan could also prove fatal to their country. In this view, India-Pakistan relations have reached a hurting stalemate that strongly resembles the cold war, during which both sides endured decades of crisis and a terrific arms burden until the Soviet Union crumbled. Any Indians who think that the rest of the world would manage a "soft" landing for a decaying Pakistan are, I believe, sorely mistaken and gambling on the future of India as well as Pakistan. Still, there remains the naïve hope that Pakistan will somehow vanish, or be peacefully reunited with India in ten or twenty years, the view of a former Supreme Court judge, Markanday Katju, the chair of the Press Council of India. Terming Pakistan a "Jurassic park" or a madhouse, he blamed Jinnah for creating a theocratic state and suggested that Jinnah was an agent of the British, who are to blame for India's Hindu-Muslim conflicts.[40] Name-calling may be gratifying, but it does not wave away the fact that Pakistan remains a potent and potentially dangerous state as far as India is concerned.

Many have argued that South Asia needs to find measures that would avert apocalyptic scenarios, permit a negotiated settlement to the Kashmir conflict, and provide a joint approach to the problem of stabilizing regional nuclear forces and preventing an all-out arms race. Unofficial diplomacy would be an essential component but cannot be a substitute for a state's determination to address these issues.

The third response I have heard is that the South Asian cold war does not have to drag on forever, and that a failed Pakistan is not politically acceptable—both outcomes are risky to India and to the international community. This view would support some form of normalization and thus call for a more activist policy, either out of optimism or a concern that the first two options are too risky. India could attempt to solve its Pakistan problem by helping Pakistan emerge from its miasma and by joining it in a normal relationship that would include cooperation in the region's strategic defense. Pakistan itself, now in the midst of a major political upheaval, could continue its domestic reforms once the India threat is stabilized or removed. The latter would reduce the influence of the army in Pakistan as well.

Could Pakistan be a long-term partner for India? Very few Indians believe that Pakistan is stable, that its recent crises are superficial, and that the underlying strengths of the country will allow it to muddle through. It may be able to hobble along for the next few years—but anything after that is a mystery. *Hoping* that Pakistan becomes a more normal state is not a policy. For Pakistanis, accepting Indian hegemony—backed up by superior force—is a strategic defeat. But what does the use of force mean in an era of nuclear weapons? Can it mean cultural hegemony, or the subtle transformation or dominance of one's culture by another society? These are universal questions being asked and answered in different ways by Indians and Pakistanis, albeit rarely in dialogue with each other.

It is essential to recognize that India-Pakistan hostility is *not* best viewed as a subject-by-subject problem relating to Kashmir, terrorism, religious conflict, the absence of democracy, or sometimes to too much democracy and not enough statecraft. Instead, the problem has to be redefined, not in terms of subjects such as Kashmir, or water, or terrorism. These are all important, but the conundrum of hostility contains three basic elements: (1) territorial, economic, and environmental issues; (2) the rivalry between two states (and now China) claiming the same strategic space; and (3) the different chosen identities that pit the rivals against each other in many fundamental ways.

In my view, a top-down approach is necessary, but it may not be sufficient; the same is true of bottom-up approaches. Efforts to improve trade and people-to-people contacts may yet be part of the solution to one of history's biggest experiments in state normalization, but they will not be decisive.

Indecision and ambiguity are likely to characterize the future. Relations between these two states are likely to oscillate within a band: it is unlikely to go to the nuclear level, nor is steady normalization in sight. A crisis in early 2012 was prototypical: after allegations that Pakistan beheaded an Indian officer, war drums began beating in India. These soon grew silent after more became known of the history of atrocities committed over the years by both sides along the Line of Control, and as the futility of escalating against a nuclear Pakistan became clearer. Indeed, the more Indians demonized Pakistan the more effective was the latter's deterrent force; by emphasizing Pakistan's reckless and dangerous side, Indian hawks also made its deterrent more credible.

For many decades India and Pakistan have been moving in the wrong direction—digging the hole deeper, talking more about insecurity than about opportunity. The slightly paranoid worldview of the strategist ensures that new threats will supplant old ones, and that institutions will devote their energies to discovering and planning to meet such new threats. Indeed, the armies and many civilian institutions on both sides are threat-generating machines. For Pakistan, mere survival will be a problem for at least several years, perhaps indefinitely. For India, its recent economic achievements are significant, and its democratic system—for all of its flaws—is able to contain new and disruptive forces, while the dream of an Indo-centric security system in South Asia is still beyond reach. For India, the danger is that Pakistan, while economically enfeebled and confused about its identity, remains capable of mortally hurting India through its growing nuclear capability and by rubbing salt in Kashmir's wounds. Normalization is as much in India's interests as in Pakistan's. New Delhi will have difficulty "rising," "emerging," or becoming one of the major powers of Asia if it has to haul a wounded Pakistan around; self-interest if not moral principles should impel it to help Pakistan, even if many of the latter's wounds have been self-inflicted.

In 2010 a young female student in Kolkata asked me, "Why should I help Pakistan—it is a country that has done terrible things to me—I hate it, I am not going to help it." My answer was this: "If your neighbor's house is on fire, isn't it in your interest to help put out the fire, rather than let it go up in flames?" I am skeptical that the Indian leadership is prepared to lead a neighborhood fire brigade and even that its neighbor's fire can be easily doused. More likely, it will try to create a firebreak and hope for the best.

CHAPTER SEVEN

American Interests and Policies

Many Americans believe that the India-Pakistan dispute is both inevitable and unsolvable, that it reflects the immaturity, deep cultural differences, or racial or geopolitical qualities of these two states. On the contrary, this is not a hopeless dispute, although engagement requires more than a simplistic understanding of its causes. Moreover, the United States can do little directly to address the core identity and strategic disputes between the two states, but it can do much indirectly.

The prime virtue of recent U.S. policy—summarized as "dehyphenation"—was that it abandoned symmetry; however, it could not cope directly with India-Pakistan quarrels. The United States cannot do much about identity issues (an appropriate subject for universities and foundations to address), but in other respects, such as promoting trade and regional economic cooperation, its input could have positive outcomes for both sides, as explained in this closing chapter. There may also be room for cooperation on strategic issues—not the ultrasensitive Kashmir—but perhaps in Afghanistan.

Recent U.S. Policies toward India and Pakistan

The United States took twenty years to shed its cold war orientation toward South Asia but is still without a comprehensive policy framework here. The process of change started at the beginning of the first Reagan administration—but this was interrupted by events that placed nonproliferation at the center of U.S. relations with India and Pakistan.

Just before Ronald Reagan came into office in 1980—by which time the Soviet Union was a military presence in Afghanistan and Pakistan was a front-line state—some memos had circulated in the Department of State calling for a truly regional policy. With the Soviet invasion, however, these were put aside and a new regional policy developed. From New Delhi, U.S. ambassador Harry Barnes advocated a policy of rapprochement with India wherever possible to supplement the emerging military alliance with Pakistan.[1] Barnes's "game plan" had a remarkably contemporary ring, said Howard E. Schaffer, who was his counterpoint as deputy assistant secretary of state for South Asia. Dennis Kux, the eminent chronicler of U.S. relations with both India and Pakistan, noted that Barnes aimed "to look for things that India and the United States could do together, could cooperate on, as a way to build a bilateral relationship that could eventually stand on its own feet."[2] Quoting Barnes, Kux wrote that "basically the thrust was to look at the whole range of the relationship and try to find those aspects that might be susceptible of some development in order to try to put the relationship . . . in a broader, fuller context without so much focus on our relationship with Pakistan." Others also proposed normalizing with India even as the United States was entering into a new military alliance with Pakistan. One such figure was Shirin Tahir-Kheli, a member of the State Department's policy planning staff, while in the White House Donald Fortier vigorously pursued the policy.

In a 1997 study on South Asia for the Council on Foreign Relations, Tahir-Kheli summed up the lesson from that period: "Washington's efforts to settle the differences must be part of an overall package of policy options towards India and Pakistan taking U.S. involvement into the next century. The basic premise for U.S. engagement must be the desire to help solve the crises that stand in the way of a permanent and productive peace between India and Pakistan."[3] Tahir-Kheli's analysis took a refreshingly long-term perspective on the South Asian conundrum, and enough has happened in the interim to make her advice still pertinent.

The new policy had something for everyone, except those still suspicious of India. The policy could be justified in a cold war framework, making it acceptable to Reaganite hawks. Since Pakistan was still vulnerable to pressure from India, one of its purposes was to protect Islamabad's eastern border. This was the obverse of the 1962 Kennedy policy, when the goal was to protect India's west from Pakistan. Other aspects envisioned a democratic and increasingly powerful India, which some day might "emerge" as a major state in Asia, if it could normalize its relations with Pakistan and revamp its dysfunctional economic policies.[4] A third goal was to "wean" the Indians away from the Soviet Union; although Soviet penetration of India was exaggerated, those who favored normalization at the time went along with such cold war arguments.[5] As a result, by 1984 a steady stream of officials was visiting Pakistan in support of the anti-Soviet effort. Many such visits incorporated a stop in India to discuss a growing list of issues, while "all American conversations at the senior level actively encouraged good relations between India and Pakistan."[6] South Asian leaders from both countries had unusual access to Washington's top leadership. In one arena, however, Americans may have misread the region: contrary to expectations, the military aid program to Pakistan did little to encourage reconciliation between Pakistan and India. Most Indians did not see the weapons America supplied to Pakistan in a positive light, whereas Zia ul-Haq personally agreed with the new American opening to New Delhi.

In the Reagan years, Indian motives were clear. Except for the pro-Soviet factions in the Congress Party and government, Indians realized that they had to reduce dependency on the Soviet Union, the first superpower to have actually invaded South Asia, and they welcomed this new attention, whatever the reason for it. Furthermore, this relationship improved Indian leverage over the U.S. aid program to Pakistan. Although Pakistani officials were skilled in raising the India bogey, this tactic did not lead the United States away from India; instead, it made the U.S. government engage more deeply with New Delhi.

As already mentioned, nuclear proliferation dominated American policy in the aftermath of cold war containment. Between 1989, when President George H. W. Bush sanctioned Pakistan for its covert nuclear military programs, and 1998, when India and Pakistan detonated nuclear weapons, the United States made a large-scale but belated attempt to get the two rivals to terminate their nuclear activities. In response, Pakistan professed agreement with every American proposal but in a classical *pahelee aap* (Urdu-Hindi for "you go first") approach claimed that India had to go first, knowing full well that India would refuse any outside prying into its (covert) nuclear plans. When the Clinton administration pushed for a policy that would "cap, roll back, and eliminate" nuclear weapons, this effort backfired, and instead it convinced both South Asian states that they did need nuclear weapons. Heavy and naïve American pressure led India to test first, followed immediately by Pakistan, both events being unpredicted by American experts.

In this period American engagement with both countries featured a wide range of official and unofficial dialogues, with and between Indian and Pakistani interlocutors, some of them described in chapter 5. Seminars and courses were held in India and Pakistan decrying the dangers of "going nuclear" and reiterating the importance of confidence-building measures (CBMs). American lectures to the effect of "do as I say, not as I do" did not go down well in either state, and Americans who pushed for the abolition of regional nuclear programs were dubbed "nuclear Ayatollahs" by leading

Indian strategists. Partly to deflect American pressure, the two countries agreed on modest CBMs such as hotlines, and they still engage in the ritual of an annual and unverified declaration of civilian nuclear sites.

The attempt to keep nuclear weapons out of South Asia had failed. When the two states tested in 1998, both removed the veil of ambiguity by declaring themselves full-fledged nuclear weapons states. In great frustration, Americans imposed sanctions on both states, which made some Americans feel good but had no impact on their nuclear policies or on two emerging nuclear candidates, Iran and North Korea.

Three years later, with a new administration and the trauma of 9/11 still widely felt, the United States became—with good reason—concerned about the confluence of nuclear weapons and the rise of Islamist terror groups, especially in unstable Pakistan. Two successive administrations, beginning with that of George W. Bush, have put these concerns at the top of their policy agendas. Although each tried to defuse various crises, all of which had a nuclear tinge, much of this engagement occurred after the fact.[7]

The Bush administration lifted most of the sanctions against Pakistan and began building on the good relations with India established under Bill Clinton.[8] The resulting strategy, formally known as dehyphenation, treated India and Pakistan separately, each for its own virtues and assets.[9] This was a very Aristotelian approach, echoing the view that justice meant "to each according to his own qualities," but it did not address the reality that India and Pakistan were still each other's main threat. Under dehyphenation, the United States would handle relations with India and Pakistan separately, with no undue effort to address their bilateral disputes, except to encourage them to continue their dialogue and stand ready to facilitate any agreements. Kashmir remained out of bounds for American policy, even though Clinton had called it the most dangerous place on earth.[10] The crux of such a policy is how far the U.S.-India relationship can go without damaging Washington's ties to Pakistan.

Over the next few years, the Bush and then the Obama administrations learned that for Pakistan the U.S.-India nuclear deal, without a corresponding acceptance of Pakistan's nuclear status, was evidence that the United States was not a reliable ally. India greeted dehyphenation warmly, because it meant the end of comparisons with Pakistan and the inference that it was now paired with China, like itself, a major rising power.

Dehyphenation enabled America to work with India without having to burden its diplomats and soldiers with the Pakistan tie, and it facilitated seemingly close cooperation with Pakistan on terror-related issues.[11] As I have noted, this also gave India a voice in America's Pakistan policy, something it never had before. This approach bore striking similarities to the early Reagan attempt to have good relations with both states, making Pakistan again a "front-line" state (now in the war against terror, not the Soviet Union).

The closer relationship with India under the rubric of dehyphenation was based on an understanding that China was a new Asian strategic factor. Washington treated India as one possible piece in the larger puzzle of containing what *might* be a hostile threat. The irony of the policy was that Pakistan had exactly the opposite view of China—seeing it as a trusted friend and a more genuine ally than the United States. In reality, it is not an either/or choice for the United States: "In the short term it is India-Pakistan, in the long-term it is India-China."[12]

As a presidential candidate, Barack Obama was the first leading American politician to advocate American engagement in the India-Pakistan dispute. In a 2007 *Foreign Affairs* article, he proposed a crackdown on Pakistani toleration of terrorists but also said he would encourage dialogue between Pakistan and India to resolve the Kashmir dispute.[13] In an interview with *Time* magazine, he acknowledged that "Kashmir in particular is an interesting situation . . . that is obviously a potential tar pit diplomatically." Obama wanted to

> get a special envoy in there, to figure out a plausible approach, and essentially make the argument to the Indians, you guys are on the brink of being an economic superpower, why do you want to keep on messing with this? To make the argument to the Pakistanis, look at India and what they are doing, why do you want to keep on being bogged down with this particularly at a time where the biggest threat now is coming from the Afghan border? I think there is a moment where potentially we could get their attention. It won't be easy, but it's important.[14]

To implement these policies, two days after taking office Obama announced the appointment of former Clinton administration diplomat Richard Holbrooke to be special representative to Afghanistan and Pakistan (SRAP). Nine months before his appointment, Holbrooke had urged upon Pakistan more democracy, domestic political reconciliation, the removal of the military from politics, and a new policy for the tribal area.[15] This ignored known Pakistani strategic concerns and was based upon unrealistic assumptions about Pakistan.

Holbrooke knew Afghanistan well, Pakistan a little, and India-Pakistan relations not at all. His job had to be defined narrowly because of Indian pressure. At one point Indian officials were so irritated with his mandate that they made it inconvenient for Holbrooke to visit New Delhi. Although India had interests in Afghanistan and had been a major player there for decades, the American system had no way of accommodating or even understanding them.[16]

One full Obama term passed without any significant American initiative—in effect this was the continuation of the dehyphenation policy. Relations with Pakistan were badly strained because of the spillover from the Afghan war while relations with India boomed.

Former Foreign Service officer Howard Schaffer accurately saw that "for the balance of its current term the Obama administration will not change its approach to the Kashmir issue. . . . Should another serious Kashmir-related India-Pakistan crisis develop, Obama will no doubt resume the crisis-management efforts which have been so central to America's role in Kashmir in the quarter-century dating back to the George H. W. Bush administration."[17]

Candidate Obama seemed to be looking for deeper causes, but President Obama quickly learned how difficult it was to be a go-between for the two countries when Washington's own relationship with at least one of them—this time Pakistan—was strained. If Obama thought the many conflicts between India and Pakistan were symptomatic of an underlying pathology, he was correct. But in terms of policy prescriptions, his view was the conventional one, that Kashmir was the place where a breakthrough might be possible. It was not, and given the military and political problems facing the administration in Afghanistan, Kashmir remained a sideshow. The Obama administration failed to develop a South Asia policy that would have encompassed both India-Pakistan relations (including Kashmir) and the grinding war in Afghanistan.

Toward a Comprehensive South Asia Policy

In mid-2012 President Obama approved a classified national decision directive for India, but there was no such directive for South Asia, or for Pakistan. The foreign policy process could not manage more: too many Pakistan policies were (and still are) circulating in the government with no coherent view of South Asia in the background. If such a South Asia policy were to emerge in his current administration, it would have to (a) address the organizational dysfunctionality that handicaps American policy toward this quarter of the world, (b) *not* place Kashmir at the center of America's regional policy, (c) expand existing collaborative and integrative programs, (d) explore the possibility of India-Pakistan strategic cooperation in Afghanistan, and (e) retain some elements of dehyphenation. Above all, American policy should be based on an understanding of the deeper antagonisms that have driven the India-Pakistan conundrum for sixty-five years. While doing everything possible to promote regional rapprochement, American policymakers must remain aware that the present state of cold peace between India and Pakistan can quickly break down, with outcomes worse than having the dispute continue for many years more.

Organizational Pathologies

Administrative restructuring is not a substitute for strategic thinking but may become necessary when such thinking is inhibited by the lack of a comprehensive policy framework, as in the case of South Asia.[18] That is why the second Obama administration should reorganize how it deals with South Asia. The U.S. government has for decades failed to see the region as a whole, with its shared environment, shared cultural system, and its own strategic logic. Ignoring the region or parceling it out conceptually and organizationally might have been an adequate response during the cold war, but its new importance demands a rethinking of both strategy and the way the U.S. government is organized to deal with Afghanistan, Pakistan, and India. This region, including the Indian Ocean, is too important now to be left to segmented and uncoordinated policymaking.[19]

To correct this, and to take advantage of new opportunities in South Asia, the United States must revise the civilian and military framework with which it approaches the region. It took forty-five years to create a freestanding South Asia bureau—and even then only at congressional prompting.[20] The bureau's focus was diluted by the addition of Central Asia to its portfolio, and debilitated by the creation of SRAP.

Equally troubling, major departments in the U.S. government differ markedly as to how they deal with India and Pakistan. These include the Departments of State and Defense, and the different military commands within Defense, each of which maintains its own foreign, intelligence, and military strategies. This makes it difficult, for example, to factor the impact of the India-Pakistan competition into America's Afghanistan policy. The disjoint is such that U.S. Central Command (CENTCOM) and the bulk of the Pentagon are increasingly wary of Pakistan's role in Afghanistan, while U.S. Pacific Command (PACOM) cheers on India's Afghan projects. Occasionally, the separate visions become temporarily fused, but U.S. policy remains rudderless and the region's history, including the still-relevant impact of the Raj, overlooked. Instead, the Department of State should have taken the initiative in crafting an Afghan policy that would have placed less emphasis on the North Atlantic Treaty Organization (NATO) and America as intervening forces and more on regional capabilities in training, development, and coercion.

The chief virtue of the about-to-be-abandoned SRAP office is that its staff came from different government agencies. When it is broken up and the Pakistan desk returns to the South Asia bureau, it should be physically adjacent to the India desk and retain the liaison with other agencies so that the interagency process can begin where strategic policy should first be developed. This also suggests strongly that the Department of State, as formulated at present, is ill equipped to think strategically about region-wide phenomena.

Reorganization along these lines would stimulate holistic thinking about the region. It would improve U.S. deployment capacity in the Indian Ocean and South Asia, one of the world's most important geopolitical theaters. Like good intelligence, good organization does not guarantee good policy. However, a poorly constructed bureaucracy is almost always a recipe for bad policy.

Kashmir Is/Is Not the Problem

In the past, Kashmir was shorthand for South Asia's strategic problems. Some well-informed experts have called for a fresh look at Kashmir. They are right, but it must not be at the center of American policy.[21]

Administration after administration has attempted to deal with Kashmir only to become discouraged, usually by Indian recalcitrance. As Daniel Markey, senior fellow at the Council on Foreign Relations, has noted, many American presidents thought that solving Kashmir was a sure road to a Nobel Peace Prize, but when they found out how difficult it was, they went back to politically more rewarding tasks such as reconciling Israeli and Arab demands.[22]

Putting any policy into action will require a clearer understanding of the several causes of India-Pakistan rivalry described in this book. It will also require a more nuanced use of American diplomatic, economic, and political assets. Of course, even if nothing is done and America remains aloof, an improved understanding of the regional tensions epitomized in the Kashmir dispute is of value.

As pointed out in chapter 5, no single theory explains the larger rivalry. America's many efforts to resolve the Kashmir question and several important private initiatives all failed because Kashmir is both a cause and an effect. It touches the identities, self-images, and geostrategic ambitions of both sides and remains a critical source of water and potentially energy.

Kashmir is really a host of identity, strategic, and economic issues. These include the Raj's legacy of geostrategic concerns, such as the disposition of the northern area, Siachen, and the ill-fitting Line of Control, but also difficult economic and environmental issues. There needs to be a fresh look at the Indus Basin agreement of 1960. Kashmir also encompasses the minority rights of Hindus, Buddhists, and Muslims, which no just solution can ignore. It has an international facet as well in that China controls part of the state. China reportedly tried to suppress a European assessment of the region mentioning the lack of freedom in those parts of Kashmir that were ceded to China by Pakistan.

In the short run the prescription for Kashmir is bypass surgery—go around it, approach it after other disputes are settled, but don't ignore it. New, indirect approaches may be called for, involving India, Pakistan, and perhaps international donors, one model being the International Fund for Ireland.[23]

As for water and energy, recent studies show significant changes in the Himalayan watershed because of environmental changes and man-made influences.[24] These should be treated as technical and scientific matters, as was the Indus water agreement, and America should offer its expertise in the expectation that the normalization process between India and Pakistan will make such initiatives politically acceptable. However, they should not be regarded as the "key" to unraveling the Kashmir knot. If feasible, reconstructing the water systems would be very important symbolically, though costly. The deeper problems of identity, minority rights, and the linkage of the two Kashmirs to India and to Pakistan are best left to the two states—and to the Kashmiri population—to grapple with. Foreign involvement in any but technical and scientific issues would be counterproductive.

Finally, the United States should begin to change past policy regarding Kashmir. While it should still treat the two Kashmirs as an unsettled issue—following the original UN resolution—it should indicate support for making the present Line of Control (LoC) the international boundary, subject to agreement by the two states and the Kashmiris themselves. The polls indicate that if the LoC were normalized, most Kashmiris would accept it, and I know of no serious official in either country who does *not* believe that the two states will wind up with such an agreement. It was part of Musharraf's plan, and it was an early proposal of the Indians. While history would suggest that partitioning can have bad consequences, in this case an agreed-upon partition, with the restoration of normal trade and movement between the two Kashmirs, would be a singular achievement. Of course, since it might involve water, rivers, and Siachen, such a proposal will necessarily involve dealing with these other issues, and might also involve China. Nevertheless, the United States should begin the process by raising the LoC as the likely final border between the two states. Such a U.S. initiative might lead to a fuller and more realistic dialogue within each country (and inside Kashmir) about the settlement of this dispute.

Promote Integrative/Ameliorative Programs

Instead of focusing on Kashmir as the key to regional peace, the United States can contribute to normalization by modifying its many existing programs within each country. These include antipiracy operations and training, agricultural research on crop and animal diseases, a shared interest in refugee and disaster relief operations, and medical research on a variety of diseases. These and other programs can serve various purposes.

First, through them the United States can actively support developments that promote South Asian regional cooperation, especially between India and Pakistan. Policies that currently make it more difficult for the two to partner should therefore be altered. For example, America could withdraw its opposition to pipelines that transit South Asia or could offer incentives to imports coming from two or more South Asian states. The latter might provide additional stimulus to India-Pakistan trade. When both states announced plans for "global centers" for nuclear safety following the Seoul nonproliferation summit, America began a dialogue with India to see what kind of technical assistance would be useful, but it could also approach Pakistan with a similar offer, so as to encourage the two to share information on nuclear safety, going beyond their current agreement on the location of extant civilian nuclear reactors.

America's many exchange and educational programs should also be rethought to expand the degree to which they support dialogue and collaborative research. The tone should not be hectoring or lecturing, as in the case of U.S.-encouraged nuclear dialogues, but more supportive, with the emphasis on university-based research focusing on common hydrology, agriculture, and environmental concerns. Indeed, the diseases that kill crops and animals in India and Pakistan pay no attention to the border between them.

To the extent feasible, the nonprofit and university programs operating in one or the other country should also encourage shared Indian-Pakistani (and American) research into issues that affect them both. In January 2012 Mark Kenoyer of the University of Wisconsin organized an unprecedented international workshop on Taxila, one of the oldest sites of Buddhist scholarship in the world, now located in Pakistan. The conference was held at Taxila itself, and Indian participants marveled at seeing a 2,000-year-old site that they had only read about.

Indian scholars, historically protectionist about allowing outsiders into their research domains—it is sometimes more difficult to obtain research visas to India than to China—are becoming interested in greater regional access themselves. They know that their knowledge of Pakistan is abysmal in large part because of governmental restraints.[25]

An appropriate model here is Sri Lanka's Regional Centre for Strategic Studies (RCSS), founded in 1993. It serves in effect as the strategic studies center of the South Asian Association for Regional Cooperation (SAARC). The RCSS hosts meetings and workshops for regional (and Chinese) scholars not only in Colombo but also in every South Asian state. It also offers fellowships for younger South Asians so that they can work together on a variety of political, economic, and social projects that affect their countries.

Strategic Cooperation in Afghanistan

Given that South Asia provides 40 percent of the world's peacekeeping forces, the United States would have been wise to invite regional powers to help stabilize Afghanistan. Instead, it called in Europeans and sent its own forces halfway around the world in a difficult if not futile effort at peacemaking and state-building.

While any Indian role in Afghanistan was vetoed by Pakistan, few have made the case for a cooperative venture, perhaps under UN auspices, that would have portioned out Afghanistan to regional powers after the Taliban was routed. The time for such a truly regional approach was after the Bonn conference of December 2011.[26] However, a new opportunity arises in 2014 when the United States is scheduled to withdraw most of its forces from Afghanistan.[27]

Throughout this book Afghanistan is referred to as one of the strategic legacies of the Raj's policy of India's security perimeter. America made three major policy errors in Afghanistan, all of which have had an impact on Pakistan and India. First, Washington expressed studied disinterest in the consequences for Pakistan of the latter's support for the war against the Soviet invaders in Afghanistan—consequences in the form of massive quantities of guns, drugs, and refugees flowing into Pakistan and beginning the social destabilization that continues today. Second, the United States failed to engage in Afghanistan when the Soviet forces withdrew, leaving the country open to warlord predations. Third, it did not place Afghanistan in a regional framework after the 2011 Bonn meeting, which is the only way in which India and Pakistan, and Iran and Russia, can agree to leave the Afghans to their own devices and not use that country as a base to pressure others. In Afghanistan cooperation between two pairs of states is essential: the United States and Iran, and India and Pakistan. While the Bush administration did work with Iran closely to expel the Taliban from Afghanistan, it disregarded Iran's potential role in Afghanistan, labeling it a member of the "axis of evil." It also lacked a vision that would have encouraged India and Pakistan to cooperate there, both of which had a vital interest in what were once the Raj's western marches.

Even today it is not too late to encourage such cooperation. The rationale has been laid out by Pakistani economist Sadika Hameed in a comprehensive exploration of the risks as well as the economic and political advantages of India-Pakistan teamwork in Afghanistan.[28] Acknowledging some skepticism about its prospects, Hamid nonetheless argues that the benefits would be significant for all the countries involved. Several Indian analysts are in favor of a similar joint arrangement, one suggestion being closer cooperation between the two armies.[29] Another cooperative effort might revolve around the transformational possibility of an expanded rail network in Afghanistan, which would also be in India's regional interests.[30]

During a recent trip to New Delhi, some Indian officials dismissed such ideas as a "pipe-dream" because of Pakistani hostility to India. They may be right, but their Pakistani counterparts might say the same thing about them. Despite such talk, I disagree that it is too late for Afghanistan's neighbors to come to an accord that ensures they will not use that country for the purpose of pressuring each other.[31] A pact of this nature is a nineteenth-century idea whose time may have come again in a world where nuclear weapons lessen the importance of classic arms races. Pakistan may have vetoed cooperation with India in the past, but its own record in Afghanistan is questionable: it has not been able to impose a stable government there, and its support for the Taliban ensures that this will not happen. In the absence of cooperative efforts, one of the likely outcomes for Afghanistan after 2014 (and not the worst) could be a civil war, with Pakistan supporting its Taliban clients in the south while India backs a revived Northern Alliance, perhaps in conjunction with Iran, in the north.

In the past the United States never attempted to integrate Indian efforts into those of NATO or its own operations, but such expanded cooperation should be attempted. A critical issue for Pakistan has been the belief that the Indians have a much larger and more assertive role in Afghanistan than they actually do. Will Pakistan's new strategic approach to India change this, making India-Pakistan cooperation in Afghanistan possible? India can allay Pakistani concerns by being more transparent about what it is doing in Afghanistan, while the United States too can help make the Indian role more visible and directed toward the stabilization of the Afghan government, both in the interest of facilitating cooperation. It should also promote covert meetings between the two intelligence services to assist in verification. For its part, Pakistan has to recognize that its interests are not served by a Taliban client. Such recognition should be a condition of American assistance.

The lack of a creative U.S. role in developing a viable strategic framework for Afghanistan—one that would include both India and Pakistan, as well as Iran—has always been a problem, but never an issue. It should be so now.

Afghanistan was the undoing of the U.S. policy of dehyphenating Pakistan from India. Afghanistan had for years been an arena of direct India-Pakistan strategic competition, each rival supporting its own proxies, including armed forces during the civil war that followed the Soviet departure. Later, after the defeat of the Taliban government, each used policy tools derived from its own special qualities: India supported the Karzai government with aid and development projects, while Pakistan eschewed aid but became the base from which the medieval and authoritarian Taliban assumed power. Pakistan justified this support on the grounds of Pushtun solidarity. This mixture of ethnicity and religion was toxic to Pakistan itself, now embroiled in a struggle against its own Islamist-Pushtun Taliban, who have the backing of most of the radical Islamist parties in Pakistan.

Events in Afghanistan have unduly shaped America's Pakistan policy. In turn, Pakistan's concerns about Indian encroachment in Afghanistan, which are as exaggerated but as understandable as its fear of India's dominance, must be worked into American policy calculations. Instead, U.S. officials talk privately of the U.S.-India relationship helping to "stabilize" Pakistan, a term that Pakistanis take to mean their "containment."

Redefine Dehyphenation

Dehyphenation clearly needs to be redefined. I would not go so far as to call for "rehyphenation," but selective engagement in regional issues is called for. The dehyphenation policy had antecedents in the Reagan administration, where it was still linked to cold war strategies. It was a conscious policy (although not called that) after the Clinton administration adjusted to the regional nuclear program, while its name came into being under the Bush administration. Dehyphenation was heartily endorsed by India and tolerated by Pakistan. The policy said nothing about India-Pakistan relations. There was merely a non-policy of hope that the two would not push their crises very far. Kashmir was off bounds, except for diplomatic urgings for normalcy, while other regional issues were addressed through a dysfunctional division of responsibility.

A more active engagement would have to have the tacit consent of both India and Pakistan. It should not treat them identically—but it should help the two transform their sixty-five years of sometimes cordial, mostly dysfunctional conflict into something more than somewhat less official malice.

At present trend lines seem to be very positive—largely because of India's restraint and Pakistan's publicly announced change of strategy to the point where it seeks good relations with all of its neighbors. This trend is reflected in the 2012 visa and trade agreements.

In South Asia's past, periods of relatively normal relations were followed by renewed bitterness and the occasional crisis—some of them involving the threat or movement of nuclear assets. These were often triggered by terror attacks, while still others were the outcome of political turmoil in India, sometimes fomented by Pakistan.

For one side, normalization may make strategic sense; for the other, it may represent important economic benefits. For some, the cultural and ideological benefits of normalization will be reason enough. But it is a mistake to think that there will be a shared payoff and thus that India and Pakistan should be treated alike. India is under less compulsion to normalize with Pakistan than it was a few years ago, but its strategic gains might be substantial. Pakistan needs to again become a South Asian country and must tie its economy to India's, but it fears a loss of strategic autonomy. Undoubtedly, the payoff structure—the gains and losses associated with normalization—will change in the future, as will the ease with which India or Pakistan can deal with the political barriers of normalization.

This means that the United States should not treat Pakistan and India alike, whether in terms of blame or virtue, nor should it assume that they view their relationship in the same way. For normalization to work, it must happen in both countries, not just one. Furthermore, the right people have to be talking to each other at the same time, which is not happening now.

Outside powers, especially those halfway around the world, should be wary of adding very much to the process. Yet for a number of reasons India-Pakistan relations are more important now than in the past, when the South Asian conflict seemed less strategically significant than U.S. relations with each of the two, invariably in the context of cold war politics and later when nuclear concerns became the centerpiece of American regional strategy.

One lesson from past diplomatic efforts is that the frontal approach is counterproductive. Yet given that regional ambitions exist alongside deep unresolved grievances, a more energetic U.S. policy is called for. India and Pakistan are no longer bit players in a global cold war. They are part of a region that is one of the world's four or five economic and military power centers, even if greater South Asia remains weakly integrated. To add to the urgency for a more vigorous policy, a rising India and a slipping Pakistan are likely to continue to stumble into crises in years to come.

It Can Get Worse

As already mentioned, South Asia could suffer a worse future than a nagging dispute that dragged on for years. Since 1965 Americans have worried about another all-out war between India and Pakistan, and after 1998 about it escalating to the nuclear level. Much worse would be the revival of an intense military rivalry, with the full use of nuclear weapons. This worst-case scenario may not be inevitable or even likely, but it would be strongly shaped by events in Pakistan.[32]

Nurturing a moderate Pakistan is not unlike patiently waiting for the Soviet leadership to recognize that the old structure of its state was dysfunctional and opt to become Europeans, albeit with Asian interests. This event was the peaceful triumph of the West's policy of containment and is the proper scale with which to measure Pakistan's progress in becoming a normal state with South Asian qualities.

Estimates of Pakistan's viability as a state range from zero to forty years. In truth, it is impossible to see beyond the next five or six years with any precision.[33] This suggests a policy time frame for action: anything that has to be done to promote greater India-Pakistan normalization must have a medium-term horizon. Pakistan's power is fading: its economy is in shambles, it is struggling politically, and its federal system is under attack from the smaller provinces. Above all, its elites remain doubtful about the ideas that created Pakistan. Unlike other failing states, however, it is politically and economically weak but militarily strong, having acquired two instruments that threaten the surrounding region and ultimately itself. The first of these is the capacity to foment insurrection in its neighbors, which it has perfected over the years; the second is its nuclear capability. India, like the United States, does not want to see Pakistan come apart, spewing nuclear weapons throughout the region. Pakistan is too nuclear to fail. Although the failure of normalization would be unwelcome, even more frightening would be the failure of the Pakistani state. This possibility offers a new common ground for the United States, India, and moderates in Pakistan to come together on.

Crises and Nuclear Risks

Ironically, the one fear that steered U.S. policy after the end of the cold war—nuclear proliferation—turns out to have important implications for India-Pakistan normalization and suggests further modification in American policy. Just as nuclear weapons brought about a kind of peace after 1998, even though their management presented new problems, India and Pakistan could reduce further the risks of a thermonuclear war if their overall relations were more normal. That is precisely what happened in the case of the United States and Russia, and Russia and China.

Indian and Pakistani strategists are in the process of learning what American and Soviet strategists worked out during the cold war: namely, that nuclear weapons have changed the nature of the military threat.[34] America should help the two countries move the learning process a step further so as to avoid the mistake Washington and Moscow made in overbuilding weapons, assuming that a nuclear war was winnable, and placing the fate of the nation in the hands of unproven and untrustworthy technologies.

The United States should encourage the two states to take advantage of the reality of deterrence and work toward a stable nuclear regime, while maintaining the tightest control over the use of the weapons. Washington went part way down this road when it entered into a civilian nuclear deal with India that legitimized New Delhi's nuclear status; it should find a formula that does the same for Pakistan, with the caveat that being a full member of the nuclear club means that Pakistan—and India—must assume the obligations set forth for nuclear weapons states under the Nuclear Nonproliferation Treaty (NPT). Such a deal outside the NPT could build on Rajiv Gandhi's idea of regional nuclear regimes that anticipated the ultimate objective of global nuclear disarmament. This is a far more realistic goal than chimerical demands that India and Pakistan disarm and sign the NPT as non-nuclear weapons states.

Washington should not punish these two states for past "bad" behavior but should incentivize responsible policy. Some specific steps could be to help Pakistan and India develop their respective regional nuclear safety centers. It could fund the exchange of scientists with each country and perhaps offer courses on nuclear safety to both in its own laboratories or in the region. It could also offer to share monitoring technology with each and establish a protocol, perhaps under the aegis of the International Atomic Energy Commission or some other international body, for organizing nuclear forensic teams to assist in determining the origin of a nuclear detonation should a catastrophe strike. Washington can also offer to work with the national disaster mitigation centers of each state, providing advice on the protection of vulnerable populations and associated technology to those who ask for it.

U.S. Policy: Do No Harm, But Do Something

The United States has a strong interest in the normalization of India-Pakistan relations that goes far beyond normal "good" ties to each of them. Their normalization is more important than Afghanistan's stabilization or building India up as a barrier to an expanding China. Normalization would solidify the world's largest block of democratic countries, would link the thriving Indian economy with the staggering one in Pakistan, and create a strategically cooperative South Asia that would be the best barrier against Chinese expansion, should Beijing turn in that direction. Some in India might greet a new American initiative with skepticism, but the recently completed American policy document on India actually encourages regional cooperation, and a carefully crafted U.S. initiative might be more welcome in New Delhi than previous efforts. Doubts will exist on the Pakistan side, but America has stuck by Pakistan despite several provocations, and its interest, like that of India's, is to see a stable democratic Pakistan emerge over the next decade. Part of the new approach would be to confirm Pakistan's identity as a South Asian state.[35]

For all its benefits, regional normalization remains a possibility, not a probability. Compounding this uncertainty are the complexities of the dispute, which suggest it could end in several unpleasant ways. Although not in America's interests, the India-Pakistan stalemate could go on indefinitely. This is a conflict that Pakistan cannot win and India cannot lose. India and Pakistan are like two gladiators locked together, each holding a nuclear weapon that cannot be used at close quarters and their relationship suffused with the psycho-political dynamic of a paired minority conflict. Both countries even support national projects that exaggerate their differences rather than reduce them. The best that can be said about their agreements to work together in various confidence-building arrangements so far is that neither has boasted of breaking them. Even so, there is a strong feeling in both countries that they can avoid a major clash and that South Asia is not as unstable as outsiders believe.

The best way to address (not "solve") the India-Pakistan conflict is to rely on a mixed strategy that takes into account not only the drivers of the conflict but also the challenges to effective intervention. Focusing on single causes will keep India and Pakistan shooting at each other for another century.

Because theirs is a paired minority conflict, India and Pakistan will find it difficult to sustain a dialogue directed at regional normalization. This does not mean that war will break out or that the conflict, like other paired minority conflicts, cannot be moderated. The United States, for example, should encourage India and Pakistan to cooperate in Afghanistan, by showing support for the present cease-fire line as an international boundary while recognizing the human rights abuses on both sides of the line. It should do everything it can to use its current cooperative programs with each state to encourage them to work together, and it should support all measures to bring about regional economic agreement and cooperation. Its guiding principle should be this: the pace of normalization and cooperation must be dictated by the two regional states, not by America. At the same time, all parties must understand that American help is a necessary but not sufficient condition for regional normalization to come about.

NOTES

PREFACE

1. Best exemplified recently by Charles A. Kupchan, *How Enemies Become Friends* (Princeton University Press, 2010).

2. Rafiq Dossani, Daniel C. Sneider, and Vikram Sood, *Does South Asia Exist? Prospects for Regional Integration* (Stanford, Calif.: Shorenstein Center, 2010), p. 16.

3. There are, however, several useful efforts. The following have as their main focus the larger problem of normalization: Shirin R. Tahir-Kheli, *India, Pakistan and the United States* (New York: Council on Foreign Relations Press, 1997); Stanley Wolpert, *India and Pakistan: Continued Conflict or Cooperation* (University of California Press, 2010).

CHAPTER 1

1. See Peter T. Coleman, *The Five Percent: Finding Solutions to Seemingly Impossible Conflicts* (New York: Public Affairs, 2011). For a broader study of global conflict, see Paul Diehl and Gary Goertz, *War and Peace in International Rivalry* (University of Michigan Press, 2010).

2. Karim Mehtab, "Effects of Migration, Socioeconomic Status and Population Policy on Reproductive Behaviour," London School of Economics Asia Research Centre (www2.lse.ac.uk/asiaResearchCentre/_files/ARCWP04-Karim.pdf). See also Prashant Bharadwaj, Asim Khwaja, and Atif Mian, "The Big March: Migratory Flows after the Partition of India," *Economic and Political Weekly*, March 20, 2008 (www.hks.harvard.edu/fs/akhwaja/papers/Big%20March%20EPW%20Publish08.pdf).

3. For an analysis of the causes of Hyderabad's relatively stable politics, see Benjamin B. Cohen, *Kingship and Colonialism in India's Deccan: 1850–1948* (New York: Palgrave Macmillan, 2007).

4. The expansion and contraction of Chinese imperial systems is one model, but so is that of Europe. See Norman Davies, *Vanished Kingdoms: The History of Half-Forgotten Europe* (London: Allen Lane, 2011).

5. For depictions of these trends over the centuries, see W. M. Day, "Relative Permanence of Former Boundaries in India," *Scottish Geographical Magazine*, vol. 65 (1949), pp. 113–22, reproduced in Graham P. Chapman, *The Geopolitics of South Asia*, 3rd ed. (London: Ashgate, 2009), p. xiv. See also Joseph Schwartzberg, *A Historical Atlas of South Asia* (University of Chicago Press, 1978), esp. chap. 14, "A Geopolitical Synopsis: The Evolution of Regional Power Configurations in the Indian Subcontinent." A digital version of the atlas can be found at http://dsal.uchicago.edu/reference/schwartzberg/pager.html?object=293.

6. Calculations based on the Pakistan federal budget 2012–13 (www.finance.gov.pk/budget/Budget_in_Brief_2012_13.pdf).

7. For an excellent overview of these and other conflicts during the Nehru years, see Srinath Raghavan, *War and Peace in Modern India* (New York: Palgrave Macmillan, 2010).

8. Robert J. McMahon, *The Cold War on the Periphery: The United States, India, and Pakistan* (Columbia University Press, 1996), pp. 274, 282.

9. Stephen Philip Cohen, *The Idea of Pakistan* (Brookings, 2004), p. 73.

10. The commission went moribund, meeting only five times, but was revived in 2012 after a visit to Pakistan by India's foreign minister, S. M. Krishna. It has had eight technical subgroups since 2005. Jayanth Jacob, "India, Pak Joint Commission May Get New Lease on Life," *Hindustan Times*, September 5, 2012.

11. For definitive histories of American relations with India and Pakistan, see Dennis Kux, *Estranged Democracies: India and the United States 1941–1991* (New Delhi: Sage, 1993); and Kux, *The United States and Pakistan, 1947–2000: Disenchanted Allies* (Washington: Woodrow Wilson Center Press, 2001).

12. For an overview of these crises, see P. R. Chari, Pervaiz Iqbal Cheema, and Stephen P. Cohen, *Four Crises and a Peace Process: American Engagement in South Asia* (Brookings, 2007); for a study of a subsequent crisis, namely, the terror attack on Mumbai, see Michael Krepon and Polly Nayak, *The Unfinished Crisis: U.S. Crisis Management after the 2008 Mumbai Attacks* (Washington: Stimson Center, 2012).

13. W. H. Auden, "Partition," May 1966, *Collected Poems* (1976), p. 604 (http://markcnewton.com/2009/05/11/partition-by-w-h-auden/). Auden's poem and other partition poetry are discussed in a review article by historian Ramchandra Guha: "Poems of Partition: Bad Poetry Can Sometimes Tell Us More than the Finest History," *The Telegraph* (Calcutta), April 28, 2007 (www.telegraphindia.com/1070428/asp/opinion/story_7706992.asp).

14. Memorandum to the viceroy, reprinted in John Connell, *Auchinleck: A Biography of Field-Marshal Sir Claude Auchinleck* (London: Cassell, 1959), p. 877.

15. Field Marshal Claude Auchinleck, interview in London, October 1963.

16. The Jamaat-i-Islami pursued a higher goal than a mere rump state called Pakistan—it envisioned the unification of the entire subcontinental Muslim community. Once partition took place, Pakistan army troops escorted JI's founder, Maulana Maudoodi, from Deoband in India to Pakistan, but many JI members stayed behind.

17. Ashis Nandy, "The Fantastic India-Pakistan Battle, Or the Future of the Past in South Asia," *Futures* 29, no. 10 (1997): 909–18. I encountered Nandy's article after this book was essentially finished; it parallels many of the arguments I present.

18. See Sumatra Jha and Steven Wilkinson, "Does Combat Experience Foster Organizational Skill: Evidence from Ethnic Cleansing during the Partition of South Asia," Working Paper 2092 (Stanford University Graduate School of Business, April 2012) (http://ssrn.com/abstract=1739812); and Stuart Corbridge, Nikhila Kalra, and Kayoko Tatsumi, "The Search for Order: Understanding Hindu-Muslim Violence in Post-Partition India," *Pacific Affairs* 85 (June 2012).

19. Teresita C. Schaffer and Howard B. Schaffer, *How Pakistan Negotiates with the United States: Riding Roller Coaster* (Washington: United States Institute of Peace, 2011), chap. 8.

20. Sadiq Ahmed and Ejaz Ghani, *South Asia, Growth and Regional Integration* (Delhi: Macmillan, 2007), p. 4.

21. Saja Lahiri, *Regionalism and Globalization; Theory and Practice* (London: Routledge 2001).

22. Ahmed and Ghani, *South Asia, Growth and Regional Integration*, p. 194.

23. Ibid., p. 31.

24. Ibid., p. 38.

25. Shaheen Rafi Khan and others, *Regional Integration, Trade and Conflict in South Asia* (Winnipeg: International Institute for Sustainable Development, January 2007), p. 24.

26. Shaheen Rafi Khan and others, "Quantifying Informal Trade between India and Pakistan," in *The Challenges and Potential of Pakistan-India Trade*, edited by Zareen Fatima Naqvi and Philip Schuler (Washington: World Bank, June 2007), chap. 5.

27. Ahmed and Ghani, *South Asia, Growth and Regional Integration*, p. 40.

28. All available years are at www.visionofhumanity.org.

29. Conversations with one Pakistani pollster indicate that Pakistani attitudes have shifted by as much as 79 percent—from minus 20 percent to plus 50 percent—and that Pakistanis no longer blame India for their problems; they now blame the United States and Pakistani politicians. Apparently this shift has occurred across all age groups and all regions. This attitude is encapsulated in a book by General Mohammed Arif, Mohammed Zia ul-Haq's closest military adviser and a classic Pakistan hawk on India and Pakistan; whereas Arif devotes a very small chapter to India, he directs most of his anger at Pakistan's political and upper-class leaders, calling Pakistan "a wounded nation, hurt by both friends and foes. Her national body is riddled with injuries of insult, neglect and arrogance inflicted by dictators and democrats;

judges and generals, the bureaucrats and media. None of them are blame-free." General K. M. Arif, *Estranged Neighbors: India-Pakistan, 1947–2010* (Islamabad: Dost, 2010), pp. 315–16.

30. Andrew Kohut and others, "Pakistani Public Opinion Ever More Critical of the U.S.," Pew Research Center Global Attitudes Project, June 2012 (www.pewglobal.org/2012/06/27/pakistani-public-opinion-ever-more-critical-of-u-s/).

31. C. Christine Fair, Clay Ramsay, and Steve Kull, "Pakistani Public Opinion on Democracy, Islamist Militancy, and Relations with the U.S.," working paper (Washington: United States Institute of Peace, February 2008), p. 36 (www.usip.org/publications/pakistan).

32. Steve Kull and others, "Pakistani and Indian Public Opinion on Kashmir and Indo-Pakistan Relations" (Washington: World Public Opinion and Program on International Policy Attitudes, July 16, 2008), p. 7.

33. "A Win for Communalism," *Express Tribune* (Lahore), December 20, 2012. The editorial expresses a common theme in Pakistani official and nonofficial thinking, that Modi's victory represents a continuing communal threat to India—and therefore to all subcontinental Muslims; six decades after partition and despite all the talk about "secularism" in India, it should be alarming to Pakistan (http://tribune.com.pk/story/482105/in-india-a-win-for-communalism/).

34. Kohut and others, "Pakistani Public Opinion Ever More Critical of the U.S.," p. 36.

35. Kull and others, "Pakistani and Indian Public Opinion on Kashmir and Indo-Pakistan Relations," p. 17.

36. Ibid., p. 12.

37. Kohut and others, "Pakistani Public Opinion Ever More Critical of the U.S.," p. 38.

38. Fair and others, "Pakistani Public Opinion on Democracy," p. 22.

39. Pew Research, "On Anniversary of bin Laden's Death, Little Backing of al Qaeda" (www.pewglobal.org/2012/04/30/on-anniversary-of-bin-ladens-death-little-backing-of-al-qaeda/).

40. Kull and others, "Pakistani and Indian Public Opinion on Kashmir and Indo-Pakistan Relations," p. 6.

41. Gallup Pakistan, "Majority of Pakistanis Supported Emergency Aid to Victims of Earthquake in India," released on March 2, 2001 (www.gallup.com.pk/Polls/2-3-2001.pdf).

42. Fair and others, "Pakistani Public Opinion on Democracy," p. 35.

43. Peter Bergen, Patrick C. Doherty, and Ken Ballen, "Public Opinion in Pakistan's Tribal Regions," New America Foundation and Terror Free Tomorrow Public Opinion Survey, September 2010, p. 8.

44. A recent review of World Values Surveys shows a surprisingly similar (low) level of support for democracy as a good form of government in India and Pakistan, at around 65 percent. Only 5 of close to 100 other countries surveyed had lower

levels of support for democracy. See Jonathan Reilly and L. J. Zigerell, "Don't Know Much about Democracy: Reporting Survey Data with Nonsubstantive Responses, *PS: Political Science and Politics* 45 (July 2012): 464. For a classic study on the sources of democracy and authoritarianism in South Asia, see Ayesha Jalal, *Democracy and Authoritarianism in South Asia: A Comparative and Historical Perspective* (Cambridge University Press, 1995). On the surprising success of India's democracy, see Atul Kohli, ed., *The Success of India's Democracy* (Cambridge University Press, 2001).

45. State of Democracy in South Asia (SDSA, 2008), p. 13, quoted in Philip Oldenburg, *India, Pakistan, and Democracy: Solving the Puzzle of Divergent Paths* (New York: Routledge, 2010), p. 6.

46. Krishna Kumar, *Prejudice and Pride: School Histories of the Freedom Struggle in India and Pakistan* (New Delhi: Viking, 2001), p. 9.

47. Sumita S. Chakravarti, "Fragmenting the Nation: Images of Terrorism in Indian Popular Cinema," in *Terrorism, Media Liberation*, edited by John David Slocum (Rutgers University Press, 2005), p. 236.

48. Jon Dorschner and Thomas Sherlock, "The Role of History Textbooks in Shaping Collective Identities in India and Pakistan," in *Teaching the Violent Past: History Education and Reconciliation,* edited by Elizabeth A. Cole (Lanham, Md.: Rowman and Littlefield, 2001), p. 291.

49. Iqbal Rehman, "Enemy Images on Pakistani Television," Transnational Institute Online, December 1996.

50. Ibid.

51. Chakravarti ("Fragmenting the Nation"), for instance, sees the Muslim figure in Indian cinema as only questioning and problematizing the state's integration of minorities, but points out that ultimately the unity of the Indian state is reaffirmed by the patriotic Muslim figure.

52. See Roshni Sengupta, "Muslims on Television: News and Representation on Satellite Channels," in *Television in India: Satellites, Politics, and Cultural Change,* edited by Nalin Mehta (Abingdon: Routledge, 2008).

53. Chakravarti, "Fragmenting the Nation," p. 238.

54. Kumar, *Prejudice and Pride*, p. 41.

55. Ibid., p. 46.

56. J. N. Dixit, *India-Pakistan in War and Peace* (London: Routledge, 2002), p. 83.

57. For a running survey of talks, see the publications of the Pakistan Institute of Legislative Development and Transparency (PILDAT), Lahore and Islamabad, available at www.pildat.org.

58. This was the special express train between India and Pakistan. The attack, plus many earlier assaults on Muslim symbols and places of worship, shows the depth of religious fanaticism in India—better contained than in Pakistan—but still present.

59. For a brief discussion of the role of cricket and cinema as unifying factors in state integration in South Asia, see Swarna Rajagopalan, *State and Nation in South Asia* (Boulder, Colo.: Lynne Rienner, 2001), p. 13.

60. The team broke up in 2011. See its Facebook page (www.facebook.com/pages/Stop-War-Start-Tennis/106020146117304).

61. For at least one or two months in early 2010, the UN secretary-general's special representative in Sudan, Ashraf Qazi from Pakistan, had an Indian officer, Jasbir Singh Lidder, as his deputy, though technically he was answerable to the UN secretary-general (http://sudanwatch.blogspot.com/2010/01/indias-jasbir-singh-lidder-heads-un.html).

62. The South Asian Free Media Association (SAFMA) publishes an excellent quarterly journal, *The South Asia Journal*; the website (http://safma.net) contains information about other regional groupings.

63. "India and Pakistan to Cooperate in Science," *Daily Times* (Pakistan), January 18, 2012 (www.dailytimes.com.pk/default.asp?page=2012%5C01%5C18%5Cstory_18-1-2012_pg7_13).

64. "India Allows Pakistan Investment," *BBC News India*, August 1, 2012 (www.bbc.co.uk/news/world-asia-india-19090467).

Chapter 2

1. For an overview, see Mohsin S. Khan, *India-Pakistan Trade: A Roadmap for Enhancing Economic Relations*, Peterson Institute Policy Brief, July 2009 (www.iie.com/publications/pb/pb09-15.pdf).

2. P. Vaidyanathan Iyer, "India Set to Cut Sensitive List of Pak Imports by 30 Percent," *The Indian Express*, April 3, 2012 (www.indianexpress.com/news/india-set-to-cut-sensitive-list-of-pak-imports-by-30-per-cent/931818/0).

3. See, for example, the editorial in the Urdu *Jang* calling on political leaders and religious groups to play a positive role in "bringing the people closer." *Jang*, May 27, 2012 (http://jang.com.pk/jang/may2012-daily/27-05-2012/idaria.htm).

4. "Talks is a welcome step towards easing tension but establishing normal relations without resolution of Kashmir would be impossible," *Khabrein*, May 27, 2012 (www.khabraingroup.com/column-corner-detail2.htm).

5. Pakistan should take "extreme steps" to resolve outstanding issues instead of "talks," according to *Nawa-e-Waqt*, editorial, May 27, 2012 (www.nawaiwaqt.com.pk/pakistan-news-newspaper-daily-urdu-online/Op...).

6. Zareen F. Naqvi, "Pakistan-India Trade: Overview and Key Issues," in *The Challenges and Potential of Pakistani India Trade*, edited by Zareen Fatima Naqvi and Philip Schuler (Washington: World Bank, June 2007), p. 2.

7. Eugenia Baroncelli, "The 'Peace Dividend,' SAFTA, and Pakistan-India Trade," in *The Challenges and Potential of Pakistani India Trade*, edited by Naqvi and Schuler, p. 62.

8. Nisha Taneja, "Informal Trade in SAARC Region," *Economic and Political Weekly*, March 17, 2001, p. 959.

9. Ibid., p. 960.

10. Sadiq Ahmed and Ejaz Ghani, *South Asia, Growth and Regional Integration* (Delhi: Macmillan, 2007), p. 194.

11. Ibid. p. 196.

12. Sajal Lahiri, *Regionalism and Globalization: Theory and Practice* (London: Routledge, 2001), p. xix.

13. Ahmed and Ghani, *South Asia, Growth and Regional Integration,* p. 31.

14. Ibid., p. 4.

15. Ibid., p. 38.

16. For examples and details, see Shaheen Rafi Khan, Moeed Yusuf, and S. Aziz, "Quantifying Informal Trade between India and Pakistan," in *The Challenges and Potential of Pakistan-India Trade,* edited by Naqvi and Schuler. See also Craig Fagin, "Evidence of Illegal Cross-Border Flows of Funds, Goods and Services in South Asia and Their Impact on Corruption," Report 282 (Berlin: Transparency International and the Anti-Corruption Resource Center, April 28, 2011), p. 2; and Nisha Taneja, "India-Pakistan Trade," Working Paper 18 (New Delhi: Indian Council for Research on International Economic Relations, June 2006), p. 17.

17. Warren Weinstein, conversation with the author, March 23, 2011, Washington, D.C.

18. Khan and others, "Quantifying Informal Trade between India and Pakistan," p. 89.

19. Fagin, "Evidence of Illegal Cross-Border Flows."

20. These goods include bicycles, electronic goods, tires, cosmetics, cloth, jewelry, and razor blades. The estimated value of this substitution is around $0.5 billion to $1 billion.

21. Anwar Iqbal, "Pakistan Seeks New IMF Loan," *Dawn* (Karachi), April 23, 2012 (http://dawn.com/2012/04/23/pakistan-seeks-new-imf-loan/).

22. For an incisive overview of the critical nature of the water crisis between (and within) India and Pakistan, see Stimson Center, Observer Research Foundation, and Sustainable Development Policy Institute, *Connecting the Drops: An Indus Basin Roadmap for Cross-Border Water Research, Data Sharing, and Policy Coordination* (Washington: Stimson Center, 2013).

23. M. A. Salman and Kishore Uprety, *Conflict and Cooperation on South Asia's International Rivers: A Legal Perspective* (Washington: World Bank, 2002), p. 37.

24. Ibid., p. 44.

25. David Lilienthal, "Another 'Korea' in the Making," *Collier's,* August 4, 1951. Lilienthal was advised by a distinguished American scholar of India, Henry C. Hart, who later wrote the first major study of Indian water systems. See Henry C. Hart, *New India's Rivers* (Bombay: Orient Longmans, 1956).

26. Salman and Uprety, *Conflict and Cooperation on South Asia's International Rivers,* p. 45.

27. K. Warikoo, "Indus Waters Treaty: View from Kashmir," June 1, 2006 (www.jammu-kashmir.com/insights/insight20060601a.html).

28. John Briscoe, interview with Kari Lifschutz, "Global Insider: The India-Pakistan Water Dispute, Interview," *World Politics Review*, June 10, 2010 (www.worldpoliticsreview.com/trend-lines/5756/global-insider-the-india-pakistan-water-dispute).

29. Salman and Uprety, *Conflict and Cooperation on South Asia's International Rivers*, p. 56.

30. Karin Brulliard, "Rhetoric Grows Heated in Water Dispute between Pakistan and India," *Washington Post* Foreign Service, May 28, 2010.

31. A retired four-star Pakistani general titles one chapter of his book on India-Pakistan relations "Loaded Water Bomb." See General K. M. Arif, *Estranged Neighbors: India-Pakistan, 1947–2010* (Islamabad: Dost, 2010), chap. 8.

32. Niharika Mandhana, "Water Wars: Why India and Pakistan Are Squaring Off on Their Rivers," *Time*, April 16, 2012 (www.time.com/time/world/article/0,8599,2111601,00.html).

33. "JI Demands Judicial Probe against India's Water Aggression," *Pakistan Today*, July 23, 2012 (www.pakistantoday.com.pk/2012/07/23/city/lahore/ji-demands-judicial-probe-against-indias-water-aggression/).

34. Amer Sial, "PM Urged to Take Notice of Nine New Indian Dams on Indus, Chenab Rivers," *Pakistan Today*, January 12, 2012 (www.pakistantoday.com.pk/2012/01/12/news/profit/pm-urged-to-take-notice-of-nine-new-indian-dams-on-indus-chenab-rivers/).

35. Ibid.

36. See www.business-standard.com/india/news/indias-soft-stance-in-troubled-waters-dispute/454700/.

37. See articles.economictimes.indiatimes.com/2010-03-15/news/27611827_1_terror-outfits-terror-attacks-indus-water.

38. See www.bgverghese.com/Indus.htm.

39. For a good introduction to the water problem in the context of South Asia's larger energy crisis, see Charles K. Ebinger, *Energy and Security in South Asia: Cooperation or Conflict?* (Brookings, 2012).

40. See Group of Interlocutors for Jammu and Kashmir, "A New Compact with the People of Jammu and Kashmir," May 2012 (http://mha.nic.in/pdfs/J&K-InterlocutorsRpt-0512.pdf). For a discussion of the report by two members of the group, see Howard Schaffer and Teresita Schaffer, "The Kashmir Interlocutors Report—But Who Will Listen?" June 1, 2012 (http://southasiahand.com/kashmir/the-kashmir-interlocutors-report-but-who-will-listen/).

41. For the director's court statement, see Syed Ghulam Nabi Fai, "Why Kashmir Is Important to Me," Alexandria Court House, Virginia, December 7, 2011. Fai is now incarcerated in a federal prison.

42. For its studies, see http://kashmirstudygroup.com/.

43. For a rare balanced account, see Navnita Chadha Behera, *Demystifying Kashmir* (Brookings, 2006). See also International Crisis Group, "Pakistan's Relations with India—Beyond Kashmir?" Asia Report 224, May 3, 2012 (www.crisisgroup.org/en/regions/asia/south-asia/kashmir.aspx).

44. Wajahat Qazi, blog, September 12, 2012 (http://akrasia-akrasia.blogspot.in/2012/09/india-pakistan-rapprochement-strategic_16.html).

45. Muzamil Jallel, "Building Bridges in Air," *Indian Express*, October 3, 2012, p. 3.

46. Steve Coll, "Kashmir: The Time Has Come," *New York Review of Books*, September 30, 2010.

47. See Schaffer and and Schaffer, "The Kashmir Interlocutors Report—But who will Listen?"

48. Bahukutumbi Raman, "Now, For Political Normalisation, *Times of India*, June 2, 2012 (http://timesofindia.indiatimes.com/home/opinion/edit-page/).

49. One famous literary representation of the syndrome appears in Prem Chand's short story "Shatranj ke Khilari," in which two Muslim princes keep deferring to the other; meanwhile their lands are taken over by the British. See Prem Chand, *The Chess Players*, first published in 1924. Also, see the fine film by the same name by Satyajit Ray, 1977.

50. Sisir Gupta, *Kashmir: A Study in India-Pakistan Relations* (Bombay: Asia Publishing House, 1966), p. 460.

51. Kanti Bajpai, "Symbols over Substance in India-Pakistan Ties," *Times of India*, August 6, 2012 (timesofindia.com).

52. Personal communication to the author, May 2012.

53. Ahmed Mukhtar, "Egos, Armies of India, Pakistan Biggest Hurdle to Siachen Peace," *Express Tribune* (Lahore), June 3, 2012 (http://tribune.com.pk/story/388052/).

54. Jyoti Malhotra, "Breaching the Final Frontier," *Times of India* blog, June 14, 2012 (http://blogs.timesofindia.indiatimes.com/ist/entry/ [July 27, 2012]).

55. Morton Deutsch, Peter T. Coleman, and Eric C. Marcus, eds., *The Handbook of Conflict Resolution*, 2nd ed. (New York: Jossey-Bass, 2006), p. 33.

56. In the case of the United States, 9/11 contributed to the shift in American policy from openly supporting Muslim "freedom fighters" who resisted Soviet forces in Afghanistan to opposing "terrorists" from Pakistan in the 1999 Kargil conflict and, especially, Pakistan's blatant use of proxy terrorist groups in the 2008 Mumbai terror attacks in which Americans and Jews were murderously singled out.

57. For my views on this, see Stephen P. Cohen, "U.S. Security in a Separatist Season," *Bulletin of the Atomic Scientists* 48 (July 1992): 28–32.

Chapter 3

1. Letter to Dwight Eisenhower, May 14, 1958, in *Selected Works of Jawaharlal Nehru*, quoted in "So Said Nehru to Eisenhower," *Economic Times*, November 2010 (http://articles.economictimes.indiatimes.com/2010).

2. This is the title of a report on Kashmir by two leading Indian and Pakistani experts, P. R. Chari and Hasan Askari Rizvi: see the U.S. Institute of Peace, "Making Borders Irrelevant," Special Report (Washington, September 2008) (www.usip.org/publications/making borders irrelevant in kashmir).

3. A. G. Noorani, "The Partition of India," *Frontline* 18, no. 26 (December 22, 2001–January 4, 2002) (www.frontlineonnet.com/fl1826/18260810.htm).

4. For literature from a liberal Indian perspective, see Krishna Kumar, *Prejudice and Pride: School Histories of the Freedom Struggle in India and Pakistan* (New Delhi: Viking, 2001); and Navnita Chadha Behera, "Perpetuating the Divide: Political Abuse of History in South Asia," *Contemporary South Asia* 5 (July 1996): 191–207.

5. Shekhar Gupta, "Be Very Afraid," *Indian Express*, October 8, 2011(www.indianexpress.com/news/be-very-afraid/857168/0).

6. India, Census 2011, "Religious Composition" (www.censusindia.gov.in/Census_Data_2001/India_at_glance/religion.aspx).

7. "The Future of Global Muslim Population" (http://features.pewforum.org/muslim-population/index.php?sort=Pop2010).

8. The most notorious cases were the 1992 destruction of the Babri Masjid by Hindu fanatics egged on by some BJP leaders and the outright persecution of Muslims in Gujarat in 2002. In the latter case, Muslims became the "other" for middle-caste and high-caste Hindus, and a state-tolerated pogrom was mounted against them.

9. Pravin Swami, *India, Pakistan and the Secret Jihad: The Covert War in Kashmir, 1947–2004* (London: Routledge, 2007), p. 218, quoting Mohammad Abdullah's autobiography, *Flames of the Chinar*, translated by Khushwant Singh (New York: Viking, 1993), p. 90.

10. To India's credit, it has conducted a national examination of the role of its Muslim citizens. The Sachar Committee, which reported its findings in 2006, was established to evaluate the entire spectrum of Indian Muslim life (excluding the role of Muslims in the armed forces). However, some observers have argued that the Congress Party's loss in the 2012 state elections was due in large part to Muslim grievances, aired by Sachar but not pursued by the party. See Saeed Naqvi, "Why Muslims Decided to Give Congress a Drubbing" (http://naqvijournal.blogspot.in/2012/03/why-muslims-decided-to-give-congress_10.html).

11. F. S. Aijazuddin, "Divided Attentions," *Dawn* (Karachi), September 20, 2012.

12. These data come from the government of India's report on Muslims in India, the Sachar Report (http://hawkeyeindia.wordpress.com/2006/12/06/the-muslim-demography-of-india-sachar-committee-report/).

13. The committee was headed by a former Indian chief justice. While it did not include a discussion of recruitment to the armed forces, it did document the underrepresentation of Muslims in many government positions and the overall weak position of Muslims in India. The full report, *Social, Economic, and Educational Status of the Muslim Community of India*, is at http://minorityaffairs.gov.in/sites/upload_files/moma/files/pdfs/sachar_comm.pdf.

14. For an overview, see C. Christine Fair, "Students' Islamic Movement of India and the Indian Mujahideen: An Assessment" (http://home.comcast.net/~christine_fair/pubs/APX_x_IndiaIslam_111109.pdf), pp. 11–12.

15. See Christopher Hill, *The Changing Politics of Foreign* Policy (London: Palgrave Macmillan, 2003), pp.107–08.

16. K. Subrahmanyam, "A Nuclear Strategy for India," May 28, 1998, reprinted by the Federation of American Scientists (www.fas.org/news/india/1998/05/980528-et.htm). Subrahmanyam was a voluminous writer who made this argument for many years as part of his effort to make an Indian nuclear weapon acceptable to the rest of the world.

17. Aiyar has written extensively on India-Pakistan relations. See in particular Mani Shankar Aiyar, *Pakistan Papers* (New Delhi: UBSPD, 1994).

18. Nayar is a frequent visitor to Pakistan and along with Pakistani economist Mubashir Hassan was honored by the Pakistani Institute for Peace and Secular Studies in Lahore, on March 24, 2012, where they spoke on the significance of the about-to-be-relaxed Pakistan-India visa regimes.

19. Shashi Tharoor, "Peace in Kashmir," February 20, 2012 (http://beta.project-syndicate.org/commentary/peace-in-Kashmir-).

20. Kuldip Nayar, "India Cannot Always Be at Odds with Pakistan," *Express Tribune* (Lahore), September 14, 2011 (http://tribune.com.pk/story/252274/india-cannot-always-be-at-odds-with-pakistan/). He cites Wiki Leaks conversations between Narayanan and American officials.

21. K. Sundarji, conversations with the author, January 1993.

22. K. Sundarji, remarks at the Center for Strategic and International Studies, India Abroad, February 25, 1994.

23. Nitin Pai, "Trading across the Partition," *The Acorn: On the Indian National Interest,* March 2, 2012 (http://acorn.nationalinterest.in/2012/03/02/tradition-across-partition/).

24. Center for Policy Research India, "Nonalignment 2.0, A Foreign and Strategic Policy for India in the 21st Century" (New Delhi, 2012) (www.cprindia.org/sites/default/files/Nonalignment%202.0_1.pdf). The group received logistic support from the Centre for Policy Research and the National Security Advisory Board. For the most trenchant comments on this document, see Ashley J. Tellis, "Nonalignment Redux: The Perils of Old Wine in New Skins" (Washington: Carnegie Endowment for International Peace, 2012) (www.carnegieendowment.org/files/nonalignment_redux.pdf).

25. Ibid.

26. Rajiv Kumar, "Taking the Long View," International Council for Research on International Economic Relations, India, Seminar 617, January 2011.

27. For similar studies, see Rajiv Sikri, *Challenge and Strategy: Rethinking India's Foreign Policy* (New Delhi: Sage, 2009); Raja Menon and Rajiv Kumar, *The Long View from Delhi: To Define the Indian Grand Strategy for Foreign Policy* (New Delhi: Academic Foundation, 2010); and Rajiv Kumar and Santosh Kumar, *In the National Interest: A Strategic Foreign Policy for India* (New Delhi: Business Standard Books, 2010). Another attempt is the project hosted by the Institute of Defence Studies and Analyses in New Delhi, which has commissioned various papers and also released, in 2011, a draft version of its final report, "Towards a National Security Strategy for India" (www.idsa.in/nationalstrategy/index.html).

28. Tridivesh Singh Maini, "Is India Policy Pakistan-centric?" *The Diplomat* (Tokyo), September 2, 2011 (http://the-diplomat.com/Indian-decade/2011/09/02/is-india-policy-pakistan-centric/).

29. B. R. Raman, "Will There Ever Be Peace between Pakistan and India?" *Newsweek* Pakistan, October 21, 2011 (www.newsweekpakistan.com/the-take/504).

30. Yashwant Sinha, "The Future of India's Foreign Policy," transcript of talk at Brookings, May 30, 2012 (www.brookings.edu/~/media/events/2012/5/30%20india%20foreign%20policy/20120530_sinha_transcript_corrected).

31. See "Roadmap for Second-rate Power Status for India: Response to Quasi-Official Foreign Policy Document— 'Nonalignment 2.0,'" posted March 4, 2012 (Bharatkarnad.com).

32. Kanwal Sibal, "The Turmoil Within: Pakistan's Future Is Causing Concern All Over the World," *The Telegraph* (Kolkata), December 14, 2011 (www.telegraphindia.com/1111214/jsp/opinion/story_14860091.jsp).

33. U. S. Bajpai, *India's Security: The Politico-Strategic Environment* (New Delhi: Lancers, 1983), pp. 70–71.

34. For a selection of contemporary Indian writing on Pakistan, much of it by present and former police and intelligence officials, see Rajeev Sharma, ed., *The Pakistan Trap* (New Delhi: UBSPD, 2001).

35. Vikram Sood, "Trading with Pak—When Hope Is a Policy," *Mid-day* (Mumbai), March 3, 2012 (www.mid-day.com/opinion/2012/mar/209312).

36. Bajpai, *India's Security*, pp. 70–71.

37. Ibid., p. 73.

38. K. Natwar Singh, "India-Pakistan Relations Are Complex and Accident Prone," *Economic Times*, December 12, 2011 (http://articles.economictimes.indiatimes.com/2011-12-12/news/30507540_1_indo-pak-yousaf-raza-gilani-neighbourly-relations).

39. Ibid.

40. Ibid.

41. See, for example, Amarjit Singh, "Why the Existence of Pakistan Is Not in India's Interest," *Indian Defence Review*, Internet edition, June 19, 2012 (www.indiandefencereview.com/news/). Singh, who lives securely in Hawaii, calls for the destruction of Pakistan, a "thorn in the left side of India," and his article includes a map, inspired by former U.S. Army colonel Ralph Peters, showing the new "solution": independent Punjabi, Sindh, and Baluchistan; FATA and the North West Frontier Province going to Afghanistan; and Pakistan-occupied Kashmir returning to India. Rather than suffer slowly, Singh observes, India needs to "get it over with even at the cost of tens of millions of deaths."

42. For Modi's tweets, see www.twitter.com/narendramodi.

43. "In China, Modi Raises Issue of PLA Troops in PoK," *Times of India*, November 11, 2011 (www.sanghparivar.org/in-china-modi-raises-issue-of-pla-troops-in-pok).

44. *Hindustan Times*, annual youth survey, March 3, 2012 (www.hindustantimes.com/Specials/coverage/YouthSurvey2012/YouthSociety.aspx).

45. C. Raja Mohan, "Ambassadors to Pakistan," *Indian Express*, November 19, 2012 (www.indianexpress.com/news/ambassadors-to-pakistan/1030155).

CHAPTER 4

1. See Aparna Pande's interpretation of Pakistan foreign policy in terms of its ideology, *Explaining Pakistan's Foreign Policy: Escaping India* (New York: Routledge, 2011).

2. Apurba Kundu, "The Indian Armed Forces' Sikh and Non-Sikh Officers' Opinions of Operation Blue Star," *Pacific Affairs* 67 (Spring 1994): 46–69 (www.vidhia.com/Historical%20and%20Political/).

3. For an overview, see the review of Pakistan historiography by the noted historian K. K. Aziz, *The Murder of History: A Critique of History Textbooks Used in Pakistan* (Lahore: Vanguard, 1993).

4. Ayaz Amir, "With Democracy Failing What Else Is Succeeding?" *The News* (Lahore), October 7, 2011.

5. General K. M. Arif, *Estranged Neighbors: India-Pakistan, 1947–2010* (Islamabad: Dost, 2010).

6. Parvez Hasan, remarks at Pakistan Society of Development Economists (PSDE) conference, December 15, 2011.

7. Ibid.

8. Navnita Chadha Behera, "Perpetuating the Divide: Political Abuse of History in South Asia," *Contemporary South Asia* 5 (July 1996): 191–207.

9. See ibid.; and Jon Dorschner and Thomas Sherlock, "The Role of History Textbooks in Shaping Collective Identities in India and Pakistan," in *Teaching the Violent Past: History Education and Reconciliation*, edited by Elizabeth A. Cole (Lanham, Md.: Rowman and Littlefield, 2001), p. 291.

10. For an overview, see Stephen P. Cohen, "The Army," in *The Oxford Companion to Pakistani History*, edited by Ayesha Jalal (Oxford University Press, 2012).

11. See Richard Bonney, Tridev Singh Maini, and Tahir Malik, *Warriors after War* (London: Peter Lang, 2011) and the review of it by Khaled Ahmed, "Generals—Theirs and Ours," *Express Tribune* (Lahore), March 10, 2012. In his evaluation of the army, Anatol Lieven stresses its pragmatism and professionalism as well as its middle-class origins. My observation of both armies is that the ideological element has always been strong in Pakistan, and this distinguishes it from its Indian counterpart. See Lieven, "Military Exceptionalism in Pakistan," *Survival* 53 (August–September 2011): 53–68.

12. Arif, *Estranged Neighbors*, p. 263.

13. Ibid., p. 330.

14. Their article and other attempts at joint statements are discussed in chapters 5 and 6. See their plea for confidence-building measures (CBMs) that would improve crisis stability between India and Pakistan in Jehangir Karamat and Shashi Tyagi, "No Dispute about This," *Hindustan Times*, March 21, 2012. See also David Ignatius

"Defusing the India-Pakistan Standoff," *Washington Post* blog, March 21, 2012 (www.washingtonpost.com/blogs/post-partisan).

15. Aqil S. Shah provides a new overview of the army in *Out of Control: The Pakistan Military and Politics in South Asian Perspective* (Harvard University Press, forthcoming). See also the comprehensive history of the army's domestic role by Shuja Nawaz, *Crossed Swords: Pakistan, Its Army, and the Wars Within* (Oxford University Press, 2008).

16. Kurshid Anwer Mirza, "Pakistan Is Facing Covert War," *The Nation* (Lahore), March 6, 2012 (www.nation.com.pk/pakistan-news-newspaper-daily-english-online/columns/06).

17. Khaled Ahmed, "Middle Class Myths," *Express Tribune* (Lahore), December 13, 2012 (http://tribune.com.pk/story/361242/middle-class-myths/?print=true).

18. Margaret Bourke-White, *Halfway to Freedom: A Report on the New India in the Words and Photographs of Margaret Bourke-White* (New York: Simon and Schuster, 1949), pp. 91–93.

19. Ibid.

20. President Zia ul-Haq told me that he understood and appreciated the comparison—he was at one time stationed in Jordan where he gained considerable respect for Israel—but that because the comparison with Israel was so "sensitive" to the average Pakistani, he apologized for banning a book of mine where the comparison was drawn. The book, *The Pakistan Army* (University of California Press, 1984), was reprinted in Pakistan with a new foreword and epilogue after his death in 1988 (Oxford University Press, 1998).

21. Aasim Sajjad Akhtar, "Of Friends and Enemies," *Dawn* (Karachi), March 16, 2012 (http://dawn.com/2012/03/16/of-friends-and-enemies/comment-page-1/),

22. Ibid.

23. An early work to apply Charles Lindblom's phrase "muddling through" to Pakistan was Jonathan Paris, *Prospects for Pakistan* (London: Legatum Institute, 2010).

24. Maleeha Lodhi, *Pakistan: Beyond the "Crisis State"* (Columbia University Press, 2011); Anatol Lieven, *Pakistan: A Hard Country* (New York: PublicAffairs, 2011).

25. John R. Schmidt, *The Unraveling: Pakistan in the Age of Jihad* (New York: Farrar, Straus and Giroux, 2011); Ahmed Rashid, *Pakistan on the Brink: The Future of America, Pakistan, and Afghanistan* (New York: Viking, 2012); and Pamela Constable, *Playing with Fire: Pakistan at War with Itself* (New York: Random House, 2011).

26. Hamza Usman, "At Home Nowhere," Pak Tea House, February 6, 2012 (http://pakteahouse.net/2012/02/06/at-home-nowhere/).

27. The way in which Pakistan changed its leadership over the past sixty years provides a good measure of its stability. Of its civilian leaders, one died in office (Jinnah), seven were fired or banished (Benazir Bhutto and Nawaz Sharif twice each), one was hanged (Zulfikar Ali Bhutto); of the military leaders, one was killed in office (Zia), and three were fired or went into exile.

28. Reeta Chowdary Tremblay and Julian Schofield, "Institutional Causes of the India-Pakistan Rivalry," in *The India-Pakistan Conflict: An Enduring Rivalry,* edited by T. V. Paul (Cambridge University Press, 2005), chap. 10.

29. The most complete history of the Pakistani nuclear program is in Feroze Khan, *Eating Grass: The Making of the Pakistani Bomb* (Stanford University Press, 2012).

30. Quoted in "Pak to Send Satellite in Space by '11: Dr. Samar," *The Nation* (Lahore), May 31, 2009 (www.nation.com.pk/pakistan-news-newspaper-daily-english-online/politics/31-May-2009/Pak-to-send-satellite-in-space-by-11-Dr-Samar).

31. For a study of the decisionmaking processes in India and Pakistan, see P. R. Chari, Pervez I. Cheema, and Stephen P. Cohen, *Four Crises and a Peace Process* (Brookings, 2007).

32. Zafar Hilaly, "Comment: Indo-Pak Relations," *Daily Times* (Islamabad and other Pakistan cities), November 20, 2009 (www.dailytimes.com.pk/default.asp?page=2009%5C11%5C20%5Cstory_20-11-2009_pg3_3).

33. Imran Khan, *Pakistan: A Personal History* (Great Britain: Bantam, 2011).

34. See P. S. Suryanarayana, *A Pakistani Vision of Peace with India,* Special Report 10 (National University of Singapore, Institute of South Asian Studies, December 7, 2012) (isas.nus.edu.sg).

35. Even in India some orthodox Islamic organizations refuse to accept Ahmadis as Muslims. The Darul Uloom Deoband, a leading seminary, declared Ahmadis to be non-Muslim and called on the Saudi government to stop them from performing hajj. Ahmadis are also not represented on the All-India Muslim Personal Law Board. In 2012 the Kashmir grand mufti, the leading Muslim figure in India's state of Jammu and Kashmir, called for state legislation declaring Ahmadis non-Muslim. See www.atimes.com/atimes/South_Asia/NE15Df02.html.

36. Mahmud Ali Durrani, *India and Pakistan: The Cost of Conflict, the Benefits of* Peace (Washington: School of Advanced International Studies, 2000), with editions published in India and Pakistan as well. Since then several such groups have been formed.

37. Moeed Yusuf, "Things Looking Up," *Dawn* (Karachi), December, 24, 2012 (http://dawn.com/2012/12/24/things-looking-up/).

38. Munir Akram, "Reversing Strategic Shrinkage," in *Pakistan: Beyond the "Crisis State,"* edited by Maleeha Lodhi (Columbia University Press, 2011), pp. 303–04.

39. Ibid., p. 288.

40. Jamal J. Elias, "The Politics of Pashtun and Punjabi Truck Decoration," in *Under the Drones: Modern Lives in the Afghanistan-Pakistan Borderlands,* edited by Shahzad Bashir and Robert D. Crews (Harvard University Press, 2012), pp. 204–05.

41. Cohen, *The Pakistan Army.*

42. For my first impressions of the Pakistan army, including several conversations like this, see ibid. in both its 1984 and 1998 revised editions.

43. For references to "prospect theory," which deals with these kinds of worries about the future, see Jack Levy, "An Introduction to Prospect Theory," *Political Psychology* 1 (June 1992); and Daniel Kahneman and Amos Tversky, "Prospect Theory: An Analysis of Decision under Risk," *Econometrica* 47 (March 1979): 263–92.

44. For a comprehensive overview of the use of the World Wide Web and other media by extremists, including several banned groups that operate publicly and

openly, see Tufail Ahmed, "Using Twitter, You Tube, Facebook, and Other Internet Tools: Pakistani Terrorist Group Lashkar-e-Jhangvi Incites Violence against Shiite Muslims and Engenders Anti Semitism" (http://pakteahouse.net/2012/03/24/using-twitter-youtube-facebook-and-other-internet-tools).

45. See Moeed Yusuf, "Youth and the Future," in *The Future of Pakistan,* edited by Stephen P. Cohen and others (Brookings, 2011).

Chapter 5

1. One of the first attempts at a comprehensive explanation is by Sumit Ganguly, *The Origins of War in South Asia: Indo Pakistani Conflicts since 1947* (Boulder, Colo.: Westview Press, 1994). Ganguly takes a broad cultural and historical approach in explaining the causes of the India-Pakistan conflict, using the framework of the three major wars they fought, in 1947, 1965, and 1971. The book was written before the nuclear tests and the 1998 Kargil war. In a recent article the author expressed his skepticism about the prospects of India-Pakistan normalization even after the two countries resumed talks about expanded trade because they remain far apart on the critical question of Kashmir. See Ganguly, "Think Again: India's Rise," *Foreign Policy*, July 5, 2012.

2. T. V. Paul, "Causes of the India-Pakistan Enduring Rivalry," in *The India-Pakistan Conflict: An Enduring Rivalry,* edited by T. V. Paul (Cambridge University Press, 2005), p. 5.

3. Samuel P. Huntington, *The Clash of Civilizations and the Remaking of World Order* (New York: Simon and Schuster, 1996).

4. For a classic study on this division line and early interactions between the Islamic and Hindu worlds in South Asia, see Al Buruni (Muhammad Ibn Ahmad), *Alberuni's India, An English Edition* (London: Kegan Paul, 1910). For a modern Hindu revivalist narrative, see the recent edition of Vinayak Savarkar, *Hindutva: Who Is a Hindu?* (New Delhi: Hindi Sahitya Sadan, 2003). For a modern Islamic narrative of Pakistan, see Rahmat Ali, *Pakistan: The Fatherland of the Pak Nation* (Lahore: Book Traders, 1978).

5. "Foodistan: India vs Pakistan Food Fight," New Delhi Television (NDTV) (http://goodtimes.ndtv.com/foodistan/).

6. "JNU Suspends Students over Pork and Beef Festival," *Hindustan Times,* October 6, 2012.

7. "Bans and Ratings," *Gallup Cyberletter on Media Research Issues 43-48* (www.gallup.com.pk/News/cyber43-48.pdf), p. 2.

8. Elias Canetti, *Crowds and Power* (New York: Seabury Press, 1978).

9. An influential and authoritative Pakistan army interpretation of India can be found in Brigadier Javed Hussain, *India: A Study in Profile* (Rawalpindi: Army Press, 1990).

10. Freud discusses the concept in several places, observing differences among and between closely related societies. See Sigmund Freud, *Civilization and Its*

Discontents, vol. 12, *Civilization, Society and Religion* (New York: Penguin Freud Library 1991), p. 305.

11. Vali Nasr, "National Identities and the India-Pakistan Conflict," in *The India-Pakistan Conflict,* edited by Paul, p. 178.

12. Yusuf Jameel, "Declare Ahmadis Non-Muslims," *Deccan Chronicle,* May 3, 2012 (www.deccanchronicle.com/taxonomy/term/5381).

13. For excellent surveys of the Kashmir problem, see Jonah Blank, "Kashmir: Fundamentalism Takes Root," *Foreign Affairs,* November-December 1999; and Sumit Ganguly, *The Crisis in Kashmir: Portents of War and Hopes of Peace* (New York: Woodrow Wilson Center Press, 1997).

14. John A. Vasquez, "The India-Pakistan Conflict in Light of General Theories of War, Rivalry and Deterrence," in *The India-Pakistan Conflict,* edited by Paul, p. 68.

15. Parenthetically, the ecological impact on the glacier is potentially devastating to both countries: it is the repository of tons of human waste, upstream from large populations. It is also an awful place to fight. More Indians and Pakistanis were killed by frostbite and hypothermia than bullets, and 129 Pakistani soldiers and 11 civilians were gruesomely killed in a landslide that affected the geologically unstable glacier.

16. For a joint India-Pakistan proposal for a regulated withdrawal of both armies from the glacier, see Samina Ahmed and Varun Sahni, *Freezing the Fighting: Military Disengagement on the Siachen Glacier* (Albuquerque, N. Mex.: Sandia National Laboratories, Cooperative Monitoring Center, 1998); for the peace park proposal, see A. Ali, "A Siachen Peace Park: the Solution to a Half-Century of International Conflict?" *Mountain Research Development* 22, no. 4 (2002): 316–19. For a sample of the Indian military's new populism, see Air Vice Marshal Manmohan Bahadur, "Heroes on the Heights," *Hindustan Times,* May 25, 2012: "Stephen Cohen may have equated the Siachen conflict to two bald men fighting over a comb. But if the head is Indian, albeit bald, we still have a duty to protect our interests—that's what nation-building is all about."

17. Pakistan's choice of proxy war tactics since the late 1980s was dictated as much by the political hope of a Kashmiri uprising as it was the result of military necessity. For a discussion of the Pakistani view on the strategic importance of Kashmir, see Stephen P. Cohen, *The Pakistan Army* (University of California Press, 1984), p. 141 ff.

18. M. L. Chibber, "Siachen—The Untold Story (A Personal Account)," *Indian Defence Review,* January 1990.

19. For a brief UN history of the conflicts in Kashmir, plus information about the UN peacekeeping operations in the state, see the United Nations Department of Public Information, "United Nations Peacekeeping Operations: UNMOGIP" (United Nations Military Observer Group in India and Pakistan), October 31, 1997 (www.un.org/Depts/DPKO/Missions/unmogip.htm).

20. John A. Vasquez, "General Theories of War, Rivalry, and Deterrence," in *The India-Pakistan Conflict,* edited by Paul, p. 55.

21. Stockholm International Peace Research Institute (SIPRI), "Trends in International Arms Transfers, 2011," Fact Sheet, March 2012 (http://books.sipri.org/product_info?c_product_id=443), p. 5.

22. For an account of the diplomacy of the war, see Leo Rose and Richard Sisson, *War and Secession: Pakistan, India, and the Creation of Bangladesh* (University of California Press, 1990). For a detailed overview of the Simla Agreement, see the study by an Indian and a Pakistani scholar, P. R. Chari and Pervaiz Iqbal Cheema, *The Simla Agreement 1972: Its Wasted Promise* (New Delhi: Manohar, 2001). For a summary of the Simla Agreement written by Chari on the occasion of its fortieth anniversary, see "Relevance of Simla Agreement: A Close Look after Four Decades," *Chandigarh Tribune*, July 2, 2012 (www.tribuneindia.com/2012/20120702/edit.htm#4).

23. For a comprehensive overview, see Kanti Bajpai and others, *Brasstacks and Beyond: Crisis Perception and Management in South Asia* (New Delhi: Manohar, 1995; Lahore: Vanguard Publishers, 1996; Columbia: South Asia Books, 1996).

24. Vasquez, "General Theories of War, Rivalry, and Deterrence," p. 73.

25. For discussions, see Scott D. Sagan, "Nuclear Dangers in South Asia," *Forum on Physics and Society* 41, no. 6 (2004) (http://iis-db.stanford.edu/pubs/20573/sagan_nuc_sasia.pdf); and Verghese Koithara, *Managing India's Nuclear Forces* (Brookings, 2012).

26. Vasquez, "General Theories of War, Rivalry, and Deterrence," p. 79.

27. Kenneth Waltz, *Man, the State, and War* (Columbia University Press, 1959), esp. chaps. 2 and 3.

28. One of the first South Asian scholar-diplomats to argue that identities and images were critical in the relationship was Sisir Gupta, in *Kashmir: A Study in India-Pakistan Relations* (Bombay: Asia Publishing House, 1966). Sumit Ganguly's important study, *Conflicts Unending: India-Pakistan Tensions since 1947* (New Delhi: Oxford University Press, 2001), emphasizes the incompatible identities of the two. More optimistically, the Mumbai-based Sundeep Waslekar acknowledges the clash of state identity, as well as confusion among other South Asian regional groups, while pointing out how they might be modified so as to permit an overall normalization. See Sundeep Waslekar, *The Final Settlement* (Mumbai: International Centre for Peace Initiatives, 2005).

29. Editorial, *The Hindu*, October 28, 2010 (www.hindu.com/2010/10/28/stories/2010102858101400.htm for the BJP). This was part of the "holocaust" against Hindus that took place in Pakistan and Bangladesh (www.hinduholocaust.com/Articles/enemyproperty.htm).

30. Kiran Pervez, "Borders and Beliefs: Ethics, Actor Hood, and the India-Pakistan Conflict," Ph.D. dissertation, American University, 2009.

31. Paul F. Diehl, Gary Goertz, and Daniel Saeed, "Theoretical Specifications of Enduring Rivalries," in *The India-Pakistan Conflict*, edited by Paul, p. 53.

32. Marie Lall, "Educate to Hate: The Use of Education in the Creation of Antagonistic National Identities in India and Pakistan," *Compare: A Journal of Comparative Education* 38, no. 1 (2008): 103–20 (http://eprints.ioe.ac.uk/4020/).

33. Ibid.

34. A. H. Nayyar and Ahmed Salim, "The Subtle Subversion: The State of Curricula and Textbooks in Pakistan" (Islamabad: Sustainable Development Policy Institute) (www.uvm.edu/~envprog/madrassah/TextbooksinPakistan.pdf [June 3,2012)], p. 10.

35. "Pakistan Schools Teach Hindu Hatred: US Commission," *Times of India*, November 9, 2011 (http://timesofindia.indiatimes.com/world/pakistan/Pakistan-schools-teach-Hindu-hatred-US-commission/articleshow/10663967.cms [June 3, 2012]).

36. Nayyar and Salim, "The Subtle Subversion," pp. 66–67.

37. Ibid., p. 68; Lall, "Educate to Hate," p. 110.

38. Nayyar and Salim, "The Subtle Subversion," provide many examples of these and other derogatory phrases.

39. Stephen Philip Cohen, *The Idea of Pakistan* (Brookings, 2004), p. 243.

40. Lall, "Educate to Hate," p. 104.

41. Ibid., p. 106; and Krishna Kumar, "Peace Demands an Educated Imagination," *The Hindu*, May 7, 2012 (www.thehindu.com/opinion/lead/article3394664.ece [June 2012]). For more information, see Kumar, *Prejudice and Pride: Histories of the Freedom Struggle in India and Pakistan* (New Delhi: Viking, 2001), and *Battle for Peace* (New Delhi: Penguin, 2007).

42. Lall, "Educate to Hate," p. 109.

43. Sundar Nandini, "Teaching to Hate: RSS Pedagogical Programme," *Economic and Political Weekly* 39, no. 16 (2004): 1605–12.

44. Kumar, "Peace Demands an Educated Imagination."

45. Navnita Chadha Behera, *Demystifying Kashmir* (Brookings, 2006); and also the earlier study by Sisir Gupta, *Kashmir: A Study in India-Pakistan Relations* (Bombay: Asia Publishing House, 1966).

46. For the Pakistani perspective, see Pervaiz Iqbal Cheema, "Pakistan, India, and Kashmir: A Historical Review," in *Perspectives on Kashmir: The Roots of Conflict in South Asia*, edited by Raju G. C. Thomas (Boulder, Colo.: Westview Press, 1992).

47. For an extensive review of the Indian position, see Ashutosh Varshney, "Three Compromised Nationalisms: Why Kashmir Has Been a Problem," in *Perspectives on Kashmir*, edited by Thomas.

48. Waslekar, *The Final Settlement*, p. 3.

49. Paul F. Diehl and Gary Goetz, *War and Peace in International Rivalry* (University of Michigan Press, 2000), pp. 201–18.

50. This point is made by several Indian and Pakistani authors in Kanti P. Bajpai and Stephen P. Cohen, eds., *South Asia after the Cold War* (Boulder, Colo.: Westview Press, 1993). See especially the chapters by Pervaiz I. Cheema and M. L. Chibber.

51. Ashok Kapur, "Major Powers and the Persistence of the India-Pakistan Conflict," in *The India-Pakistan Conflict*, edited by Paul, pp. 152–55.

52. Ibid., p. 152.

53. I am grateful to Soumi Chatterjee, now of the University of California–Los Angeles, for comments on my work. See his unpublished manuscript, "Paired-Minority Conflicts: Exploration of the Categorization of a Potential Genus of Conflict," on file with Stephen Cohen.

54. This term is my own. For the perspective of a clinical psychologist who has studied the origins of ethnic conflict and war, see Vamik D. Volkan, *The Need to Have Enemies and Allies: From Clinical Practice to International Relationships* (New York:

Jason Aronson, 1988). See also Elias Canetti, *Crowds and Power* (New York: Seabury Press, 1978), a modern classic.

55. See also Stephen P. Cohen, "Causes of Conflict and Conditions for Peace in South Asia," in *Resolving Regional Conflicts,* edited by Roger E. Kanet (University of Illinois Press, 1998), pp. 105–33.

56. The phrase is often attributed (in Hebrew) to Levi Eshkol. See Avi Schlaim, "The Albatross of Victory," *The Guardian* (Manchester), June 7, 2002 (www.guardian.co.uk/books/2002/jun/08/featuresreviews.guardianreview4).

57. Other states have their treasured grievances, although these can vary. For some former colonial states it is the fear of the return of the colonial power; for the United States it is the metaphor of surprise attack on its seemingly invincible homeland, epitomized in the Japanese attack on Pearl Harbor and refreshed by the al Qaeda attack on New York and Washington on September 11, 2001.

58. Chatterjee, "Paired-Minority Conflicts."

59. For Jinnah's views, see his speech to the Constituent Assembly, discussed in Stanley A. Wolpert, *Jinnah of Pakistan* (Oxford University Press, 2005), pp. 333–40. For a contemporary Pakistani discussion of Jinnah's secularism, see Akbar S. Ahmed, *Jinnah and Islamic Identity: The Search for Saladin* (Oxford University Press, 1997).

60. For his early and comprehensive study of Kashmir, see Gupta, *Kashmir: A Study in India-Pakistan Relations.*

61. This image is vividly conveyed to a second and third generation of Indians (and others) by the portrayal of Jinnah in the Attenborough film *Gandhi.* This inspired a second film, produced by the polymath Pakistani academic-administrator Akbar Ahmed, dealing with the life of Jinnah.

62. The civilizational gap between Islamic Pakistan and (largely Hindu but formally secular) India was a theme of Girilal Jain, one of India's most brilliant journalists. In the last ten years of his life (he died in 1988), he wrote feelingly about Hindu-Muslim affairs and the phenomenon of Pakistan; he was, in many ways, the most successful popularizer of BJP views well before the party came to power. For an overview of his arguments, see Girilal Jain, *The Hindu Phenomenon* (New Delhi: USBSPD, 1994).

63. Lieutenant General P. N. Kathpalia, "Indo-Pak Relations: The Concept of National Security," *Indian Defense Review,* January 1989, pp. 116, 124.

64. For a definitive statement of army perceptions of India by a Pakistani officer, see Lieutenant Colonel Javed Hassan, *India: A Study in Profile* (Rawalpindi: Services Book Club, 1990).

65. Mahmud Ali Durrani, *India and Pakistan: The Cost of Conflict, the Benefits of Peace* (Washington: School of Advanced International Studies, 2000), p. xvi.

66. Joseph S. Nye, *Soft Power: The Means to Success in World Politics* (New York: Public Affairs, 2006).

67. "Indo-Pakistan Unity Inevitable: Pandit Nehru Urges Saner Thinking to End Disputes," *Times of India* (New Delhi), November 29, 1947. A passage from this address is cited out of context by one of Zia ul Haq's closest associates as indicating that Nehru was bent on destroying Pakistan. See General K. M. Arif, *Estranged Neighbors: India-Pakistan, 1947–2010* (Islamabad: Dost, 2010), p. 330.

CHAPTER 6

1. For an Indian diplomat's survey of unofficial diplomacy, see Kishan S. Rana, *Bilateral Diplomacy* (Geneva: Diplo Handbooks, 2002). Other overviews include Sundeep Waslekar, *Track-Two Diplomacy in South Asia*, 2nd ed. (University of Illinois Program in Arms Control, Disarmament, and International Security [ACDIS], October 1995); and Navnita Chadha Behera, Paul Evans, and Gowher Rizvi, *Beyond Boundaries: A Report on the State of Non-Official Dialogues on Peace, Security and Cooperation in South Asia* (York University–University of Toronto Joint Centre for Asia Pacific Studies, 1997).

2. Some of these efforts are summarized in Waslekar, *Track-Two Diplomacy in South Asia*; and in Behera and others, *Beyond Boundaries.*

3. Behera and others, *Beyond Boundaries*, p. 14.

4. The full text of the 2004 Musharraf-Vajpayee joint statement is at http://jinnah-institute.org/pak-india-pcm/pcm-archive/262-joint-statement-president-musharraf-and-pm-vajpayee.

5. For a thoughtful examination of Neemrana and other dialogues, see Aqil S. Shah, *Non-Official Dialogue between India and Pakistan: Prospects and Problems* (University of Illinois, August 1997) (http://acdis.illinois.edu/assets/docs/290/NonOfficialDialoguebetweenIndiaandPakistanProspectsandProblems.pdf).

6. The trip was sponsored by the Association of Pakistani-American Physicians of North America (APPNA) in 2005. A delegation of more than 200 members visited India and were warmly welcomed by several ministers, including Pranab Mukherjee, who subsequently became India's president. Indian American doctors and professionals generally seem to be more wary of such interactions than their Pakistani American counterparts.

7. For a respected account, see Steve Coll, "The Back Channel," *New Yorker*, March 2, 2009 (www.newyorker.com/reporting/2009/03/02/090302fa_fact_coll).

8. The KSG included a strong group of experts. Its funding by an expatriate Indian Kashmiri reduced its credibility in the eyes of some officials, and its authority was weakened when a few members went public with their own set of recommendations.

9. The Atlantic Council effort is organized by the former Pakistani journalist-bureaucrat Shuja Nawaz, the director of the council's South Asia Center, and has fostered separate dialogues between former officers of the two armies and on water issues (www.acus.org/program/south-asia).

10. Toufiq A. Siddiqi, *A Natural Gas Pipeline for India and Pakistan* (Washington: Balusa, 2003).

11. Amir Mughal, "Joint Indo-Pak School History Textbook on the Web" (chagtaikhan.blogspot.com [May 25, 2009]).

12. Behera and others, *Beyond Boundaries* p. 32.

13. For a discussion, see Mohamed Jawhar bin Hassan, "CSCAP: Its Evolution and Activities," in *South Asia Security Futures: A Dialogue of Directors of Regional Strategic Studies Institutes*, edited by Dipankar Banerjee (Colombo: Regional Centre for Strategic Studies, 2002), p. 214 ff.

14. Behera and others, *Beyond Boundaries*, p. 37.

15. This was not quite true for the United Kingdom, which after World War II saw the region as a stepping-stone to its Far Eastern possessions. This changed by the 1950s when Britain eventually became America's junior partner in several joint efforts to solve regional problems in South Asia. It joined with the United States in urging India and Pakistan to reach a Kashmir settlement after the India-China war, and it was the mediator in the 1965 Rann of Kutch crisis that let to a proposal accepted by both countries on June 30, 1965.

16. Shirin R. Tahir-Kheli, *India, Pakistan and the United States* (New York: Council on Foreign Relations Press, 1997), p. 137.

17. Wiki Leaks cited in "How India Kept Kashmir Out of U.S. Af-Pak Envoy's Brief," *The Hindu*, May 24, 2011.

18. SAARC provided a venue for meetings between Indian and Pakistani leaders and sponsors some cooperative projects on regional issues. However, security issues are not included in its remit, nor is it allowed to deal with bilateral issues. Some of these functions have been taken over by an NGO, the Regional Centre for Strategic Studies, Colombo, which is in effect the SAARC security studies program. India has twice been able to force a postponement of SAARC annual meetings when it was displeased with developments in Pakistan.

19. See Claude Arpi, "Lessons for SAARC from the European Union" (www.rediff.com/news/2007/apr/04claude.htm).

20. European Parliament, Committee on Foreign Affairs, Baroness Nicholson of Winterbourne, rapporteur, *Report on Kashmir: Present Situation and Future Prospects*, Final Report A6-0158 (Strasbourg, 2007), p. 20.

21. Institute of Defence Studies and Analyses, *POK Project Report, Pakistan Occupied Kashmir: Changing the Discourse, Report of a Roundtable* (August 19, 2010) (http://idsa.in/system/files/book_PakistanOccupiedKashmir.pdf).

22. "Inauguration of Kashmir EU Week in the European Parliament," Kashmir News Watch (London), July 13, 2011 (www.kashmirnewswatch.com/inauguration-of-kashmir-eu-week-in-the-european-parliament/).

23. Rashmee Roshan Lall, "European War of Words on Kashmir," *Times of India*, May 26, 2007 (http://articles.timesofindia.indiatimes.com/2007-05-26/europe/27883975_1_european-parliament-report-amendments).

24. Shabir Choudhry, "Emma Nicholson and EU Kashmir Report," *Asian Tribune* (Stockholm), December 14, 2006 (www.asiantribune.com/index.php?q=node/3652).

25. See www.rediff.com/news/report/european-union-not-to-interfere-in-kashmir-issue/20110513.htm.

26. Thom Shankar, "Gorbachev Address Leaves Issues behind in India," *Chicago Tribune*, November 28, 1986 (http://articles.chicagotribune.com/1986-11-28/news/8603300160_1_indo-soviet-india-and-pakistan-prime-minister-rajiv-gandhi).

27. When Musharraf (as president) was sending out feelers to India on Kashmir and trade, some very senior Pakistani army officers told me, "If it works, fine," but they were very skeptical about the chances of success, and in the end his rapprochement

strategy was too rapid for many in the military. The army chief has a constituency and must persuade it that normalization is in its interest.

28. E-mail communication to the author, May 2012, shortly after Yashwant Sinha reversed prime minister Manmohan Singh's formulation of "trust but verify."

29. Vinod Sharma, "No Point in PM Visiting Pak Anytime Soon: Officials," *Hindustan Times*, October 7, 2012, p. 8.

30. For an elaboration of my views, see Stephen P. Cohen, "Pakistan: Arrival and Departure," in *The Future of Pakistan*, edited by Stephen P. Cohen and others (Brookings, 2011); also published in India and Pakistan.

31. Sundeep Waslekar, *The Final Settlement* (Mumbai: International Centre for Peace Initiatives, 2005), p. vii.

32. Shahid Javed Burki, "Pakistan-India Detente: A Three-Step Tango," Institute of South Asian Studies Insights 179 (Singapore, August 8, 2012) (www.isas.nus.edu.sg/Attachments/PublisherAttachment/ISAS_Insight_179_-_Pakistan-India_Detente-_A_Three-Step_Tango_08082012143948.pdf).

33. This language routinely appeared in the Indian press whenever there was speculation about a visit. See Sachin Parashar, "PM Unlikely to Visit Pakistan as 26/11 Scar Yet to Heal," *Times of India*, November 17, 2012, based on comments by an MEA spokesman (http://articles.timesofindia.indiatimes.com/2012-11-17/india/35171334_1_raja-pervez-ashraf-india-salman-bashir-pakistan).

34. C. Raja Mohan, "Return of the Raj," *American Interest*, May-June 2010 (www.the-american-interest.com/article.cfm?piece=803). See also C. Raja Mohan, "Modernizing the Raj Legacy," *Seminar* 629, January 2012, pp. 80–83.

35. One caveat to this proposition that does not affect this statement is that there were sometimes differences in preferences and interests between the Raj, based in India, and British leaders in London. This was often the subject of heated politics between New Delhi (or Calcutta) and London and extended to the different perspective of British and Indian army officers such as Bernard Montgomery and Claude Auchinleck.

36. Verghese Koithara, *Managing India's Nuclear Forces* (Brookings, 2012). Also Toby Dalton and Jaclyn Tandler, "Understanding the Arms 'Race' in South Asia" (Washington: Carnegie Endowment for International Peace, September 2012) (http://carnegieendowment.org/files/south_asia_arms_race.pdf).

37. Bharat Karnad, "Tricky Waters," *Asian Age*, February 16, 2012 (www.asianage.com/columnists/tricky-waters-986).

38. Stephen P. Cohen and Sunil Dasgupta, *Arming without Aiming, Aiming without Arming: India's Military Modernization* (Brookings, 2010); and Polly Nayak and Michael Krepon, "The Unfinished Crisis: U.S. Crisis Management after the 2008 Mumbai Attacks" (Washington: Henry L. Stimson Center, 2010) (www.stimson.org/images/uploads/research-pdfs/Mumbai-Final_1.pdf).

39. Cohen and others, *The Future of Pakistan*.

40. "Pakistan Will Be Reunited with India, says Katju," *The Hindu*, March 5, 2013 (www.thehindu.com/news/national/kerala/pakistan-will-be-reunited-with-india-says-katju/article4476192.ece).

Chapter 7

1. For a discussion of Barnes's efforts by a senior State Department official and noted historian of American policy in South Asia, see Howard B. Schaffer, South Asia Hand Blog, August 21, 2012 (http://southasiahand.com/india-u-s-relations/in-memoriam-harry-barnes-in-india/).

2. Dennis Kux, *Estranged Democracies: India and the United States 1941-1991* (Washington: National Defense University Press, 1993), p. 282.

3. Shirin R. Tahir-Kheli, *India, Pakistan and the United States* (New York: Council on Foreign Relations Press, 1997), p. 141.

4. Stephen P. Cohen and Richard L. Park, *India: Emerging Country* (New York: Crane, Russak, 1979).

5. A policy of having good relations with both India and Pakistan was not universally supported. Some American ambassadors to both countries have steadfastly refused opportunities to visit the other, preferring to work hardest on improving U.S.-India relations or U.S.-Pakistan relations. The same is true of assistant secretary visits; the first "cross-visit" by respective assistant secretaries of East and South Asia took place in the Clinton administration. Cross-visiting is now accepted practice.

6. Tahir-Kheli, *India, Pakistan and the United States*, p. 42.

7. For an overview of American policy in these crises, see P. R. Chari, P. I. Cheema, and Stephen P. Cohen, *Four Crises and a Peace Process* (Brookings, 2007). For a somewhat different approach, two other studies are valuable: Polly Nayak and Michael Krepon, *US-Crisis Management In South Asia's Twin Peaks Crisis* (Washington: Stimson Center, 2006) (www.stimson.org/images/uploads/research-pdfs/USCrisisManagement.pdf); and Sumit Ganguly and Devin T. Hagerty, *Fearful Symmetry: India-Pakistan Crises in the Shadow of Nuclear Weapons* (Oxford University Press, 2005).

8. The best account of the process is Strobe Talbott, *Engaging India: Diplomacy, Democracy and the Bomb: A Memoir* (Brookings, 2004).

9. For an authoritative explanation of dehyphenation, see Ashley J. Tellis, "The Merits of Dehyphenation: Explaining U.S. Success in Engaging India and Pakistan," *Washington Quarterly* 31 (Autumn 2008): 21–42.

10. On Kashmir as "the most dangerous place on earth," see William J. Clinton, Remarks at the One America Meeting with Religious Leaders, March 9, 2000, *Public Papers of the Presidents of the United States: William J. Clinton*, Book 1 (Washington: Government Printing Office, 2000).

11. This idea goes back to the dividing line between CENTCOM and PACOM, which was drawn so that India and Pakistan would be handled by two different commanders; it was assumed that policy matters that affected them would be dealt with at a higher level. This did not happen as planned, and each became beholden to "their" South Asian state, formulating different military and political strategies with little or no coordination. See "South Asia and US Military Policy," in *The Coordination of Complexity in South Asia*, edited by Lloyd Rudolph and Susanne Rudolph, vol. 7, *Papers Prepared for the National Commission on the Organization of the Government*

for the Conduct of Foreign Policy (Washington: GPO, 1975; New Delhi: Manohar, 1978), appx. v, pp. 149–58.

12. Stephen P. Cohen, quoted by Alexander Evans, "The United States and South Asia after Afghanistan," a report sponsored by the Asia Society Advisory Group on U.S. Policy toward South Asia (New York: Asia Society, 2012), p. 64.

13. Barack Obama, "Renewing American Leadership," *Foreign Affairs*, July-August 2007 (www.foreignaffairs.com/articles/62636/barack-obama/renewing-american-leadership?page=show).

14. Joe Klein, "The Full Obama Interview," *Time*, October 23, 2008 (http://swampland.time.com/2008/10/23/the_full_obama_interview/).

15. Richard Holbrooke, "Hope in Pakistan," *Washington Post*, March 21, 2008 (www.washingtonpost.com/wp-dyn/content/article/2008/03/20/AR2008032003016.html).

16. For example, the Communist Party of India brokered the agreement between the two factions of the Afghan left (Khalq and Parcham) at the behest of the Soviet Union, and many of the Afghan elite, including President Hamid Karzai, were educated in India; others have their families residing there. While Pakistan provided no assistance to Afghanistan, India's aid program came to about a billion dollars.

17. Howard Schaffer, "U.S. Kashmir Policy in the Obama Administration and Beyond," *South Asia Journal* no. 3 (2012), p. 16.

18. For more on structural dysfunctionality, see Bruce Riedel and Stephen Cohen, "Rethinking South Asia," *The National Interest*, May 4, 2011 (http://nationalinterest.org/commentary/rethinking-south-asia-5253.i [July 21, 2011]).

19. For a good lay introduction to the strategic geopolitics of the Indian Ocean, see Robert D. Kaplan, *Monsoon: The Indian Ocean and the Future of American Power* (New York: Random House, 2010).

20. Among other things, this freed South Asia from the grip of the Middle Eastern–dominated diplomats in the old Near East and South Asia Bureau of the Department of State.

21. Steve Coll, an eminent American journalist, has suggested that Obama act upon his first instincts, which were to become more involved in Kashmir; Ambassador Howard Schaffer, the author of the definitive study of American effort to resolve Kashmir, has written that the present period provides more opportunities for a settlement of Kashmir than the aborted effort of the Kennedy administration. Steve Coll, "Kashmir: The Time Has Come," *New York Review of Books*, September 30, 2010; and Schaffer, "U.S. Kashmir Policy," p. 201.

22. Daniel Markey, *No Exit: The Future of the US-Pakistan Relationship*, draft review manuscript, chapter 4, p.158.

23. The International Fund for Ireland is financed by the United States, the European Union, Canada, Australia, and New Zealand; it encourages contact, dialogue, and reconciliation between Ireland's nationalists and unionists and tackles the underlying causes of sectarianism and violence throughout the country (www.internationalfundforireland.com/).

24. See National Academy of Sciences (NAS), Committee on Himalayan Glaciers, *Himalayan Glaciers: Climate Change, Water Resources, and Water Security* (Washington: NAS Press, 2012) (www.nap.edu/catalog.php?record_id=13449/pdf).

25. Smruti S. Pattanaik, "India-Pakistan Foreign Ministers Meet: The Hype and the Substance," September 17, 2012 (www.idsa.in/idsacomments/IndiaPakistan ForeignMinistersMeet_sspattanaik_170912).

26. The International Afghanistan Conference took place on December 5, 2011 (www.auswaertiges-amt.de/EN/Aussenpolitik/RegionaleSchwerpunkte/Afghanistan Zentralasien/Bonn_Konferenz_2011/Uebersicht_node.html).

27. For one statement of a regional approach after the U.S. withdrawal, see Haroun Mir, "Is Regional Consensus on Afghanistan Possible?" in *Afghanistan in Transition: Beyond 2014?* edited by Shanthie Mariet D'Souza (Singapore: Institute for South Asian Studies, 2012).

28. Sadika Hameed, "Prospects for Indian-Pakistani Cooperation in Afghanistan" (Washington: Center for Strategic and International Studies, August 2012) (http://csis.org/files/publication/120821_Hameed_ProspectsIndianPakistan_Web.pdf).

29. Bharat Karnad, "Brothers-in-Arms," *Asian Age*, May 10, 2012.

30. M. K. Bhadrakumar, "Indian Punch line, Reflections on Foreign Affairs: It's Time to Look beyond Afghan War," blog (http://blogs.rediff.com/mkbhadrakumar/2011/12/22/its-time-to-look-beyond-afghan-war/ Dec 22 2011). Bhadrakumar is a retired Indian diplomat.

31. For a critique of the notion of regional cooperation to help solve the Afghanistan problem, see Ashley Tellis, "Implementing a Regional Approach to Afghanistan: Multiple Alternatives, Modest Possibilities," in *Is a Regional Strategy Viable in Afghanistan?* edited by Ashley Tellis and Aroop Mukharji (Washington: Carnegie Endowment for International Peace, 2010). Chapters in this book by Frederic Grare (on Pakistan) and Gautam Mukhopadhyaya (on India) are also pessimistic, but the environment in which an India-Pakistan arrangement would be negotiated is rapidly changing as of late 2012.

32. One of the most realistic accounts of a nuclear exchange also pays close attention to the domestic politics that might drive the two states to a war. See Manil Suri's novel *City of Devi* (New York: Norton, 2013). Set in Mumbai in a post-nuclear era, this dystopia is a mixture of Orwell's 1984 and the film *Blade Runner.*

33. I have attempted this, with several colleagues, in Stephen P. Cohen and others, *The Future of Pakistan* (Brookings, 2011). See also "Pakistan's Road to Disintegration," Council on Foreign Relations, interview, January 26, 2011 (www.cfr.org/pakistan/pakistans-road-disintegration/p23744).

34. One of the finest discussions of the relevance of the American and Soviet experience is in David Smith, "The U.S. Experience with Tactical Nuclear Weapons: Lessons for South Asia" (Washington: Stimson Center, March 4, 2013) (www.stimson.org/images/uploads/research-pdfs/David_Smith_Tactical_Nuclear_Weapons.pdf).

35. There was a long American tradition of seeing Pakistan as a Middle Eastern Muslim state, which made it look relatively prosperous and stable; this exaggerated its difference from India. Washington now correctly speaks of Pakistan as a fledgling South Asian democracy that happens to have a large number of Muslims. One reason for this change was the creation of a South Asia Bureau diluting the role of the Middle East specialist in the making of South Asia policy.

Index

Page numbers followed by *b* or *f* refer to boxed text or figures, respectively.

About the Author

Stephen P. Cohen is a senior fellow in Foreign Policy at the Brookings Institution. Long considered one of America's premier experts on South Asia, he has a number of books to his credit, including *India: Emerging Power*, *The Idea of Pakistan*, and *Arming without Aiming: India's Military Modernization* (with Sunil Dasgupta).